BLURRED BORDERS

JORGE DUANY

BLURRED

BORDERS

Transnational Migration between the

Hispanic Caribbean and the United States

The University of North Carolina Press *Chapel Hill*

© 2011 The University of North Carolina Press

All rights reserved. Manufactured in the United States of America. Designed and set in Whitman and Scala Sans by Rebecca Evans. The paper in this book meets the guidelines for permanence and durability of the Committee on Production Guidelines for Book Longevity of the Council on Library Resources. The University of North Carolina Press has been a member of the Green Press Initiative since 2003.

Library of Congress Cataloging-in-Publication Data
Duany, Jorge.
Blurred borders: transnational migration between the Hispanic Caribbean and the United States / Jorge Duany.
p. cm.
Includes bibliographical references and index.
ISBN 978-0-8078-3497-8 (cloth: alk. paper)
ISBN 978-0-8078-7203-1 (pbk. : alk. paper)
1. Caribbean Area—Emigration and immigration. 2. West Indians—United States. 3. West Indians—Puerto Rico. 4. United States—Emigration and immigration. 5. Puerto Rico—Emigration and immigration. 6. Transnationalism. I. Title.
JV7321.D83 2011   304.8'30729—dc22   2011002343

cloth   15 14 13 12 11   5 4 3 2 1
paper   15 14 13 12 11   5 4 3 2 1

For my dear cousins LOURDES BLANCO PÁEZ and
CATINA SUÁREZ ROSCOE, separated by fifty years of
revolution and exile — may they soon reunite

Contents

Tables and Figures

Acknowledgments

I incurred many intellectual and institutional debts during the writing of this book. During the academic year 2009–10, I enjoyed a sabbatical leave from the University of Puerto Rico. Raquel Dulzaides and Jorge Giovannetti kindly served as witnesses to my contract with the university. I would also like to recognize the support of my colleagues in the Department of Sociology and Anthropology, especially Juan José Baldrich, Jorge Giovannetti, Luisa Hernández Angueira, Jesús Tapia, and Lanny Thompson.

During the fall of 2009, I was the Wilbur Marvin Visiting Scholar at the David Rockefeller Center for Latin American Studies at Harvard University. I am grateful to Edwin Ortiz, Anika Grubbs, Monica Tesoreiro, and Yadira Rivera for their administrative support, as well as to Merilee Grindle for her warm welcome. I am equally grateful to the students in my graduate seminar at Harvard, Melissa Deas, Maryell Hernández, and Deepak Lamba-Nieves, for helping me clarify my thinking about transnationalism.

During the spring of 2010, I was Scholar-in-Residence at the Center for Latin American and Caribbean Studies at the University of Connecticut. Guillermo Irizarry and Anne Lambright were wonderful hosts, together with their children Isis, Mobey, and Maya, who practically adopted me during my month-long stay in Hartford. I also thank Mark Overmyer-Velázquez, Samuel Martínez, Blanca Silvestrini, Ángel A. Rivera, Ruth Glasser, Odette Casamayor, Hebe Guardiola, and Alfin Vaz for their hospitality.

This book began as a paper for the conference "The Caribbean and the United States since 1898: One Hundred Years of Transformation," organized by Laird Bergad at the City University of New York on October 13–15, 1998. Several colleagues made encouraging comments on various drafts of this paper, including Silvia Pedraza, Edgardo Meléndez, Ninna Nyberg Sørensen, Ernesto Sagás, Yolanda Martínez–San Miguel, Marifeli Pérez-Stable, Vicky Muñiz, Karen Fog Olwig, and Lisa Maya Knauer.

The CUNY–Caribbean Exchange Program of the Centro de Estudios Puertorriqueños at Hunter College supported my archival research on Puerto Rico's Farm Labor Program, reported in chapter 4. Centro archivist Pedro Juan Hernández and former reference librarian Jorge Matos provided generous assistance. Edwin Meléndez, the Centro's director, invited me to present an earlier version of this essay as part of the Centro's lecture series during the spring of 2009. Ulbe Bosma, Jan Lucassen, Gert Oostindie, Eileen Findlay, and Edgardo Meléndez commented on the chapter.

I conducted fieldwork with Puerto Ricans in Orlando, the topic of chapter 5, while I was the Bacardí Family Eminent Scholar in Latin American Studies at the University of Florida during the spring of 2007. Helen I. Safa, John Dumoulin, Efraín Barradas, Carmen Diana Deere, and Carmen Meyers made my stay in Gainesville very agreeable. Vilma Quintana, of the Orlando Regional Chamber of Commerce, assisted in contacting and recruiting participants for my study. Ana Yolanda Ramos-Zayas, Patricia Silver, Luis Martínez-Fernández, and three anonymous reviewers commented on earlier versions of this chapter.

Antonio Aja, Damián J. Fernández, María Cristina García, my cousin Raúl Portuondo Duany, and Ernesto Rodríguez Chávez made constructive suggestions on previous drafts of chapter 7. The first version of chapter 9 was prepared as a report for the North America Regional Program of the Rockefeller Foundation. Rubén Puentes invited me to write the report, in collaboration with Peggy Levitt and Rubén Silié. Ginetta Candelario offered useful suggestions for revision.

Deepak Lamba-Nieves, Sergio Marxuach, and Miguel Soto-Class of the Center for the New Economy in San Juan encouraged me to initiate fieldwork on remittances in Puerto Rico, the topic of chapter 10. Their recommendations on an earlier draft of my report were very welcome. I could not have completed the project without the assistance of my wife, Diana Johnson, as well as Sonia Castro, Vivianna de Jesús, Karin Weyland, and Carlos Rutiner. In addition, my daughter, Patricia Duany, helped to enter the results of the survey into a computer database. Douglas S. Massey made helpful comments and authorized the adaptation of the survey instrument designed by the Latin American Migration Project at Princeton University. João Felipe Gonçalves invited me to discuss my findings at the Graduate Workshop on the Anthropology of Latin America and the Caribbean at the University of Chicago. I am grateful for the suggestions made by Emilia Arellano, Stephan Palmié, Agnes Lugo-Ortiz, João Felipe Gonçalves, and other workshop participants. Thanks to Katharine Donato and Douglas S. Massey for commenting on a later version of my paper.

The late Brunilda (Wiwa) Santos de Álvarez helped me obtain financial information about remittances in Puerto Rico. Wiwa was a loyal, gentle, humorous, and generous friend and will be missed dearly. As I wrote these acknowledgments, I was saddened by the news that Andrzej Dembicz had passed away. He was a dear friend, colleague, teacher, researcher, and tireless organizer of academic events. I will also miss the lively conversations I had with my late uncle, Andrés Blanco, every time I visited my relatives in Havana. I greatly admired my uncle's kindness, modesty, and commitment to his family.

At the University of North Carolina Press, Elaine Maisner has been an enthusiastic supporter for many years. I appreciate her constructive criticisms to improve the text. Paula Wald helped me prepare and edit the manuscript for publication. Alex Martin carefully and expertly copyedited the manuscript. In addition, two anonymous reviewers provided many incisive observations.

Countless colleagues and friends have expressed their solidarity with my work, including Luis Agraít, Silvia Álvarez-Curbelo, Uva de Aragón, Elizabeth Aranda, Diana Ariza, Jossianna Arroyo, César Ayala, Carmen Centeno, José A. Cobas, Jeffrey Colón, Grace Dávila, Jorge Durand, Damián J. Fernández, Myrna García-Calderón, Lawrence La Fountain–Stokes, Luis Martínez-Fernández, Yolanda Martínez–San Miguel, Félix V. Matos-Rodríguez, Nancy Morris, Nilda Navarro, Emilio Pantojas-García, Victoria Párraga, Silvia Pedraza, Vilma Quintana, César A. Rey, Carmen Haydée Rivera, Raquel Z. Rivera, Eliana Rivero, Yeidy Rivero, Irizelma Robles, Carlos Rodríguez-Vidal, Raquel Romberg, Ivette Romero-Cesáreo, María Sandoval, Betty Sasaki, Patricia Silver, Ninna Nyberg Sørensen, Marian Z. Sugano, Maura Toro-Morn, and Silvio Torres-Saillant.

As usual, I am happy to acknowledge the daily sustenance of my wife Diana, my daughter Patricia, and my son Jorge Andrés. My brothers and sisters — Rafael, Lourdes, Luis, Raúl, and María Caridad — deserve special mention for always being there. I dedicate this book to my dear cousins Lourdes Blanco Páez, who lives in Havana, Cuba, and Catina Suárez Roscoe, who lives in Julian, North Carolina. Although they have not seen each other for five decades, they both bring home to me the significance of transnational family ties as a source of emotional strength. I am glad that they are now in touch through Facebook, but I hope they will soon meet each other again in person.

Abbreviations

BUMIDOM	Bureau pour le Développement des Migrations Intéressant les Départements d'Outre-Mer
CANF	Cuban American National Foundation
COMECON	Council for Mutual Economic Assistance
DANR	Dominican American National Roundtable
FIU	Florida International University
GDP	gross domestic product
IADB	Inter-American Development Bank
INS	Immigration and Naturalization Service
IRCA	Immigration Reform and Control Act
LAMP	Latin American Migration Project
MMP	Mexican Migration Project
MODEBO	Movimiento para el Desarrollo de Boca Canasta
PIP	Partido Independentista Puertorriqueño
PLD	Partido de la Liberación Dominicana
PNP	Partido Nuevo Progresista
PPD	Partido Popular Democrático
PRC	Partido Revolucionario Cubano
PRD	Partido Revolucionario Dominicano
PRE	*permiso de residencia en el exterior*
PRFAA	Puerto Rico Federal Affairs Administration
PRLDEF	Puerto Rican Legal Defense and Education Fund
PRSC	Partido Reformista Social Cristiano
SOPROVIS	Sociedad Progresista de Villa Sombrero

BLURRED BORDERS

Introduction

Crossing Borders and Boundaries
in the Hispanic Caribbean

During the 1990s *border* became a buzzword in the social sciences and the humanities, including anthropology, sociology, history, literary criticism, and cultural studies. Scholars were increasingly disenchanted with territorially grounded concepts of nation, state, citizenship, identity, and language, which have long dominated discussions about migration. In turn, the expansion of migrant, refugee, exile, and other displaced populations dramatized the limitations of state control and surveillance over citizens. As Hastings Donnan and Thomas Wilson (1999: 4) point out, "the concept of transnationalism, which has become central to many interpretations of post-modernity, has as one of its principal referents international borders, which mark off one state from another and which sometimes, but not as often as many people seem to suppose, set off one nation from another."

In a now classic essay, Michael Kearney (1991) differentiated "borders" from "boundaries" in the contemporary world. For him, borders are the often hybrid geographic and cultural zones between nations, while boundaries are the legal spatial delimitations of states. Thus, the borders and boundaries of nation-states often do not correspond neatly to each other. In particular, the crisscrossing of cultural borders and legal boundaries by migrants disturbs the conventional dichotomy between "us" and "them." As Kearney writes, "'transnationalism' implies a blurring, or perhaps better said, a reordering of the binary cultural, social, and epistemological distinctions of the modern period" (55). Moreover, "peoples that span national borders are ambiguous in that they in some ways partake of both nations and in other ways partake of neither" (52). It is this ambiguity — or "bifocality" — of transnational migrants from the Spanish-speaking Caribbean that I am primarily interested in exploring in this book.

Building on the work of several authors, Steven Vertovec (2009: 67–68) employs the term *bifocality* to allude to the dual frame of reference through which expatriates constantly compare their home and host countries. Many migrants routinely engage in activities and relationships that bind them to both "here" and "there" in their everyday lives. Expatriates may remain attached to their places of origin even as they settle down in their new domiciles. Such bifocality not only structures the experiences of first-generation migrants but may also affect their children and grandchildren, often raised in extended transnational households. In Kearney's terms, the descendants of transnational migrants may continue to inhabit cultural borders. Yet they may never cross the legal boundaries between their ancestral homelands and current places of residence.

In this introduction, I present two of the basic concepts used throughout this book: diaspora and transnationalism. Then I explain why I have chosen to compare the Cuban, Dominican, and Puerto Rican diasporas and their transnational experiences. Furthermore, I formulate the thesis of this book, namely, that migrants' attachments to their home countries depend largely on the nature of their states' relationship to the host states. Next I argue that studying transnationalism requires new approaches to document the enduring connections between sending and receiving communities. Finally, I reflect on how my own diasporic condition as the child of Cuban exiles to Puerto Rico has shaped my intellectual project.

Defining Diaspora

Migration studies have recently experienced a semantic explosion of key terms such as *diaspora*, *transnationalism*, *exile*, and *exodus*. As the Puerto Rican cultural critic Juan Flores (2008: 15) suggests, the concept of diaspora evokes a wide range of connotations, including movement, travel, displacement, dislocation, uprooting, resettlement, hybridity, and nomadism. The proliferation of meanings, according to Rogers Brubaker (2005), has led to a "diaspora diaspora" since the early 1990s, and the term is now applied to practically any migrant group. Several scholars, such as James Clifford (1994), Robin Cohen (1997), William Safran (1991), and Khachig Tölölyan (1991), have attempted to restrain, classify, and interpret diasporas. For instance, the classical diasporas (such as the Jews, Armenians, and Greeks of antiquity) all shared collective memories and myths about the homeland; a commitment to preserve or recover it; a strong ethnic group consciousness; and a troubled relationship with their host societies.

I agree with Brubaker and Flores that it is futile to enumerate the "essential" characteristics of diasporas and then determine whether they apply to different moments and places. Instead, it might be more useful to recall the etymological origins of the Greek words *dia*, meaning "through" or "across space," and *speirein*, meaning "to sow or to scatter." Although the term *diaspora* originally referred to the Jewish exile in Babylon beginning in 586 B.C., it has broadened considerably over time. Accordingly, *Merriam-Webster's Online Dictionary* (2009) defines *diaspora* as "the movement, migration, or scattering of a people away from an ancestral homeland."

This definition of *diaspora* encompasses groups and periods as diverse as ancient Jews, African slaves, and modern-day Palestinians. It also leaves open the questions of how diasporas originate, develop, relate to their homelands, and incorporate into their new societies. Furthermore, it invites comparative analysis of the causes, forms, and consequences of the scattering of people. Finally, it overlaps substantially with current definitions of *transnationalism*, to be discussed in more detail in chapter 1, as the creation and maintenance of multiple social ties across borders and boundaries.

For now, it seems sufficient to anticipate that diasporas often sustain strong social, economic, cultural, political, and emotional bonds to their countries of origin. The enduring links to a real or putative homeland through collective memories, myths, and rituals constitute one of the basic criteria for most definitions of diaspora (Brubaker 2005; Cohen 1997; Vertovec 2009). The concepts of diaspora and transnationalism undermine the notion of the nation-state as the "natural" container of the physical and cultural spaces in which people lead their daily lives. Instead, many people — especially transnational migrants — are part of broader social networks across nations.

Three Case Studies

Of the three Spanish-speaking countries of the Caribbean islands, the Dominican Republic has sustained the most attention from transnational migration scholars. Many authors have regarded Cuba and Puerto Rico as anomalies in contemporary population movements, because Cuba is socialist and Puerto Rico remains a colony. Yet I argue throughout this book that the insular Hispanic Caribbean can profitably be visualized through a transnational lens, highlighting common patterns as well as the peculiarities of each case.

To begin with, the justification for comparing these countries is grounded in geographic and historical criteria: they are all located in the Greater Antilles and were conquered by Spain after 1492. These countries were subjected to more than three centuries of uninterrupted Spanish colonialism, which imposed the Spanish language and Catholic religion on local populations. In turn, these populations were largely the product of the mixture among indigenous groups (especially Tainos), Spanish immigrants, and African slaves. As Spain lost its American empire in the nineteenth century, the United States expanded its economic, political, and military power in the Caribbean. During the first third of the twentieth century, Cuba, Puerto Rico, and the Dominican Republic consolidated their primary economic role as sugar exporters for the U.S. consumer market. During the second half of the century, all three countries expelled large portions of their populations to the United States. Smaller numbers of Cubans and Dominicans also moved to Puerto Rico and other Caribbean, Latin American, and European countries. Thus began the Hispanic Caribbean diasporas, the subject of this book. I provide the following historical sketches with general readers in mind; those already familiar with the region will find more specialized sources in the Works Cited list.

Within Latin America and the Caribbean, Cuba has traditionally been deemed exceptional. Given its strategic location between the New and Old Worlds, and between the Northern and Southern Hemispheres, Cuba has long enjoyed a privileged position in international affairs, disproportionate to its land mass and population size (Grenier and Pérez 2003; Louis Pérez 1999). During the sixteenth century, Havana became one of the leading shipping and trading entrepôts of the Americas, especially after the *flota* system established in 1566 required all Spanish ships to rendezvous in that port. Because of Cuba's commercial and military significance, the Spanish Crown hailed it as the "key to the New World and rampart of the West Indies." Cuba and Puerto Rico were Spain's two remaining colonies in the Americas. Between 1868 and 1878, Cuban insurrectionists waged the Ten Years' War of liberation from Spain, which ended in a truce, only to reemerge in a second war of independence in 1895–98.

On June 22, 1898, the United States invaded Cuba shortly after the USS *Maine* exploded in Havana harbor, thus beginning a "splendid little war" that lasted merely three months (the so-called Spanish-American War). The United States established a military government in Cuba between 1898 and 1902, when the island became formally independent. However, the infamous Platt Amendment to the Cuban constitution allowed the United States to intervene in Cuban affairs to protect U.S. interests. Between 1906 and 1909, U.S. troops occupied the island to prevent a civil war and returned in 1912 to quell an Afro-Cuban rebellion against the local government. In effect, the Cuban republic became a protectorate of the United States, until the Platt Amendment was repealed in 1934.

After a popular uprising against the dictator Gerardo Machado, a reformist government was briefly in power between 1933 and 1934. Strongman Fulgencio Batista ruled Cuba indirectly from 1935 until he was elected president in 1940. A brief democratic interlude followed between 1940 and 1952, during which time a new constitution was promulgated. On March 10, 1952, Batista led a coup d'état that returned Cuba to military rule. On July 26, 1953, Fidel Castro launched a guerrilla movement that took power on January 1, 1959 (see Louis Pérez 2006 [1988]). The Cuban Revolution, which Castro declared to be socialist and Marxist-Leninist in 1961, has provoked the exodus of nearly 1.2 million Cubans to the United States and Puerto Rico, and thousands more to other countries, over the past five decades.

Since the early 1990s, the Dominican Republic has been touted as a classic example of transnationalism. The Dominican Republic shares the island of Hispaniola with Haiti (only one other Caribbean island is shared by Saint Martin and Sint Maarten). Although Hispaniola was the original seat of Spanish colonization in the Americas, the island quickly lost its importance to the mainland viceroyalties of Mexico and Peru in the sixteenth century. During the seventeenth century, the French settled the western third of the island, which eventually became Saint-Domingue and later Haiti after the 1795–1804 revolution. The Spanish colony, known as Santo Domingo, became independent from Spain in 1821 but was occupied by Haiti between 1822 and 1844. It returned to Spanish rule in 1861. The Dominican Republic gained its second independence from Spain in 1865.

The U.S. government made several attempts to annex the Dominican Republic beginning in the mid-nineteenth century. Although these attempts failed, the United States became the dominant external power in the Dominican Republic during the twentieth century. The U.S. government established a customs receivership in the Dominican Republic between 1905 and 1941; occupied the country between 1916 and 1924; bolstered the dictator Rafael Trujillo between 1930 and 1961; and invaded the country again between 1965 and 1966. Since then, the volume of Dominican migrants to the United States and Puerto Rico swelled to 1.2 million, while Spain and other countries received thousands more. The Dominican Republic thus illustrates the rise of mass migration in the context of U.S. hegemony. The Dominican Republic might be characterized as a neocolonial or "unsovereign state" due to its extreme dependence on U.S. markets, investment, and aid (Black 1986).

Because of Puerto Rico's continued colonial relation to the United States, the island is often judged as an anomaly in a postcolonial world. For most of the period between 1493 and 1898, the island was an isolated military outpost of the Spanish empire. As one of Spain's last overseas possessions, Puerto Rico (along with Cuba) experienced the longest period of Hispanic influence in the New World. On July 25, 1898, however, U.S. troops invaded the island during the Spanish-Cuban-American War. They have retained a strong presence there ever since.

In 1901 the U.S. Supreme Court paradoxically defined Puerto Rico as "foreign to the United States in a domestic sense," neither a state of the union nor an independent country (Burnett and Marshall 2001). The Court later ruled that the island was an "unincorporated territory" "belonging to . . . but not a part of" the United States, meaning that Congress would determine which parts of the U.S. Constitution applied to the island. In 1904 the Court declared that Puerto Ricans were not "aliens" for immigration purposes and could not be denied entry into the U.S. mainland (Erman 2008). In 1917 Congress granted U.S. citizenship to all persons born on the island but did not extend to them all constitutional rights and obligations, such as having congressional representation or paying federal income taxes.

In 1952 Puerto Rico became a U.S. commonwealth (or Estado Libre Asociado) with limited autonomy over local matters, such as taxation, education, health, housing, culture, and language. Still, the federal government retained jurisdiction in most state affairs, including citizenship, immigration, customs, defense, currency, transportation, communications, foreign trade, and diplomacy. By most accounts, Puerto Rico remains a colony because it lacks sovereignty and effective representation in the federal government. (Like the District of Columbia and other territories such as Guam and the U.S. Virgin Islands, Puerto Rico elects a delegate — called, in Puerto Rico's case, a "resident commissioner" — to the U.S. House of Representatives, but such delegates can vote only in committee.) The island's political status has facilitated the relocation of nearly 1.8 million persons to the United States since 1898. Today, more than half of all persons of Puerto Rican origin live outside the island. At the same time, 8.1 percent of Puerto Rico's population was born abroad, especially in the United States, the Dominican Republic, and Cuba.

My Thesis

Based on these three case studies, I argue that the form, frequency, and intensity of transnationalism largely hinges on the nature of the relationship between sending and receiving countries.[1] In particular, the tight political, economic, and cultural ties between the United States and the Spanish-speaking countries of the Caribbean islands forged at least since the early twentieth century nurtured growing diasporas since the midcentury. The United States has dominated all the nations of the Caribbean (as well as Central America) during the long "American century." But Cuba, the Dominican Republic, and Puerto Rico, along with Panama and Mexico, have borne the brunt of U.S. military interventions, political interference, economic hegemony, and cultural penetration. Today, the three nations of the Spanish-speaking Caribbean islands exemplify the full range of colonial, neocolonial, and postcolonial ties with the United States.

To conceptualize the relationship between the United States and the insular Hispanic Caribbean, I draw on Peggy Levitt and Nina Glick Schiller's (2004) threefold classification of migrant-sending states. The most common is the "strategically selective state," which encourages expatriates' engagement with the home country but does not grant them citizenship rights or allow their full political participation in national affairs. Examples of this stance include Haiti and Barbados. A second type is the "transnational nation-state," which defines its migrants as long-distance members, grants them dual citizenship, and incorporates them as an integral part of public policies. The Dominican Republic, El Salvador, and Mexico illustrate this category. The third and least common type is the "disinterested and denouncing state," which treats émigrés as if they no longer belonged to their homeland, often considering them suspicious and even traitors. Cuba, the former Czechoslovakia, and Vietnam (between 1975 and 1994) exemplify the exclusion of expatriates for political reasons during the Cold War.

A fourth type of state, which I elaborate throughout this book, is the "transnational colonial state." This category includes dependent territories with large migrant populations in metropolitan countries and which continue to regard them as part of the colonial nation. Although residents of the dependent territory and its metropole share the same citizenship, the former are often treated as foreigners in the "mother country." In this scenario, the legal boundaries between sending and receiving countries are blurred, while their cultural borders remain intractable to those who move back and forth. Puerto Ricans in the United States and Antilleans in the Netherlands are cases in point.

Although a transnational colonial state lacks sovereignty, it extends its reach to the metropolitan state. At the same time, it must follow metropolitan laws and regulations about immigration, citizenship rights, social benefits, and other public policies. This insider/outsider logic differentiates transnational colonial states such as Puerto Rico from independent ones such as the Dominican Republic. It also underlines the basic analogies among the overseas territories of the United Kingdom, France, the Netherlands, and the United States. For example, all citizens of the dependent Caribbean share the right of abode, as well as access to welfare and social rights, in their metropolitan countries. Not surprisingly, migration rates from nonsovereign territories are much higher than from independent states (see Cervantes-Rodríguez, Grosfoguel, and Mielants 2009; Clegg and Pantojas-García 2009; de Jong and Krujit 2005).

Each migrant-sending state in the Spanish-speaking Caribbean has developed a distinctive relation with the United States. As a result, migrants from each country have different legal statuses on arrival in the country of settlement. During the Cold War, the U.S. government defined Cubans as refugees from communism and privileged them over other groups. In contrast, the U.S. government classifies most Dominicans as economic migrants and denies entry to many of them, creating a large pool of undocumented immigrants. As U.S. citizens, Puerto Ricans enjoy free access to the United States and can fully exercise their political rights when they migrate. In this book, I appraise the long-term repercussions of the legal status of Cubans, Dominicans, and Puerto Ricans in the United States, as well as in Puerto Rico, a secondary destination for Dominicans and Cubans.

To develop my thesis, I highlight key moments and locations of transnational migration from the Spanish-speaking Caribbean islands. I first compare the historical origins and contemporary situation of the Hispanic Caribbean diasporas. Then I examine each case separately, establishing the multiple connections among the diasporic experiences of the three islands.

I scrutinize major features of each transnational flow, including the rise of Puerto Rican migration after World War II and its current reorientation toward Florida; the postrevolutionary exodus from Cuba, particularly since the disappearance of the Soviet Union in 1991; and the large-scale displacement of Dominicans to the United States and Puerto Rico after 1961. I end by contrasting migrant remittances to the Dominican Republic and Puerto Rico at the beginning of the twenty-first century.

Researching Transnationalism

Comparing the Cuban, Dominican, and Puerto Rican diasporas requires abandoning what some scholars have called "methodological nationalism" — the tendency to equate society with the nation-state. In an illuminating essay, Andreas Wimmer and Nina Glick Schiller (2002) have questioned whether the nation-state is the natural unit of the modern world and whether social processes such as migration take place only within its boundaries. Wimmer and Glick Schiller propose that migration studies take not the nation-state but transnational communities in various countries as their main objects of analysis. Methodologically, transnationalism calls for multisited ethnographies and other forms of fieldwork in the points of origin and destination, as well as for the comparison of different groups, localities, and periods (see George Marcus 1995).

More recently, Levitt and Glick Schiller (2004) have insisted that studies of transnationalism should focus, first, on the connections between those who migrate and those who stay behind. Second, researchers should approach transnational practices as historical processes that vary according to cycles, events, and crises. Finally, scholars should use qualitative techniques such as participant observation and intensive interviewing to document migrants' cultural repertoires, identities, and interactions. I follow this methodological advice whenever possible.

Unfortunately, single-case ethnographies make it difficult to generalize about transnational practices. Hence, scholars have extensively used cross-sectional surveys, comparing groups of different national origins during the same period (see, for example, Orozco et al. 2005; Portes, Escobar, and Arana 2009; Portes, Haller, and Guarnizo 2002; Waldinger 2007). This research strategy has helped determine the magnitude, frequency, variation, and intensity of activities across international boundaries, such as membership in political parties, business enterprises, remittances, telephone com-

munication, and travel to the country of origin. However, most of the literature lacks a longitudinal perspective to spell out how each of these activities
unfolds over time. Moreover, the results of the studies are often inconsistent
because they draw on different operational definitions, sampling frames, instruments, and analytical units, such as individuals, communities, regions,
and even nations.

In this book, I combine multiple sources of information on migration
from the Spanish-speaking countries of the Caribbean islands to the United
States and Puerto Rico. First, I often consult official statistics published by
the U.S. Census Bureau, the U.S. Citizenship and Immigration Services, the
U.S. Coast Guard, and other government agencies, to quantify the volume
and characteristics of Cuban, Dominican, and Puerto Rican immigrants.
Second, I cite the results of my own ethnographic fieldwork and survey
research with Hispanic Caribbean communities in the United States and
Puerto Rico to assess their ties with their countries of origin. Third, I have
scanned the historical archives of the Puerto Rican diaspora at the Centro de
Estudios Puertorriqueños at Hunter College, City University of New York,
as well as the Fundación Luis Muñoz Marín in Trujillo Alto, Puerto Rico.
Fourth, I have benefited from the comparative work of other scholars, especially those affiliated with the Latin American Migration Project (LAMP) at
Princeton University and the University of Guadalajara. Finally, I have sometimes drawn on my experiences as a "Cuba-Rican" to interpret the personal
meaning of transnational lives.

Becoming Cuba-Rican

I was born in Havana in January 1957, but left Cuba with my mother and
older brother on December 26, 1960.[2] My parents' momentous decision to
leave the island has always intrigued me, and I still do not understand it
fully. When the Cuban Revolution triumphed on January 1, 1959, my father
was temporarily working as a television director in Costa Rica. Meanwhile,
I remained in Cuba with my mother and brother. My father went back to
Havana sometime thereafter but could not find a job, so he had to move
again, this time to Panama. Among other reasons, he felt displaced by the
swift nationalization of the main Cuban television station, CMQ, where he
had worked before. My mother, who then sympathized with the Revolution
like most of her family, stayed on until she followed my father, together
with my grandmother, who returned to Cuba after three months. My young

mother must have been torn by the choice of keeping her marriage together or staying in her home country with her relatives.

Initially, we settled in Panama but moved on to Puerto Rico in 1966. I remember looking at a map of the Caribbean and wondering why on earth we were going there; I felt completely Panamanian by then. My growing family (I had two more siblings now) relocated in San Juan, where my father got a job producing and directing television programs, including *telenovelas* and game shows. Also, my *padrinos* (godparents) were living there, as were two of my parents' cousins on both sides of the family. I spent the rest of my childhood and adolescence in the San Juan metropolitan area. After graduating from high school, I continued my undergraduate and graduate education in the United States. After I finished my doctoral studies, I returned to Puerto Rico and started a full-time teaching career. I later worked for a year in Florida. Since 1988, I have lived continuously in Puerto Rico, with short absences abroad related to my academic career.

In many ways, my family's experience is typical of the Cuban diaspora to Puerto Rico. We left Cuba during the first stage of the postrevolutionary exodus (the so-called Golden Exiles).[3] My father's surname derives from Irish migrants to Santiago de Cuba in the late seventeenth century, while my mother's family, which lived mostly in Havana, was primarily of Spanish origin, especially from the Canary Islands and Galicia. My parents' occupations mirrored the concentration of Cuban exiles in the middle and upper levels of trade, communication, and other service sectors of the Puerto Rican economy (see Cobas and Duany 1997). My father became programming director at one of Puerto Rico's leading television stations, until he lost his job after a corporate takeover and had to start again in Ecuador, where he died years later. My mother worked as a cosmetics sales clerk in a department store, an itinerant clothing seller, a beautician, and an insurance agent (although she had been a schoolteacher in Cuba, she never practiced her profession in Puerto Rico).

Since I was very young, I was troubled by the constant question, "Where are you from?" I usually answered, "I was born in Cuba, but grew up in Puerto Rico." But that answer never settled which country I felt most attached to, an issue that became periodically urgent, as when Puerto Rico's national team faced Cuba's in basketball or baseball competitions. I must confess that I have to think twice when I see the flags of the two countries, with their identical layout and inverted colors, before deciding which is which. As a member of the 1.5 generation of immigrants (or perhaps 1.75, as the Cuban American sociologist Rubén G. Rumbaut would have it), my position is quite precarious.[4] If Cuba plays against Puerto Rico, I will root for the Puerto Rican team. But when Cuba faces the United States in international sports, I will usually side with the Cuban team.

One way I tried to solve the puzzle of my divided loyalties was by visiting Cuba since the early 1980s, first as part of organized groups,[5] then as a participant in academic conferences, and lately as an ordinary member of the "Cuban community abroad," as I took my wife, daughter, and son to meet my extended family in Cuba. Since 1981 I have returned more than a dozen times (I have lost track of the exact count) to Havana and once to Santiago, the city of my father's birth. My goal was to reconnect with my uncle, aunts, and cousins, as well as to better understand contemporary Cuban society and its ongoing exodus, including that of my paternal aunt and four of my cousins who left in the 1990s. Every time I have been back to Cuba I have felt differently. At first I felt very much at home, almost like a prodigal son, easily reconciled with my relatives on the island, especially on my mother's side. More recently, I have grown more distant from Cuba and increasingly convinced that I could not live anywhere but in Puerto Rico, where I have spent most of my life and where I have raised my own children. I now prefer to say that "I live in Puerto Rico, but my parents came from Cuba." Sometimes I will declare that I am Cuba-Rican,[6] rather than Cuban American, since I have never lived continuously for an extended period in the United States, even though I have been a U.S. citizen since 1985.

My diasporic condition has undoubtedly shaped my research on migration from the Spanish-speaking Caribbean. In 1983 I began to study Cuban exiles in San Juan for my doctoral dissertation. In 1987 my first postdoctoral research project focused on Dominican migration to Puerto Rico. In 1993 I conducted a field study of Dominican transnationalism in New York City. Over the past decade and a half, most of my intellectual efforts have dwelt on the Puerto Rican diaspora in the United States. Despite the shifting terminology and objects of study, I have been largely concerned with how massive population displacements impact personal and collective identities.

I hope this autobiographical disclosure will show more clearly the connections between my life history and those of many others who have left their countries of origin in the Caribbean over the last six decades. As C. Wright Mills (2000 [1960]) put it so well, capturing the intersections between biography and history is one of the hallmarks of the sociological imagination. As an anthropologist, I am primarily interested in how my experiences resonate with those of other people like myself.

I completed my doctoral dissertation in 1985, after a year and a half of fieldwork with Cubans in Puerto Rico. At the time, I thought of my work as an autoethnography, in the sense that I went back "home" to study "my people," not an exotic Other. It was clearly an autobiographical intellectual project, as I struggled to understand the community in which I had grown up but to which I no longer belonged. I felt estranged from older exiles who seemed fixed on recuperating *la Cuba del ayer* ("the Cuba of yesterday," as they often referred to prerevolutionary society). Because I was too young to remember anything about my childhood in Cuba, I had no emotional investment in that period, except through my parents' memories. Still, I retained many Cuban friends and relatives in Puerto Rico and the United States.

As I approached this sensitive issue, I sought to abandon the popular myth of the Golden Exiles — the almost instantaneous economic success of Cubans in San Juan as well as in Miami — and to explain their mode of incorporation, cultural adaptation, and ambivalent relationship with Puerto Rican society. Writing my dissertation, it was difficult to assume a "neutral" tone in describing the Cuban community in Puerto Rico, a tone that was neither celebratory nor condemnatory. It was even more difficult to insert myself in a storyline dominated by a social scientific perspective in the third person.

Placing Myself in the Narrative

Writing about Puerto Rican national identity, I am often painfully aware that I am not one of the island's native sons. My foreign birth, coupled with long-time residence in Puerto Rico, gives me an odd status somewhere between stranger and near-native. I have often felt uneasy straddling this outsider/insider dichotomy, as when I am called a "Puerto Rican sociologist" (who is neither Puerto Rican nor a sociologist, but rather an anthropologist). But being called a "Cuban-born anthropologist" does not entirely resolve the problem either. This issue emerged sharply in a February 2004 interview with a Puerto Rican graduate student, Verónica Toro Ortiz, who translated several chapters of my book, *The Puerto Rican Nation on the Move* (Duany 2002), into Spanish. Toward the end of our long and intense conversation, Toro Ortiz asked me about the use of the first person in my writing. Here is a passage from my response (translated from the Spanish original):

I've realized, in the course of writing this book, among other things, that although I generally use the third person, when I'm going to introduce myself as part of the text, as part of the environment I'm observing, then I use the first person and I make the distinction, and that has to do partly with my own biography. To give you an example, a political science professor, Ángel Israel Rivera, told me one day in the hallway: "I'm glad that you're now saying, 'we Puerto Ricans.'" And it's difficult for me to say that, because I don't feel totally Puerto Rican, since I was born in Cuba, although I grew up here. Nor do I feel very comfortable saying "we Cubans." Therefore, given that duality, that ambiguity, I normally don't say one thing or another. I resort to the third person: Cubans do this and say that, as well as Puerto Ricans. Every now and then, I use "we" when I feel part of what I'm writing. Perhaps that appears more explicitly when you're translating, the way in which sometimes I'd rather remain on the margins and don't place myself there.

Let me add a personal comment on language and identity. Someone once asked when I first "became" bilingual. I responded that my parents sent me to an all-English missionary school in the Panama Canal Zone during my third grade. Initially, I could not understand most of what was taught, except for Spanish class. But that year forced me to learn English quickly to survive academically. Moreover, I was often taken for an American because of my pale skin, blue eyes, and light hair color, and many of my classmates were children of U.S. military personnel stationed in Panama. I would try to darken my hair by dampening it with water, combing it constantly, and repeating in front of the mirror, "I don't want to be a gringo." Anti-Americanism was entrenched in Panama City during my childhood years.

After moving to Puerto Rico, I was again placed in an all-English seventh-grade group called "Continental" — referring to the children of American businesspeople on the island — because I did well in the English entrance exam. I did not like that experience, as I felt isolated from Spanish-speaking students in other classrooms. Again, many thought I was American because of my physical appearance and I was commonly associated with the "gringos." Even today, people routinely mistake me for an American, especially in public places with many U.S. tourists, such as airports, restaurants, and hotels. "But you don't look Puerto Rican," I am frequently told, and when I retort that I was born in Cuba, I may hear the rebuttal, "You don't look

Cuban either." To which I may reply rhetorically, "What does a Puerto Rican (or a Cuban) look like?" I have often pondered the irony of "looking American" while living in three of the countries where that attribution is most problematic (Cuba, Panama, and Puerto Rico), because of the long history of U.S. intervention in the Caribbean region.

A decade of study in U.S. universities gave me the opportunity to develop fluency in the English language, to the point that I feel almost (though not quite) as comfortable writing in English as in Spanish. But language is a minefield for cultural politics because of Puerto Rico's colonial relation with the United States, and the unequal status of Spanish and English. As I remarked in my interview with Toro Ortiz (cited above),

> This is the first question I'm always asked . . . "Why did you write
> this book in English?" One always feels under attack and I always
> think, noting the differences, of the case of [the noted Puerto Rican
> writer] Rosario Ferré, who decided to write a book in Spanish and
> rewrite it in English, and she's still criticized for it. When my book
> is published in Spanish, I think the audience will be similar [to the
> original one]; we'll see how the translation affects the socioeconomic
> and educational composition of the audience. I think that it'll be more
> self-reflexive; for example, some things in the English version are
> explained thoroughly, which won't be necessary in Spanish [because
> most of my readers will be Puerto Rican].

Being born in Cuba, raised in Panama and Puerto Rico, and living on and off in the United States have left an indelible imprint. One result of these experiences has been the shuttling between Spanish and English throughout my life. Although Spanish has always been the "native" language I speak at home, I now read and write in English every day. Spanish is the primary medium for my most intimate thoughts and feelings, while English is a more academic and professional mode of expression for me. I suppose this linguistic split is part of many migrants' lives, as well as a sign of increasing cultural hybridity. In an interview with the newspaper *El Nuevo Día*, I once told the Puerto Rican literary critic Carmen Dolores Hernández that being an immigrant had led me inexorably to probe my own identity and that of others, especially when the sources of identity are fragmented. Returning to Cuba, if only infrequently and briefly, has helped me regain my sense of wholeness and connectedness to my childhood past, distant homeland, and family dispersed throughout Cuba, the United States, Puerto Rico, Panama, Chile, Spain, Switzerland, Germany, and Russia.

My ailing mother's last letter to her older brother, Andrés, in Cuba is dated December 31, 1994, more than thirty-four years after we left Havana. I still keep a copy of that letter in my laptop computer. Because she could not write easily anymore, my mother dictated the following sentence to me (in Spanish): "Thank God, Jorge was able to travel to Cuba, which was a great dream of his, and that way we'll have the opportunity to see each other through him." When my mother passed away less than four months later, on April 11, 1995, I felt like I had become the main liaison between my relatives in Cuba and abroad — that they somehow had to "see each other" through me, that it was now my turn to repair the family ties that were ruptured as a consequence of the Cuban Revolution five decades ago. It is a great burden, to have inherited my mother's role as a safe keeper of those fragile links, which must continually be renewed across generations, long distances, and political differences.

Like many transnational migrants I have met throughout my research, I find it indispensable to maintain emotional, family, and cultural connections with my country of birth. Going back to Cuba every so often is a way of not burning the bridges back "home." Even though I might never go back to live there again, I would like to claim, with the exiled poet Heberto Padilla, that I have always lived in Cuba, if only in my mind.[7] Yet I have lived most of my life in Puerto Rico and cannot be anything but Cuba-Rican. Studying transnational migration has forced me to ponder how my own experiences may reverberate with ordinary people who blur borders in their daily lives. This book is an academic attempt to answer that very personal question, "Where are you from?"

Rethinking Transnationalism

Conceptual, Theoretical, and Practical Problems

In the introduction, I distinguished analytically between a nation's borders and boundaries. I also pointed out that diasporas usually remain connected to their nations of origin over long periods of time. As I stress in this chapter, transnationalism can undermine the state's legal definition of boundaries by blurring cultural borders.[1] The identities of many diasporic peoples (including my own) cannot be contained within a single nation-state, nor can their practices and discourses be completely understood from a well-bounded political, territorial, or linguistic perspective.

Since the 1990s transnationalism has spurred a minor academic industry among migration scholars, with an increasing number of books, dissertations, anthologies, journal issues, articles, conferences, workshops, courses, and research centers devoted to its study. Together with the closely related concept of diaspora, transnationalism has captured the imagination of social scientists and humanists. However, persistent problems plague the field of transnationalism, including the operational definition of the concept; the classification of various types; the explanation of its causes and consequences; its alleged novelty; its relationship with assimilation; and its future beyond the first generation of immigrants. In particular, scholars have engaged in lively debates as to whether Puerto Rico, Cuba, and the Dominican Republic are exemplars of transnationalism.

This chapter delves into some of the main issues in the study of transnationalism. This exercise will set the stage for the comparative analysis of Cubans, Dominicans, and Puerto Ricans in the United States and Puerto Rico. Focusing on three very different diasporas from the same region (the

Hispanic Caribbean) and to the same countries (the United States and Puerto Rico) reveals both the underlying parallels and range of variation in contemporary transnationalism. Preexisting ties between sending and receiving countries, whether colonial, neocolonial, or postcolonial, shape the size, composition, settlement patterns, and incorporation of migrant flows. A comparative transnational perspective entails suspending the illusion that the nation-state can entirely encapsulate a citizen's thoughts, loyalties, and actions.

A Brief Intellectual Genealogy

In 1916 the U.S. journalist Randolph Bourne coined the expression "transnational America" to challenge the myth of the melting pot, which justified the assimilation of immigrants into Anglo-Saxon culture. Instead, Bourne posited that newer European groups (such as Germans, Scandinavians, and Poles) in the United States retained vigorous connections to their homelands, rather than becoming unhyphenated Americans. He then argued that the United States should be more cosmopolitan in accommodating ethnic groups with origins other than Anglo-Saxon. Bourne's essay was a passionate plea for cultural pluralism, which later writers would elaborate under the banner of multiculturalism.

Unfortunately, the term *transnationalism* fell out of common and academic use for decades, while the assimilation model prevailed in migration studies, at least in the United States. In the 1950s economists began to write about "multinational" and later "transnational" corporations simultaneously operating in several countries, usually headquartered in industrialized North America, Western Europe, and Japan. During the 1970s scholars in the field of international relations extended the term *transnationalism* to nongovernmental organizations that cut across boundaries between countries (Levitt and Waters 2002: 7). By the 1980s social scientists widened the concept to groups that move across international boundaries yet remain attached to their home communities (Glick Schiller, Basch, and Szanton Blanc 1995). When applied to migrants rather than corporations, transnationalism suggests that people may transgress borders and boundaries, inhabiting the interstitial social spaces between them; hence such migrants have been called "borderless people" (Michael Peter Smith 1994).

The earliest and most influential formulation of the transnational migration paradigm was in the volume edited by Nina Glick Schiller, Linda Basch, and Cristina Blanc-Szanton, *Towards a Transnational Perspective on Migration* (1992). Shortly thereafter, their coauthored work, *Nations Unbound* (Basch, Glick Schiller, and Szanton Blanc 1994), spelled out more systematically the conceptual and methodological implications of the new model. Later, other scholars expanded, refined, or criticized the transnational perspective on migration (see, among others, Cordero-Guzmán, Smith, and Grosfoguel 2001; Levitt and Nyberg-Sørensen 2004; Olwig 1997; Pessar and Mahler 2003; Portes, Guarnizo, and Landolt 1999; Portes, Haller, and Guarnizo 2002; Rouse 1995; Vertovec 2009; and Waldinger and Fitzgerald 2004). By now, transnationalism has become entrenched in migration studies, heralded as "one of the most promising potentials for social research for the twenty-first century" by its proponents (Guarnizo 1997: 287) but derided as an "intellectual fashion" by its detractors (Waldinger and Fitzgerald 2004: 1176).

Several writers have argued that the contemporary phase of the world economy, which has accelerated the volume and speed of international population flows, requires a new approach to migration. Many have sought to rethink conventional categories for social analysis — such as nation, state, citizenship, race, ethnicity, class, gender, and identity — in light of globalization. One of the basic problems is to define, describe, and explain the lasting connections of various migrant settlements to their home countries. A key intellectual puzzle for contemporary scholars is how people reconstruct their identities and imagine their communities across borders and boundaries. The cultural dimensions of globalization have been conceptualized as transnationalization, hybridization, Creolization, syncretism, *bricolage*, and even "mondialization" (from the French *monde* or world) (Appadurai 1996; Hannerz 1996; Renató Ortiz 1996, 1997). The earlier term, *transculturation*, coined by Cuban anthropologist Fernando Ortiz (1947), has also been recovered to capture the mixture of cultural practices of different origins in migrant flows.

Defining Transnationalism

Glick Schiller, Basch, and Blanc-Szanton (1992: 1) approach transnationalism as "the processes by which immigrants build social fields that link together their country of origin and their country of settlement," including "multiple relations — familial, economic, social, organizational, religious, and political — that span borders." These authors call those who develop and maintain such relations "transmigrants." For instance, Hispanic Caribbean migrants may simultaneously participate in several political systems, send money to their countries of origin, and define themselves in culturally hybrid terms, such as Dominican American or Cuban American. Glick Schiller, Basch, and Blanc-Szanton's conceptualization encompasses the constant movement of people across nations as well as occasional practices such as sending gifts and packages back home. Although this approach allows one to compare transnational actors and practices with variable scales and distributions, it runs the risk of diluting the character of the "transnational."

In contrast, Alejandro Portes, Luis Guarnizo, and Patricia Landolt (1999: 219) limit transnationalism to "occupations and activities that require regular and sustained social contacts over time across national borders for their implementation." This definition applies well to transnational enterprises as an "alternative form of economic adaptation," which requires investments in capital, labor, and markets in more than one nation (see also Portes and Guarnizo 1991; and Portes, Haller, and Guarnizo 2002). Thus, for Portes, Guarnizo, and Landolt, some economic activities — such as trading ethnic goods between the Spanish-speaking Caribbean and the United States — are transnational, while others — such as sporadic shopping trips to Miami or New York — are not. These authors also reject the neologism *transmigrant* because it adds little to the standard term *migrant*. Other cumbersome expressions such as *deterritorialized nation-state* and *transborder citizenship*, proposed by Glick Schiller and her colleagues, can be similarly critiqued (Basch, Glick Schiller, and Szanton Blanc 1994; Fouron and Glick Schiller 2001).

Unfortunately, the definition of *transnationalism* in Portes, Guarnizo, and Landolt (1999) leaves out many practices that bind people in different countries, such as purchasing clothes and cars from the United States in the Caribbean, and consuming Caribbean food and music in the United States. Indeed, most Latin American and Caribbean immigrants participate in "nostalgic trade," importing home-country products such as beer, rum, coffee, cigars, bread, cheese, and other foodstuffs. This practice is connected to other transnational activities such as telephoning, traveling, and sending money to the country of origin (Orozco et al. 2005). When such activities are taken into account, the scope of transnationalism becomes much more expansive.

In this book, I use *transnational* as a middle-ground concept. By *transnationalism*, I mean the construction of dense social fields through the circulation of people, ideas, practices, money, goods, and information across nations. This circulation includes, but is not limited to, the physical movement of human bodies as well as other types of exchanges, which may or not be recurrent, such as travel, communication, and remittances. Such exchanges may involve direct state intervention — as in government attempts to promote and profit from remittances — or they may take place in the absence of the state — as in smuggling undocumented migrants. To quote Peggy Levitt and Nina Glick Schiller (2004: 1009), transnationalism "connect[s] actors through direct and indirect relations across borders between those who move and those who stay behind." This definition provides an intermediate stance between nearly all-inclusive and extremely exclusive approaches (see Goldring 1996; Levitt and Nyberg-Sørensen 2004; Sørensen and Olwig 2002; and Vertovec 2009). Furthermore, the definition comprises different types of linkages across various kinds of borders (not just state boundaries), including widely dispersed kinship networks and households.

Cataloging Transnationalism

Some of the earliest scholars of transnationalism portrayed it as an undifferentiated global phenomenon. For instance, Roger Rouse (1995: 366–67) states that "Third World migrants" serve as "conduits for the further movement of money, goods, information, images, and ideas across the boundaries of the state." Aside from the dubious validity of the Third World category, such a blanket statement tends to homogenize transnational migration from Latin America, the Caribbean, Asia, and Africa. It also restricts transnationalism to movement across state boundaries. But each migrant group develops a distinctive brand of transnationalism based on its own historical legacy, cultural practices, settlement patterns, and mode of incorporation into the host society, as well as the policies of sending and receiving governments and other factors.

I consider the Dominican, Puerto Rican, and Cuban diasporas to be transnational, but the three cases vary greatly in their citizenship status, relationship to the homeland, possibility of return, timing of the flows, length of stay abroad, and so on. As the Cuban American sociologist Silvia Pedraza (2007) has observed, irregular contacts between Cuban émigrés and their homeland have stunted a transnational Cuban community in the United States. Since 1959 U.S. and Cuban policies — as well as the politics of exile — have curtailed the exchange of people, goods, and ideas between Havana and Miami. In contrast, migrants, money, and cultural practices circulate much easier and more frequently among Puerto Rico, the Dominican Republic, and the United States. To invert the title of a chapter by Basch, Glick Schiller, and Szanton Blanc (1994), "Different Settings, Same Outcomes," similar settings may produce different outcomes for transnationalism.

One way to solve the puzzle of transnationalism is to distinguish various kinds of the phenomenon. Luis Eduardo Guarnizo and Michael Peter Smith (1998) propose a basic contrast between transnationalism "from above" and "from below." Transnationalism from above refers to the actions of powerful elites and institutions, such as transnational corporations, military bodies, the mass media, supranational political movements, and interstate entities. This type of transnationalism includes global companies such as Microsoft, CNN, MTV, McDonald's, and Disney, as well as the United Nations, the World Bank, the International Monetary Fund, and the Catholic and evangelical churches with a worldwide reach.

Transnationalism from below refers to the grassroots initiatives of ordinary people, small businesses, some nongovernmental organizations, and nonprofit institutions, such as migrant workers and refugees, the ecological and indigenous movements, human rights groups, and hometown associations. It is unclear exactly where some "transnational" actors, such as traffickers of illegal drugs and undocumented migrants, would fit into this typology. Furthermore, some authors refer to "transnationalism of the middle" as an intermediate location in the global-local continuum, such as many informal religious practices occupy (Mahler and Hansing 2005b). In any case, most scholars have been primarily concerned with labor migration as a form of "transnationalism from below."

Building on Guarnizo's and Sarah Mahler's suggestions (see Guarnizo and Smith 1998; and Mahler 1998), José Itzigsohn and his colleagues (1999) have contrasted "narrow" and "broad" transnational practices. Narrowly defined, transnationalism consists of highly institutionalized activities and constant population flows between two countries, such as membership in Dominican political parties in the United States. Broadly defined, transnationalism involves a low level of institutionalization and sporadic physical displacement between two countries, such as carrying bags full of merchandise back home when returning from infrequent trips abroad (which some anthropologists have called "suitcase trading"). Although this classification does not spell out the causes and consequences of each form of transnationalism, it helps locate transnational practices along a wide continuum of intensity and regularity.

Guarnizo (2000) also sees two forms of transnational activities, the "core" and the "expanded." Core transnationalism comprises an individual's habitual practices, while expanded transnationalism involves occasional responses to, for example, political crises or natural disasters. Again, this typology does not explain why some groups engage transnationally more often than others. It is also unclear just how frequent a practice has to be in order to be deemed core or expanded. A similar analytical problem arises when trying to disentangle the economic, political, and sociocultural dimensions of transnationalism, which often reinforce each other (Portes, Guarnizo, and Landolt 1999).

Explaining Transnationalism

Scholars have enumerated several causes of contemporary transnationalism (Basch, Glick Schiller, and Szanton Blanc 1994; Glick Schiller, Basch, and Blanc-Szanton 1992; Guarnizo and Smith 1998; Portes, Guarnizo, and Landolt 1999). The expansion of global capitalism since World War II accelerated the worldwide integration of financial and labor markets. In turn, the search for cheap labor in developing economies intensified the movement of people seeking employment abroad. In addition, the technological revolution in mass transportation and electronic communications has compressed time and space, especially through jet airplanes, cellular phones, fax machines, videotapes, cable and satellite television, the Internet, and e-mail. Consequently, it has become less expensive and time-consuming to travel to, trade with, and communicate with other countries.

Scholars disagree, however, about the local effects of globalization on people's everyday lives. According to its critics, globalization has deepened inequality among regions, countries, classes, races, and genders (Guarnizo and Smith 1998). To more optimistic analysts, the rise of transnational networks has multiplied cosmopolitan practices (Hannerz 1996) and even created the possibility of a postnational or diasporic citizenship (Laguerre 1998). Certainly, the neoliberal discourse of globalization celebrates borderless states and consumer markets, as well as the free flow of capital, if not labor, across formerly insurmountable boundaries.

Regardless of how one defines transnationalism, it usually entails the movement of workers between countries. Technical innovations, such as the microchip revolution, have greatly reduced the time and cost of circulating people, images, and ideas among the Caribbean, the United States, Europe, and other parts of the world. In this context, the transnational movement of people is only one aspect — albeit a crucial one — in the worldwide exchange of capital, commodities, technology, information, ideology, and culture (see Appadurai 1996; Basch, Glick Schiller, and Szanton Blanc 1994; Guarnizo and Smith 1998; Hannerz 1996; and Renato Ortiz 1996, 1997).

Transnationalism is as much a political as an economic phenomenon. During the 1990s six Latin American countries (Brazil, Colombia, Costa Rica, the Dominican Republic, Ecuador, and Mexico) amended their constitutions to extend dual citizenship and political rights to their growing diasporas. Furthermore, social institutions bridging several nations (such as confederations of political parties, churches, grassroots movements, and other nongovernmental organizations) have proliferated. Nation-states have surrendered much of their sovereignty to global and regional forces by establishing common markets, free trade, and other international agreements. In many countries, public policies have moved toward "de facto transnationalism," accepting the limitations of strictly national approaches to the movement of capital, labor, and even controlled substances (Sassen 1999).

Why Does Transnationalism Matter?

Contemporary transnationalism has many theoretical and practical implications. Among them is the challenge to the "straight-line assimilation" model that dominated immigration research in the United States during the first half of the twentieth century (Pedraza 2006; Portes and Rumbaut 2006). This model posited the inevitable absorption of immigrants into their host societies, through gradual elimination of their linguistic, religious, and other cultural differences. Instead, transnationalists have shown that contemporary migrants may develop multiple identities, lead bifocal lives, express loyalties to more than one nation, and practice hybrid cultures (Basch, Glick Schiller, and Szanton Blanc 1994; Duany 2008a [1994]; Glick Schiller, Basch, and Blanc-Szanton 1992; Glick Schiller, Basch, and Szanton Blanc 1995; Itzigsohn et al. 1999; Levitt 2001; Portes, Guarnizo, and Landolt 1999; Vertovec 2009). Current strategies of immigrant adaptation do not always lead to complete assimilation by the second or third generation, as earlier theories had predicted. Alejandro Portes and Min Zhou (1993) have argued that "segmented assimilation" includes various forms of incorporation, depending on the immigrants' human capital, context of reception, community of residence, and other variables. Rather than assimilate into mainstream U.S. culture, some groups might adopt the lifestyle of a racial or ethnic minority such as African Americans, Hispanics, or "people of color."

Even more broadly, Glick Schiller, Basch, and Blanc-Szanton (1992) claim that transnationalism subverts established concepts in the social sciences, including nation, ethnicity, race, class, and gender. In their view, nation-states can no longer capture (if they ever could) people's multiple and over-lapping identities (such as local, regional, racial, ethnic, translocal, or even postnational allegiances). Contemporary migrants often combine their experiences in their societies of origin and settlement to create a new kind of self-awareness.

Scholars may themselves promote or hinder the interests of transnational actors when engaging in public debates about immigration, multicultural-ism, bilingualism, or remittances (Glick Schiller, Basch, and Szanton Blanc 1995). For instance, Steven Vertovec (2009) has assessed recent efforts by national and international organisms to facilitate circular migration. Con-temporary transnationalism has hastened the back-and-forth movement between people's homelands and other countries, as I have documented for Puerto Rico (Duany 2002: chap. 9). Whether circular migration can be managed effectively to meet labor shortages, ensure remittance flows, and promote the "brain gain" of skilled workers is debatable. Furthermore, the political implications of promoting the short-term circulation of people without full citizenship rights are problematic. It is often difficult for aca-demics to make practical recommendations to policy-oriented institutions without qualifying their research findings.

Let me give a personal example. In March 2001 I was invited to partici-pate in a roundtable, "Transnational Civic Movements," at the conference in New York City of the community organization Dominicanos 2000. One of the central questions posed in that meeting was how transnational organi-zations could contribute to empowering Dominicans in the United States. At the time, I could not answer in a satisfactory manner, because I was pri-marily concerned with transnationalism as a cultural phenomenon. I then suggested that the wider scope and resources of transnational organizations could strengthen local institutions and grassroots initiatives. This claim still needs elaboration and documentation. But transnationalism clearly has con-crete repercussions for people labeled as transnational. That is one of the main issues of contention in recent discussions about whether Dominicans are better deemed "transnational" or "diasporic" subjects (see chapter 8).

Problematizing Transnationalism

Beyond the Nation-State

Although scholarly understanding of transnationalism has advanced swiftly since the early 1990s, several issues merit further reflection. I have already noted that transnational research has tended to concentrate on cross-national exchanges regulated by states, overlooking other "in-between" spaces where people live their daily lives. As Portes (2001) points out, many transnational activities take place outside the limits of state control. For instance, a large share of the remittances sent to Cuba from the United States relies on an informal network of travelers, known as *mulas*, who are difficult to track by both governments (Orozco 2003). Most of these remittances escape official records such as Cuba's balance of payment accounts.

Another neglected issue in transnationalism is the role of dependent territories as major sources of migration. Much of the available literature assumes that transnationalism occurs between sovereign nations. In particular, academic discussions of transnationalism have tended to exclude Puerto Ricans, who do not cross international boundaries when they move to the United States. Consequently, the Puerto Rican diaspora seems anomalous (see Crespo-Soto 2009).[2]

However, citizenship rights are defined differently on the island and in the United States. Only when Puerto Ricans reside in one of the fifty states do they acquire the full privileges of U.S. citizenship, such as voting for the president and vice president. They also assume new legal and economic obligations, such as paying federal income taxes. Moreover, they cross significant geographic, linguistic, cultural, and even racial borders when they migrate. Regardless of their political ideology, most Puerto Ricans on the island and in the diaspora see themselves as part of a distinctive Puerto Rican nation (see de la Garza et al. 1992; Morris 1995; and Rivera Ortiz 1996). Even on the mainland, few Puerto Ricans identify themselves primarily as American, Latino, Hispanic, or even Caribbean. The vast majority of Puerto Ricans imagine themselves as part of a broader community that meets all the standard criteria of nationhood — such as a historic territory, language, and culture — except sovereignty.

Applying the concept of transnationalism to Puerto Rico must take into account that the island is not a sovereign state, and therefore the analytical distinction between state and nation must be made carefully. For example,

U.S. government authorities do not police Puerto Ricans' movements between the island and the U.S. mainland, unlike migrants who cross international boundaries. However, the subjective experience of migration for many Puerto Ricans as a dual process of deterritorialization and reterritorialization has been well documented (Aranda 2007; Gina Pérez 2004; Ramos-Zayas 2003; Whalen 2001). As Puerto Ricans commonly say, moving abroad involves *irse pa' fuera*, literally "going outside" — their island-country, that is. For most Puerto Ricans, the United States is culturally as foreign as the Dominican Republic or Venezuela — perhaps more so. Even the colonial legislature of Puerto Rico called the United States an "ethnologically alien" setting in 1947 (Asamblea Legislativa 1947a: 386).

In addition to Puerto Ricans, contemporary movements of people include massive flows from the dependent Caribbean and other regions to their U.S. and European metropoles, such as the United Kingdom, France, and the Netherlands. The Puerto Rican sociologists Clara Rodríguez (1989) and Ramón Grosfoguel (1994–95) have argued that Puerto Ricans have more in common with colonial migrants than with citizens of independent countries such as the Dominican Republic or Cuba. For instance, colonial migrants need not apply for a visa or change their legal status to participate in metropolitan elections. Both Puerto Ricans in the United States and Antilleans in France occupy subordinate positions as "people of color," even though they hold the same citizenship as their metropolitan counterparts (see Daniel 2000; Giraud 2002; Grosfoguel 2003, 2004; and Milia-Marie-Luce 2002). The differences and similarities among transnational migrants therefore should be spelled out, depending on whether or not they cross state boundaries.

How New Is Transnationalism?

Another problem with the transnational standpoint is that it tends to be historically shortsighted. For many writers, contemporary transnationalism represents a radical departure from previous population movements. Yet a large body of scholarship shows that past migrants maintained transnational connections over long stretches of time, including returning en masse and sending remittances to their homelands (see Foner 2005; Morawska 2001; Pedraza and Rumbaut 1996; and Portes and Rumbaut 2006). A longitudinal perspective that highlights both temporal changes and continuities therefore should temper analyses of recent transnational flows. It is revealing to compare the current practices of Dominicans or Puerto Ricans in the United States with those of Russian, Italian, or Irish immigrants at the beginning of the twentieth century. Although not entirely new, transnationalism has assumed a greater scale, intensity, diffusion, and velocity at the turn of the twenty-first century, as a result of air transportation and electronic communications. Again, this trend is strongly correlated with globalization.

Many of the first essays on contemporary transnationalism interpreted it as a complete break with the past. Several contributors to Glick Schiller, Basch, and Blanc-Szanton's (1992) compilation suggested that transnationalism, not assimilation, better explains the cultural dilemmas of today's immigrants. Scholars have often celebrated transnationalism as a viable alternative to merging into mainstream U.S. society. Many have privileged what is new in contemporary transnationalism rather than what is old — even though they often allude to earlier stages of European immigration in the United States (see Glick Schiller 1999; and Portes, Guarnizo, and Landolt 1999). In any case, much of the first wave of transnational research underlined that contemporary migrants differed from previous migrants.

In hindsight, earlier ethnic groups often engaged in what are now called transnational practices. For example, about 15 percent of all Italian immigrants between 1899 and 1910 had already lived in the United States. Between 1900 and 1906, immigrants in the United States sent US$69 million in money orders to Russia and Austria-Hungary (Foner 2005: 64, 67). Many preserved strong attachments to their nations of origin, well beyond the first generation, as Irish and Polish Americans illustrate. Some groups organized transnationally through political parties, economic enterprises, and cultural institutions that bridged home and host countries. Finally, Southern and Eastern Europeans (notably Italians and Jews) were not considered fully white in the United States until the mid-twentieth century. In response, they often asserted their ancestral cultures and resisted Americanization as fiercely as some recent immigrants do.

Still, contemporary transnationalism is not exactly the same phenomenon it was a hundred years ago (Foner 2005; Glick Schiller 1999; Glick Schiller, Basch, and Blanc-Szanton 1992; Glick Schiller, Basch, and Szanton Blanc 1995; Morawska 2001; Pedraza 2006; Portes, Guarnizo, and Landolt 1999). First, because of advances in transportation and telecommunications, especially telephones, migrants now have more immediate contacts with families, friends, and communities back home. Second, today's migrants participate more frequently in transnational activities than before, including sending money and visiting relatives. Third, some migrants engage in many different kinds of practices — economic, political, and cultural — in both home and host countries. Fourth, migrants may become incorporated into their societies of settlement while remaining involved with their societies of origin, as exemplified by dual citizenship and voting abroad. Finally, the reduced cost of long-distance communication has made transnationalism more available to people worldwide.

Will Transnationalism Survive the First Generation?

Studies of transnational migrants have centered on the first generation — those who were born and raised in one country and moved to another as adults. Recent debates about the future of transnationalism have dwelt on the differences between the first and second generations. The publication of two collections of essays (Levitt and Waters 2002; Portes and Rumbaut 2001) has elucidated the options for second-generation immigrants, those who were born and raised in the United States. One of the most powerful concepts to emerge from this literature was Portes and Zhou's (1993) "segmented assimilation": the proposition that impoverished and racialized groups, like Dominicans, could follow the path of "downward assimilation" of African Americans, Puerto Ricans, and other minorities, rather than adopt mainstream values and customs. In contrast, most second-generation Cubans (at least those whose parents arrived before the 1980 Mariel exodus) experience "selective acculturation" and upward mobility in the United States (Portes and Rumbaut 2006). Nancy Foner (2005: 124–25) has argued that the segmented assimilation model exaggerates the negative outcomes of identifying with African Americans; and that some groups labeled as black, such as West Indians, may also experience upward mobility.

Whether second-generation immigrants will preserve ties with their parents' country is an empirical question that recent studies have sought to answer among Dominican Americans (see Bailey 2002; Itzigsohn 2006; Levitt and Waters 2002; López 2004; and Pantoja 2005). In my appraisal, second-generation immigrants tend to decrease their transnational engagements (such as remitting), but they do not break completely with their ancestral homelands (for instance, most continue to describe themselves based on national origin). Many Dominican Americans (if that is the term they prefer) retain much of their parents' language, music, religion, and foodways. Second-generation Dominicans insist on their national and panethnic affiliations to distinguish themselves from African Americans and ally themselves with other Hispanics (Bailey 2002; Itzigsohn and Dore-Cabral 2000). At the same time, many embrace the consumer habits, speech patterns, dress, haircut, and fashion styles of African American and Hispanic teenagers in New York and other U.S. cities where they concentrate. It is premature to characterize the second generation as entirely disconnected from Dominican culture and absorbed by U.S. culture. A similar argument can be made, with different nuances, for both Puerto Ricans and Cubans born in the United States. Hybrid practices and identities may well be the rule rather than the exception in the second generation.

Transnationalism as Resistance

At first glance, transnational migration may subvert globalization and assimilation. For some authors, transnationalism can transform nation-states and their ideologies of national identity and citizenship. According to Vertovec (2009: 88), "transnational migrants challenge nation-state ideals of belonging in both sending and receiving countries. They do this not least by moving back and forth between states, sometimes circumventing state controls over borders and taxes." David Fitzgerald (2000: 10) phrases it more dramatically: "Transnational migrants often live in a country in which they do not claim citizenship and claim citizenship in a country in which they do not live." According to Roger Waldinger and David Fitzgerald (2004: 1183), "Population movement across state boundaries is inherently a *political* matter: it threatens to sever the alignment of territory, political institutions, and society that states try so hard to create."

However, the counterhegemonic potential of transnationalism should not be overstated. Although the large-scale mobility of the population may weaken national identities "from the bottom up," crossing an international boundary does not erase it. As Hastings Donnan and Thomas Wilson (1999: 10) recognize, "borders may serve as useful metaphors for understanding the rootlessness of many populations today, but this should not obscure the fact that everyone lives within or between the boundaries of nation-states, and these boundaries are always more than metaphorical." In other words, nation-states have not relinquished their power to regulate the daily lives of ordinary migrants.

On the contrary, state policies in advanced industrial countries (such as the United States, France, Germany, and Japan) are increasingly hostile to migrant workers. While migrant-sending governments may promote transnationalism, laws and regulations in the major receiving countries seek to reassert, control, and protect their boundaries (Sassen 1998). Although expatriates often transgress such boundaries, the latter continue to define citizenship rights and duties. Furthermore, rather than embody subaltern resistance to existing structures of domination (whether between states, classes, ethnic groups, or genders), transnationalism may reinforce global inequality (Guarnizo and Smith 1998). Thus, one should not romanticize the territorial extension of migrant households, social networks, economic resources, political activities, and cultural practices, which often express power asymmetries.

Bringing Gender In

Much of the early writing on transnational migration neglected gender, focusing instead on class, race, ethnicity, and nationalism. Feminist scholars have advocated a gendered approach to transnationalism since the late 1990s (see, for example, Alicea 1997; Hondagneu-Sotelo 2003; López 2004; Pessar and Mahler 2003; and Toro-Morn and Alicea 2003). Some of this research has focused on the key role of women, especially mothers, in transnational households (Hondagneu-Sotelo and Avila 1997). Women are largely responsible for the emotional, caring, and ritual work required to maintain kinship bonds between home and diaspora communities. Through constant visiting, writing, and talking on the phone, women often keep transnational households in touch with each other across long distances and stretches of time. More so than men, women frequently travel back and forth to take care of relatives, raise children, and participate in their family's rites of passage, such as baptisms, birthdays, weddings, and funerals (Alicea 1997; Aranda 2007).

Patricia Pessar and Sarah Mahler (2003) have elaborated a useful model to "bring gender into" transnationalism. First, gender ideologies and relations operate simultaneously on multiple spatial and social scales, including across state boundaries. Second, gender hierarchies affect an individual's or group's social locations at national and supranational levels. Finally, gender differences structure people's access to resources and power over mobility. These "gendered geographies of power" help map how gender shapes transnational experiences.

Transnationalism in the Hispanic Caribbean

The transnational framework helps scholars gauge the socioeconomic impact of migration at home and abroad in four ways. First, it emphasizes that sending and receiving communities have been bridged through long-standing webs of social, economic, political, and cultural exchange. Second, transnationalism calls attention to migrants' bifocality — the experience of two (or more) interconnected spaces, markets, polities, and often languages. Third, this framework situates population movements within the worldwide circulation of capital, labor, commodities, and technology. Fourth, thinking transnationally encourages the interrogation of discourses on statehood, nationality, citizenship, ethnicity, race, class, gender, and other master narratives in the social sciences.

In the rest of this book, I substantiate these four propositions. Massive migration has strengthened the bonds between the Spanish-speaking Caribbean and the United States. In particular, many migrants' kinship and friendship networks span two or more countries. Since the 1950s Hispanic Caribbean people have moved abroad en masse in response to changes in the global economy and their local repercussions. This exodus has deepened the region's dependence on the United States. In addition, transnationalism intensifies disparities between countries, regions, classes, ethnic groups, and genders (Guarnizo 1997). Documenting the internal rifts *within* Hispanic Caribbean diasporas (such as those produced by regional, racial, generational, or gender differences) remains an important intellectual project.

At the same time, studying Hispanic Caribbean diasporas can help scholars rethink transnationalism. On the one hand, extensive linkages between the sending and receiving countries were established prior to large-scale migration, as a consequence of U.S. hegemony in the region since 1898. On the other hand, the dispersal of the Puerto Rican, Cuban, and Dominican populations began well before the current phase of globalization. The Spanish-speaking countries of the Caribbean islands have developed various forms of transnationalism as a result of their political, economic, and cultural entanglements with the United States. Massive population displacements have contributed to blurring — without erasing — the borders between the Spanish-speaking Caribbean and the United States. Since the 1990s stricter U.S. immigration policies have made it painfully clear that borders (and boundaries) matter. Many Dominicans and Cubans have responded by shifting their travel routes and destinations, including European and other Caribbean countries.

Finally, transnationalism has had far-reaching effects on collective identities in the Spanish-speaking Caribbean. Throughout the twentieth century, Caribbean nationalism evolved largely in opposition to U.S. hegemony: being a nationalist almost automatically meant being anti-American. But the emergence of diasporic communities "in the entrails of the monster," in the well-worn phrase of Cuban poet and patriot José Martí, has complicated matters. Hispanic Caribbean migrants participate simultaneously in two or more political systems that define them as members of a nation, an ethnic minority, or a panethnic and quasi-racial group called Hispanic or Latino. The émigrés may accept, contest, or negotiate such definitions of their identity, as they have on countless occasions. But at least one thing is certain: the diaspora has expanded the contours of the Puerto Rican, Cuban, and Dominican nations. In the past hundred years, the Caribbean region has been thoroughly Americanized, just as the diaspora has Caribbeanized (and Latinized) parts of New York, Miami, and San Juan. As globalization generates both local and translocal notions of cultural identity, transnational migrants negotiate the two competing claims, thereby redrawing the lines between home and host societies. In the next chapter, I examine how each Hispanic Caribbean diaspora evolved over time.

In the Entrails of the Monster

*A Historical Overview of Hispanic Caribbean
Migration to the United States*

At the end of the nineteenth century, few people of Caribbean origin lived in the United States.[1] Between 1890 and 1899, the United States admitted 31,480 immigrants from the "West Indies." More than four-fifths came from Cuba. According to the 1900 census, only 0.3 percent of the foreign-born population of the United States was born in the Caribbean. Between 1900 and 1909, when U.S. immigration first peaked at 8.2 million people, Caribbean migrants merely represented 1.6 percent of the total (Ruggles et al. 2010; U.S. Citizenship and Immigration Services 2009). At that time, Miami was a small town with few Cuban residents, while in New York the terms *Spanish* and *Hispanic* referred to Spaniards as much as to Latin Americans. No one could then imagine that both cities would be Caribbeanized during the second half of the twentieth century.

After World War II Puerto Ricans began to move en masse to the U.S. mainland. In 1959 the Cuban Revolution unleashed the largest refugee flow in the history of the United States. Since 1961 hundreds of thousands of Dominicans have relocated abroad, especially in the United States, Puerto Rico, and Spain. During the 1960s Puerto Rico and Cuba became the second- and third-largest sources of the Hispanic population in the United States, after Mexico. By the mid-1990s the Dominican Republic was among the top five migrant-sending countries to the United States from any region in the world. At the beginning of the twenty-first century, the three countries of the Spanish-speaking Caribbean islands have multiple and large-scale diasporic communities.

TABLE 2.1 Basic Demographic Features of the Hispanic Caribbean Population
in the United States, 2009

Feature	Cubans	Dominicans	Puerto Ricans
Number of persons claiming ancestry	1,696,141	1,356,361	4,426,738
Percentage of population with this ancestry[a]	12.9	12.3	52.7
Number of persons born abroad	992,684	777,689	1,552,397[b]
Percentage of group in United States	58.5	57.3	35.1
Number of persons born in United States	703,457	578,672	2,874,341
Percentage of group in United States	41.4	42.7	64.9

Sources: Central Intelligence Agency 2009; U.S. Census Bureau 2010.

[a]Includes estimated population of sending country in 2009.

[b]Includes all persons born in Puerto Rico and Puerto Ricans born in the United States.

This chapter documents the rapid growth of Hispanic Caribbean migration to the United States since the mid-twentieth century. Then it charts the historical trajectories of the Cuban, Puerto Rican, and Dominican diasporas. In each case, an entangled web of political, economic, and cultural connections led most of the migrants to the United States. Comparing the three migrant flows shows recurring themes as well as important differences among them. Among other factors, legal status, class and regional origins, settlement patterns, and racial composition varied from one group to another and over time. A particular form of transnationalism thus arose in each of the Spanish-speaking countries of the Caribbean islands.

The Demography of Hispanic
Caribbean Diasporas

One of the most impressive differences among Cuban, Dominican, and Puerto Rican migrants is their proportion relative to the sending populations (table 2.1). In 2009 approximately one out of eight Cubans and Dominicans lived in the fifty United States, compared to more than one out of two Puerto Ricans. Furthermore, roughly two-fifths of U.S. Cubans and Dominicans, and nearly two-thirds of Puerto Ricans, were born stateside. Puerto Ricans have become more mobile than Cubans and Dominicans, as measured by their places of birth and residence. As U.S. citizens, all Puerto Ricans can move freely between the island and the fifty United States, as well as the nation's overseas territories. This legal status helps explain the higher number

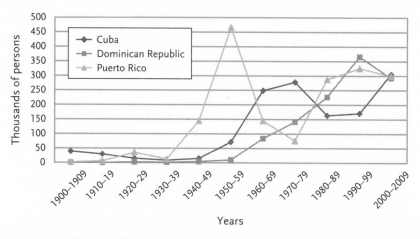

FIGURE 2.1 Migration from the Hispanic Caribbean to the United States, 1900–2009

Sources: Banco Gubernamental de Fomento 2010; Junta de Planificación 1970–89, 2001; Larson and Sullivan 1989; Senior 1947; U.S. Census Bureau 1933–50; U.S. Citizenship and Immigration Services 2002–9; U.S. Commissioner-General of Immigration 1893–1932; U.S. Department of Justice 1942–77, 1978–95, 1996–2001.

Note: The available data for Puerto Rico refer to the net balance between inbound and outbound passengers between Puerto Rico and the fifty United States. For Cuba and the Dominican Republic, the data refer to immigrants born in these countries.

of Puerto Ricans abroad than either Cubans or Dominicans, who enter the United States as foreigners.

Each diasporic community from the Spanish-speaking Caribbean emerged at a different juncture. The Cuban exodus dates back to the late nineteenth-century struggles of liberation from Spain, beginning in 1868. In the twentieth century, Cuban migration concentrated in two periods: between 1900 and 1920 and after 1960 (figure 2.1). During the first two decades, Cubans dominated Caribbean population movements to the United States; their numbers dwindled thereafter, only to rise again during the 1940s and 1950s. The triumph of the Cuban Revolution in 1959 prompted an extensive refugee movement to the United States.

The number of Puerto Ricans leaving the island took off during the 1940s, intensified during the 1950s, decreased during the 1970s, and regained strength during the 1980s. In the 1940s, Puerto Ricans surpassed Cubans as the main Caribbean group in the United States. The Puerto Rican diaspora has become one of the most unrelenting movements of people since the mid-twentieth century. The proportions of this exodus are even more staggering when one recalls that Puerto Rico's population was roughly 3.7 million in 2010. (The island actually lost 2.2 percent of its population between 2000 and 2010.) No country in recent memory has exported a larger share of its people than Puerto Rico.

The volume of Dominican migrants was relatively small until the 1960s, but it has increased swiftly since then. By the 1980s, Dominicans had become one of the fastest growing segments of the foreign-born population in the United States. In the 1990s the Dominican flow continued unabated, while the Cuban and Puerto Rican flows decreased temporarily. Between 2000 and 2009, Cuba and the Dominican Republic were respectively the fifth- and seventh-leading sources of foreign migrants to the United States (U.S. Citizenship and Immigration Services 2009). During the first decade of the twenty-first century, around three hundred thousand residents of each of the Spanish-speaking countries of the Caribbean islands relocated to the United States. In addition, thousands of Dominicans and Cubans have settled in other Caribbean countries (including Puerto Rico), Canada, and Western Europe, especially Spain.

All three population movements took place primarily after World War II. Before 1965 migration from Puerto Rico, Cuba, and elsewhere in the Americas provided the United States with much-needed cheap labor during the era of national origin quotas. To a large extent, the Hispanic Caribbean diasporas are part of the post-1965 migrant wave to the United States, predominantly from Latin America, the Caribbean, and Asia. This wave gained strength with the 1965 Hart-Celler Act, which amended the U.S. Immigration and Nationality Act and abolished national origin quotas. Since then, various immigrant communities — from places as varied as Guatemala, Haiti, the Philippines, and China — have consolidated their transnational connections with their home countries.

The spectacular growth of Hispanic Caribbean migration over the past five decades is reflected in the number of U.S. residents born in the region. U.S. census data confirm a relatively small but expanding number of Cuban-born people between 1850 and 1930, and its rapid increase between 1960 and 1980 (figure 2.2). During the 1940s and 1950s, the number of U.S. residents born in Puerto Rico rose dramatically, and it has continued to grow faster than the island's population. Finally, the Dominican-born population of the United States has continued to increase since the 1960s. Of the three groups, Dominicans added the most immigrants during the 1990s. Let me now trace the trajectories of each population movement.

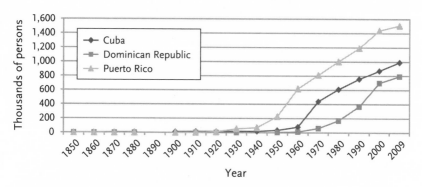

FIGURE 2.2 U.S. Residents Born in the Spanish-Speaking Caribbean, 1850–2009

Sources: Ruggles et al. 2010; U.S. Census Bureau 2009a, 2010.

The Cuban Exodus

Before the Revolution

Migration from Cuba to the United States can be roughly divided into two major stages: before and after the Cuban Revolution of 1959. A steady stream of Cubans had been coming to the United States, beginning in the early nineteenth century. By the 1820s small numbers of professionals, merchants, and landowners had settled in New York City, Philadelphia, and New Orleans (Poyo 1989). Prominent advocates of Cuba's independence from Spain sought political refuge in the United States, notably Félix Varela, José María Heredia, and José Antonio Saco. Some, like Gaspar Cisneros Betancourt and Cirilo Villaverde, promoted Cuba's annexation to the United States.

Large-scale migration from Cuba began with the Ten Years' War (1868–78) and continued well after the Spanish-Cuban-American War (1895–98). (See table 2.2.) The late nineteenth century was a period of political upheaval and economic hardship in Cuba, including rising unemployment and an increasing cost of living (Louis Pérez 2006 [1988]: 99–102). Between 1868 and 1898, the United States admitted 55,749 Cubans (U.S. Bureau of Statistics 1868–92; U.S. Commissioner-General of Immigration 1893–98). Among them was the exiled poet, journalist, and politician José Martí, who founded the Partido Revolucionario Cubano (PRC), or Cuban Revolutionary Party, in New York City in 1892, embracing armed struggle against Spain. In an unfinished 1895 letter, written a day before he died in battle in Cuba, Martí used the phrase "the entrails of the monster" to refer to his longtime residence in the United States.

TABLE 2.2 Cuban Diaspora to the United States, 1868–2009

Years	Number of Migrants	Related Historical Events
1868–69	2,215	The Ten Years' War begins in Cuba (1868).
1870–79	8,676	Carlos Manuel de Céspedes is the first Cuban elected mayor of Key West, Florida (1875). The Pact of Zanjón ends the Ten Years' War (1878). An armed rebellion against Spain, dubbed "the Little War," fails in Cuba (1879–80).
1880–89	20,134	The Cuban patriot José Martí is exiled in New York City (1881–95). Slavery is abolished in Cuba (1886). Ybor City is founded near Tampa, Florida, attracting Cuban cigar workers (1886).
1890–99	26,098	Martí establishes the Partido Revolucionario Cubano (PRC) in New York City (1892). The Cuban war of independence from Spain begins (1895). U.S. troops intervene in the Cuban war (1898). The United States sets up a military government in Cuba (1898–1902).
1900–1909	39,506	The Sociedad La Unión Martí-Maceo is established in Ybor City (1900). The Platt Amendment to the Cuban constitution is approved (1902). Cuba gains its independence (1902). U.S. troops occupy Cuba to prevent a civil war (1906–9).
1910–19	29,658	The United States intervenes in an armed rebellion by black Cubans (1912).
1920–29	14,996	Gerardo Machado is reelected president of Cuba through unconstitutional means (1929).
1930–39	8,516	A military coup led by Fulgencio Batista deposes Machado (1933). The United States abrogates the Platt Amendment (1934).
1940–49	14,084	A new Cuban constitution is promulgated (1940). Batista is elected president (1940).
1950–59	71,962	Batista deposes President Carlos Prío Socarrás (1952). Fidel Castro leads an attack on the Moncada barracks in Santiago, beginning the Cuban Revolution (1953). The Cuban Revolution triumphs (1959).
1960–69	248,718	The United States breaks diplomatic ties with Cuba (1961). The U.S. government establishes the Cuban Refugee Program (1961).

TABLE 2.2 *(continued)*

Years	Number of Migrants	Related Historical Events
		The Bay of Pigs invasion fails (1961).
		The U.S. government establishes a trade embargo of Cuba (1962).
		The Cuban Missile Crisis takes place (1962).
		Castro opens the port of Camarioca for migration (1965).
		The United States and Cuba organize the "Freedom Flights" (1965–73).
		The U.S. Congress approves the Cuban Adjustment Act (1966).
1970–79	278,064	The city of Sweetwater, Florida, elects the Cuban Jorge Valdés as mayor (1975).
		Castro begins a dialogue with Cuban exiles (1978).
		The first exiles return to Cuba for short family visits (1979).
1980–89	163,666	The Mariel exodus takes place (1980).
		The Cuban American National Foundation (CANF) is established (1981).
		The United States and Cuba sign migration accords (1984).
		Xavier Suárez is the first Cuban elected mayor of Miami (1985).
		Robert Menéndez is the first Cuban elected mayor of Union City, New Jersey (1986).
		Ileana Ros-Lehtinen is the first Cuban elected to the U.S. House of Representatives (1989).
1990–99	170,675	The Special Period in Peacetime officially begins (1990).
		The *balsero* crisis takes place (1994).
		The United States and Cuba renew their migration accords (1994).
		The U.S. Congress tightens the Cuban embargo through the Helms-Burton Act (1996).
		Pope John Paul II visits Cuba (1998).
		The *balsero* child Elián González arrives in Miami (1999).
2000–2009	305,989	The Bush administration restricts Cuban American travel and remittances to Cuba (2004–8).
		Fidel Castro retires as Cuba's president (2006).
		Raúl Castro is elected president (2008).
		The Obama administration lifts restrictions on Cuban American travel and remittances to Cuba (2009).
Total	1,402,957	

Sources: U.S. Bureau of Statistics 1868–92; U.S. Census Bureau 1933–50; U.S. Citizenship and Immigration Services 2002–9; U.S. Commissioner-General of Immigration 1893–1932; U.S. Department of Justice 1942–77, 1978–95, 1996–2001.

By the end of the nineteenth century, Cubans had established sizable colonies in Key West, Tampa, and New York City (see Lisandro Pérez 1994; and Louis Pérez 1978). These communities were all connected to cigar manufacturing, which benefited from a protective U.S. tariff on cigar imports. Several cigar entrepreneurs — including Vicente Martínez Ybor, Eduardo Hidalgo Gato, and Cayetano Soria — located their factories in Florida, attracting skilled Cuban, Spanish, and Italian laborers. By 1885 one-third of Key West's population was Cuban, mostly employed in the tobacco industry (Poyo 1989: 53). In 1910 nearly 41 percent of Tampa's cigar workers were Cuban; almost 15 percent of all the Cuban residents of Hillsborough County, which includes Tampa, were black (Greenbaum 2002: 98, 115).

With the decline of Tampa's and Key West's cigar industries during the 1930s, New York City emerged as the epicenter of Cuban immigration because it offered more employment opportunities, particularly in manufacturing. By 1950 nearly twice as many Cubans lived in New York as in Florida (Ruggles et al. 2010). Miami became an important exile destination during the Gerardo Machado dictatorship (1929–33). (Machado himself was later exiled to and buried in Miami.) During the 1940s and 1950s, thousands of Cubans moved abroad seeking better jobs and civil liberties. In 1958, on the eve of the Cuban Revolution, more than fifty-three thousand persons of Cuban birth lived in the United States (U.S. Department of Justice 1959).

The Postrevolutionary Phase

THE "GOLDEN EXILES"

The exodus of Cuban refugees began with the dismantling of Fulgencio Batista's dictatorship, which lasted from 1952 to 1958. In 1959 Fidel Castro's overthrow of Batista's government launched the first socialist revolution in the Americas and a large wave of exiles. The first to leave Cuba were military officers, government officials, large landowners, and businesspersons associated with the Batista regime. As the revolution became more radical, the exodus drew increasingly on disillusioned members of the middle class, such as professionals and managers, especially those who had been employed by U.S. corporations. As many as 150,000 Cubans had worked for such companies, which were nationalized by the revolutionary government after 1960 (Louis Pérez 1999: 394).

The first postrevolutionary migrant wave between 1959 and 1962 has been dubbed the "Golden Exile," because most refugees came from the upper and middle strata of Cuban society (Portes 1969). The majority were urban, well-educated, and white-collar workers. Most were born in the island's largest cities, particularly Havana (Fagen, Brody, and O'Leary 1968). The exiles also overrepresented the lighter-skinned sectors of the population, especially descendants of earlier Spanish immigrants to Cuba. Many fled for political or religious reasons, fearing persecution by the revolutionary government. Between 1959 and 1962, the U.S. government admitted 248,070 Cubans (Clark 1975: 75).

On January 3, 1961, the United States broke diplomatic relations with Cuba. Until then, the U.S. embassy in Havana and the U.S. consulate in Santiago issued regular visas to those who wanted to leave the island. Afterward, Cubans qualified for visa waivers in the United States for "urgent humanitarian reasons." On arriving in U.S. territory, they could apply for parole and obtain refugee status, claiming they were escaping "communist oppression." Most eventually became permanent residents of the United States.

The refugees settled primarily in Miami (Boswell and Curtis 1984: 72–85). During the early 1960s they quickly occupied the Riverside and Shenandoah neighborhoods, at the time a decaying area near the central business district between Flagler and Southwest Eighth Streets, and later rechristened Little Havana or Calle Ocho (Price 2007). Another city that attracted working-class refugees was Hialeah, north of Miami, which became known as Little Marianao, after a Havana suburb. Subsequently, middle-class Cubans tended to move to suburban neighborhoods in southwest Miami and nearby cities such as Sweetwater and Westchester. Still, Little Havana remains the symbolic core of Cuban America (García 1996: 86).

Between 1961 and 1981, the federally funded Cuban Refugee Program provided more than US$1.4 billion in assistance with health care, professional and vocational retraining, English-language instruction, and college tuition loans. The program also relocated thousands of exiles outside South Florida to areas with better employment opportunities. By 1966 the U.S. government had resettled 130,599 Cubans in other states and territories, especially New York, New Jersey, California, and Puerto Rico (Masud-Piloto 1996: 67; Pedraza-Bailey 1985: 40–52). Many exiles later returned to Miami because of the city's proximity to Cuba, increasing concentration of Cuban residents, and expanding economy.

The Cuban Missile Crisis in October 1962 interrupted commercial travel between Cuba and the United States. Clandestine migration rose correspondingly, mostly by small craft and makeshift vessels. According to U.S. sources, 6,698 "boat people" from Cuba arrived in Florida between 1962 and 1965 (Ackerman and Clark 1995: 14). In addition, 55,916 Cubans were admitted to the United States from other countries, such as Mexico and Spain (Clark 1975: 75).

On September 28, 1965, Castro announced that he would permit anyone wishing to leave the island to do so. On October 10, he opened the port of Camarioca in northern Matanzas, allowing 4,993 persons to depart the country before November 15 (Clark 1975: 86). Camarioca ushered in a second migrant wave from revolutionary Cuba.

Diplomatic negotiations between Washington and Havana established a regular air bridge between Varadero (a tourist resort east of Havana) and Miami, beginning on December 1, 1965. The U.S. government touted the chartered planes as the Freedom Flights, evoking the Cold War ideology that gave rise to the effort. The airlift became the largest and longest refugee resettlement program in U.S. history, as twice-daily flights transported 260,561 Cubans to the United States (Masud-Piloto 1996: 68). On April 6, 1973, Castro canceled the flights, reducing the migration to a mere trickle.

By then, the exodus had become more representative of the island's population. As the number of professionals and managers decreased, the number of blue-collar and service workers increased. Skilled and semiskilled workers, salespersons, and small farmers were the bulk of the immigrants between 1965 and 1973. Shifts in the refugee flow mirrored the impact of revolutionary programs on wider segments of the Cuban population, such as small-scale merchants and artisans.

Although most of the Freedom Flights' refugees were white city dwellers, they were predominantly female, older, and less educated than earlier refugees, reflecting travel restrictions imposed by the Castro government. Moreover, economic motives loomed larger during this stage than before (Portes, Clark, and Bach 1977). The Freedom Flights thus expanded the socioeconomic diversity of Cubans in the United States.

Like their predecessors, the immigrants settled primarily in Miami, Hialeah, and other cities in South Florida. A secondary concentration emerged in the adjacent New Jersey towns of West New York and Union City. This area became known as Little Santa Clara because many exiles were from the province of Las Villas, now called Villa Clara (Prieto 2009). Smaller numbers established themselves in Puerto Rico, Venezuela, and Spain.

In 1966 the U.S. Congress passed Public Law 89-732, better known as the Cuban Adjustment Act. This legislation allowed Cuban citizens admitted or paroled into the United States to qualify for permanent residence a year later. Henceforth, most Cubans arriving in the United States have been authorized to stay.

THE MARIEL EXODUS

The third migrant wave, from Mariel harbor to Key West, Florida, took place between April 21 and September 26, 1980. One reason for the Mariel boatlift was that in 1979, more than one hundred thousand exiles had visited Cuba, renewing contacts with relatives and familiarizing them with economic opportunities abroad. The immediate cause of the exodus was the takeover of the Peruvian embassy in Havana by more than 10,800 Cubans who wanted to migrate. In a reprise of Camarioca, the Cuban government opened the port of Mariel, near Havana, for those who could be picked up by relatives living abroad.

Thus began what became known as the "Freedom Flotilla" in the United States. When exiles arrived in Mariel aboard private boats and ships, Cuban officials forced them to take unrelated persons, some of whom had been inmates at prisons or psychiatric hospitals, while others had been identified as prostitutes and homosexuals. Consequently, the Mariel exodus tarnished the reputation of the entire Cuban American community. The boatlift ended abruptly when Castro closed Mariel for further emigration.

The Mariel exodus brought 124,779 Cubans to Key West. Most of the "Marielitos" (as they were pejoratively labeled) were young, single men with a working-class background and an elementary education. Approximately 20 percent classified themselves as black or "other" (most likely mulattos), compared to only 7 percent of the Cubans who had arrived between 1960 and 1964 (Pedraza 2007: 158). Contrary to media reports, less than 2 percent of the Marielitos were common criminals, though 25 percent had been imprisoned in Cuba for various reasons, including ideological differences with the Cuban government and "antisocial" behavior such as public displays of homosexuality (Clark, Lazaga, and Roque 1981: 7; see also Hernández and Gomis 1986). The socioeconomic profile of the Mariel exodus thus departed significantly from the profiles of previous refugee waves, especially those of the early 1960s.

The 1980 boatlift deepened the rifts between "old" and "new" Cubans in Miami, where most of the latter group settled. The inverse relationship between date of departure from Cuba and social status became more visible than ever. The diminutive term Marielito itself signaled the public scorn of the new arrivals. Initially, Mariel Cubans faced unemployment, low-paid work, and welfare dependence. Most ended up working for themselves or their compatriots (Portes, Clark, and Manning 1985; Portes and Jensen 1989).

In the United States, Mariel Cubans were labeled "entrants (status pending)," an ambivalent legal category that did not provide the benefits of political asylum. To qualify as refugees, applicants had to prove a "well-founded fear of persecution" for political or religious reasons in their home country. Yet dissidence from the Castro regime was increasingly difficult to verify. In December 1984 the U.S. and Cuban governments reached an agreement allowing a minimum of twenty thousand Cubans to emigrate, but the Cuban government suspended the agreement in May 1985 and reinstated it in November 1987. Accordingly, the exodus slowed. Between 1981 and 1989 the United States admitted only 148,612 Cubans (U.S. Department of Justice 1981–89).

THE *BALSEROS*

The fourth migrant wave began during the Special Period in Peacetime, the official euphemism for Cuba's prolonged economic crisis after the fall of the Berlin Wall in 1989 and the collapse of the Soviet Union in 1991 (Ackerman 1997; Martínez et al. 1996; Pedraza 2000). In the latter year, the U.S. Interests Section in Havana stopped granting new visas because of a backlog in applications. Hence, unauthorized exits became the primary means of leaving the island during the early 1990s. Migratory pressures accumulated rapidly, including broad sectors of the population.

Material deprivation and family reunification became increasingly salient reasons for leaving Cuba, although ideological factors continued to be important. When interviewed in Cuba, would-be migrants said they wanted to move primarily for economic or personal reasons, especially to reunite with relatives living abroad. Once detained in the U.S. naval base in Guantánamo, most rafters claimed that their chief motivation was the desire for freedom and release from state control (Ackerman and Clark 1995; Martínez et al. 1996).

Cubans increasingly resembled economic migrants from other Caribbean countries, such as Haiti or the Dominican Republic, driven abroad by their quest to improve their living standards. Most were unskilled laborers and service workers, reflecting the occupational distribution of Cuba's population more accurately than ever before. In addition, most were relatively young, male, light-skinned, urban in origin, and born in Cuba's western provinces, especially Havana (Aja Díaz 1999, 2009; Martínez et al. 1996). This pattern continued during the first decade of the twenty-first century.

In 1994 migratory pressures in Cuba erupted into the *balsero* crisis. The Spanish term *balseros* (rafters) refers to people attempting to sail across the Straits of Florida in rafts, inner tubes, small boats, and other improvised vessels. At least 63,175 Cuban rafters arrived in the United States between 1959 and 1994 (Ackerman and Clark 1995: 2). During the fall of 1994 unauthorized migration from Cuba broke all the records established during the Mariel boatlift. The immediate cause of the exodus was the decline in the material conditions of daily life in Cuba, including food and water shortages, power blackouts, deteriorating public health, and a decaying infrastructure, particularly in housing and transportation.

President Bill Clinton refused to accept the rafters as refugees, however. On August 19 he instructed the U.S. Coast Guard to detain Cubans at sea and take them to the U.S. naval base in Guantánamo, Panama, and other safe havens. Between August 13 and September 13, the U.S. Coast Guard interdicted 30,879 Cubans (Rodríguez Chávez 1997: 112). On September 9 Washington and Havana renewed their 1984 agreement, allowing the migration of at least twenty thousand Cubans per year and creating a special lottery for five thousand new visa applications.

The *balsero* crisis led to a major change in U.S. policy toward Cuban migrants. On May 2, 1995, the Clinton administration announced that the United States would not give automatic asylum to Cubans interdicted at sea. Since then, the U.S. government has treated those leaving Cuba without visas as undocumented immigrants subject to deportation. As the Cuban American sociologist Max Castro (2002: 5) notes, "Recent immigration from Cuba does not enjoy a privileged position relative to other large Caribbean nations, at least quantitatively." However, the Cuban Adjustment Act still allows Cubans to remain in the United States if they reach U.S. territory (the "wet foot/dry foot" policy) (see Henken 2005). In chapter 7 I assess recent trends and projections in the Cuban exodus.

The Puerto Rican Exodus

The Nineteenth Century

THE "PILGRIMS OF FREEDOM"

At the end of the nineteenth century, most Puerto Rican migrants went to other Caribbean and Latin American countries, especially the Dominican Republic, Cuba, Panama, and Venezuela. Since then, working-class Puerto Ricans have migrated primarily for economic reasons, such as chronic unemployment and persistent poverty. Some political exiles also sought refuge in the United States, particularly in New York City, after the Grito de Lares, the island's aborted insurrection against Spanish colonialism in 1868 (see table 2.3). Between 1868 and 1895 the United States admitted only 690 Puerto Ricans (U.S. Bureau of Statistics 1868–92; U.S. Commissioner-General of Immigration 1893–95).

This small group of exiles has been called "the Pilgrims of Freedom" because they supported the island's independence from Spain (Ojeda Reyes 1992). In 1895 they created the Puerto Rican Section of the Partido Revolucionario Cubano (PRC) in New York City, advocating an "Antillean Confederation" of the Cuban, Puerto Rican, and Dominican republics. Most of the expatriates were light-skinned, affluent, and well-educated professionals such as physicians, teachers, and journalists. Among them were prominent intellectuals such as Eugenio María de Hostos, Ramón Emeterio Betances, Segundo Ruiz Belvis, Lola Rodríguez de Tió, Sotero Figueroa, and Arturo Alfonso Schomburg. Immediately after 1898, when the United States took over the island, few Puerto Ricans moved to the U.S. mainland. The 1900 U.S. Census counted only 703 persons born in Puerto Rico (Ruggles et al. 2010).

The Twentieth Century

THE "PIONEERS"

The second phase of Puerto Rican migration started when thousands of islanders sought work abroad. The U.S. occupation of the island facilitated the relocation of Puerto Ricans to other Caribbean and Pacific territories under U.S. hegemony. Between 1898 and 1930 at least thirty-one thousand moved to Cuba, the Dominican Republic, Hawaii, and the U.S. Virgin Islands

(History Task Force 1979; Mustelier Ayala 2006; Rosario Natal 1983; Senior 1947).

Beginning in 1900 the first major migrant stream of Puerto Ricans under U.S. rule was directed to Hawaii, another recently acquired U.S. territory. Most were recruited to cut sugarcane. Until 1920 Hawaii had the highest concentration of Puerto Rican migrants of any U.S. territory. Smaller settlements appeared in states like California and Arizona, along the travel routes to Hawaii. Others relocated across the U.S. mainland, especially after 1917, when Congress granted U.S. citizenship to Puerto Ricans. The U.S. armed forces recruited nearly eighteen thousand islanders during World War I, including four thousand to guard the Panama Canal (Whalen 2005: 14). Hundreds worked in mainland military bases and industries. Thousands went back to the island during the Great Depression of the 1930s.

The largest mainland Puerto Rican settlements emerged in New York City, the U.S. seaport with the best transportation and trade links with San Juan since the nineteenth century. Also, the city offered abundant employment opportunities in manufacturing and services after European immigration dwindled in the 1920s. Until the 1940s, most Puerto Ricans traveled on steamships such as the *Marine Tiger*, the *Borinquen*, and the *Coamo* (Matos-Rodríguez and Hernández 2001). About seventy-one thousand Puerto Ricans moved to the mainland between 1900 and 1944.

During the first two decades of the twentieth century, thousands of skilled Puerto Rican workers, especially cigar makers, arrived in the United States. Among them were labor leaders Bernardo Vega, Jesús Colón, and Joaquín Colón and anarchist and feminist Luisa Capetillo. Between 1917 and 1944, Puerto Ricans settled primarily in working-class neighborhoods of New York City, such as Chelsea, East Harlem, the Lower East Side and West Side of Manhattan, and the Brooklyn Navy Yard. By the 1920s the immigrants concentrated in East Harlem, especially between East 96th and 125th Streets, which quickly became known as Spanish Harlem or simply El Barrio (Sánchez Korrol 1994). Many Puerto Rican communities (or *colonias*, as they were called then) developed alongside African American neighborhoods such as Harlem in Manhattan or Bedford-Stuyvesant in Brooklyn. These compact settlements incorporated other Spanish-speaking groups, especially Cubans and Spaniards, and were racially diverse. In the 1940s two-thirds of New York's Puerto Ricans were classified as white and one-third as black or mulatto (Mills, Senior, and Goldsen 1950: 25).

TABLE 2.3 Puerto Rican Diaspora to the United States, 1868–2009

Years	Number of Migrants	Related Historical Events
1868–69	13	The Lares revolt for Puerto Rican independence fails (1868). The Puerto Rican patriots Ramón Emeterio Betances and Eugenio María de Hostos flee to New York City (1869).
1870–79	202	Slavery is abolished in Puerto Rico (1873).
1880–89	234	Spain suppresses the autonomist movement in Puerto Rico (1887).
1890–99	241	The Puerto Rican Section of the Partido Revolucionario Cubano (PRC) is established in New York City (1895). Spain grants autonomy to Puerto Rico and Cuba (1897). U.S. troops occupy Puerto Rico during the Spanish-Cuban-American War (1898).
1900–1909	2,000	The United States sets up a civilian government in Puerto Rico through the Foraker Act (1900). The first expedition of Puerto Rican contract workers to Hawaii begins (1900). The U.S. Supreme Court rules that Puerto Ricans are not aliens in the United States for immigration purposes (1904). The Club Social Puertorriqueño is founded in San Francisco (1906).
1910–19	5,580	The Jones Act extends U.S. citizenship to Puerto Ricans (1917). The Club Demócrata Puertorriqueño is founded in New York City (1918).
1920–29	35,638	The Liga Puertorriqueña e Hispana and the Club Caborrojeño are founded in New York City (1922).
1930–39	12,715	The Puerto Rican government establishes the Bureau of Employment and Identification in New York City (1930). Oscar García Rivera is the first Puerto Rican elected to the New York State Assembly (1937).
1940–49	144,930	The Puerto Rican government launches Operation Bootstrap to promote the island's industrialization (1947). The Puerto Rican government creates the Employment and Migration Bureau (1947). Puerto Rico's Farm Labor Program begins recruiting workers for the U.S. mainland (1947). Luis Muñoz Marín is the first elected governor of Puerto Rico (1948).

TABLE 2.3 *(continued)*

Years	Number of Migrants	Related Historical Events
1950–59	460,826	Puerto Rico's Labor Department establishes the Migration Division (1951). The constitution of the Commonwealth of Puerto Rico is promulgated (1952). The Puerto Rican Day Parade is founded in New York City (1958).
1960–69	144,725	Radical Puerto Ricans form the Young Lords Organization in Chicago (1969).
1970–79	76,198	Herman Badillo is the first Puerto Rican elected to the U.S. House of Representatives (1970). New York City enters a financial crisis (1975).
1980–89	287,451	The Puerto Rican government creates the Department of Puerto Rican Community Affairs in the United States (1989).
1990–99	325,875	The Department of Puerto Rican Community Affairs in the United States is eliminated (1993). The phaseout of Section 936 of the Internal Revenue Code begins (1996).
2000–2009	299,700	The Puerto Rico Federal Affairs Administration (PRFAA) is downsized (2005–6). The Commonwealth government shuts down for a month (2006). Puerto Rico experiences a prolonged recession (2006–11).
Total	1,791,217	

Sources: Banco Gubernamental de Fomento 2010; Junta de Planificación 1970–89, 2001; Senior 1947; U.S. Bureau of Statistics 1868–92; U.S. Commission on Civil Rights 1976; U.S. Commissioner-General of Immigration 1893–98; Vázquez Calzada 1979.

THE "GREAT MIGRATION"

The third stage of the Puerto Rican exodus took place roughly between 1945 and 1964 (Clara Rodríguez 1989). Net migration between the island and the mainland peaked at more than 650,000 persons during this period. The island's agricultural economy, particularly in sugar, coffee, and tobacco, had plummeted since 1930. After World War II the government's industrialization program, Operation Bootstrap, displaced thousands of rural workers to urban areas. Especially hard-hit was the central mountainous region, including the coffee-growing municipalities of Utuado, Lares, Jayuya, and Maricao, which suffered large population losses. Insufficient jobs on the island, combined with a growing demand for cheap labor on the mainland, sparked the first massive emigration in the 1940s and 1950s.

Agricultural laborers were an important component of the postwar Puerto Rican diaspora (see chapter 4). During the 1960s an average of 17,600 workers traveled to the mainland each year under Puerto Rico's Farm Labor Program (Monserrat 1991). Several migrant communities originated as former contract workers resettled in cities such as Philadelphia, Lancaster, Camden, Buffalo, Hartford, Boston, Milwaukee, Detroit, and Miami. Most of the migrants were young, male, unskilled workers with little education and knowledge of the English language. They were largely incorporated into the lower rungs of the U.S. labor market, particularly in seasonal agriculture, light manufacturing, and domestic service. Because many Puerto Ricans had African ancestry, they were often treated as black and denied access to better jobs, housing areas, and schools.

After 1946 most Puerto Ricans arrived in New York City in commercial airplanes, making them the first large-scale airborne migration in history. Pan American, Eastern, and later American and other U.S. airlines transported increasing numbers of passengers between San Juan and New York City. In a classic short story, Luis Rafael Sánchez (1994) coined the metaphor of a "flying bus" (la guagua aérea),[2] suggesting that Puerto Ricans shuttle between the island and the mainland as if they were just taking a brief bus ride. As flights between San Juan and New York became cheaper, shorter, and more frequent, Puerto Ricans became a "nation on the move" (Duany 2002). Moreover, air transportation eased back-and-forth movement between the island and the mainland. Thus began the circulation of Puerto Ricans that continues today.

Postwar Puerto Rican communities in New York City spread across the Harlem and East Rivers into the South Bronx and South Brooklyn, transforming neighborhoods such as Williamsburg and Sunset Park. Most of the immigrants settled in dilapidated inner-city housing areas abandoned by other ethnic groups such as the Irish, Italians, and Jews. Puerto Ricans became the second-largest minority in New York City, after African Americans; the second-largest Hispanic population in the United States, after Mexicans; and one of the most disadvantaged groups, together with American Indians and later Dominicans.

From New York, Puerto Ricans expanded to New Jersey, Connecticut, and Pennsylvania. A Puerto Rican nucleus emerged around Philadelphia, Camden, Lancaster, and other cities along the Delaware River Valley (Whalen 2001). A secondary concentration developed in the Midwest during the 1950s, particularly in Chicago, Cleveland, and smaller industrial cities such as Lorain, Ohio, and Gary, Indiana. During the 1970s, more Puerto Ricans began to move to the South, principally to Orlando, Florida (see chapter 5).

THE "REVOLVING DOOR"

A restless circulation of people characterized the fourth period of the Puerto Rican exodus, roughly between 1965 and 1980. In several years, more Puerto Ricans went back to the island than left for the U.S. mainland, especially as a result of minimum-wage hikes on the island and the fiscal crisis in New York City, the historic core of the Puerto Rican diaspora (Edwin Meléndez 1993). During the 1970s, net migration to the mainland reached its lowest point (less than 76,200) since World War II (table 2.3). Among the main causes of the return flow were declining living conditions and employment opportunities in New York City, Chicago, and Philadelphia.

Consequently, the movement of first- and second-generation Puerto Ricans to the island took massive proportions. The 1980 census found that 6.2 percent of Puerto Rico's population was born in the fifty United States, mostly of Puerto Rican parents (U.S. Census Bureau 1984). The presence of hundreds of thousands of Puerto Ricans raised in the United States and speaking English as their first language raises important issues about the island's cultural identity, notably the role of the Spanish language as a symbol of that identity. The island has also received a smaller but growing number of foreigners, mostly from the Dominican Republic and Cuba (see chapter 9). As I argue in chapter 10, Puerto Rico has become a "transnational migrant crossroads."

THE POST-NUYORICAN PHASE

High emigration rates resurged in the 1980s, largely because of the persistent discrepancy between wages in Puerto Rico and the United States. In 1989 island workers earned on average less than half as much as their U.S. counterparts. The gap was much higher in some occupations, such as police officers, construction workers, electricians, nurses, and physicians (Sotomayor 2000). Beginning in 1996 the phaseout of Section 936 of the Internal Revenue Code wreaked havoc on the island. (Section 936 allowed U.S.

corporations to operate in Puerto Rico and other U.S. possessions without paying federal taxes.) In 2009 poverty levels on the island (45 percent) more than tripled those in the fifty United States (13 percent). That same year, Puerto Rico's unemployment rate (18.9 percent) nearly doubled that of the United States (9.9 percent) (U.S. Census Bureau 2010). Largely because of such economic woes, more than 913,000 Puerto Ricans moved to the mainland between 1980 and 2009.

Today, most Puerto Rican migrants continue to be blue-collar and service workers, who are more likely to be unemployed and earn lower wages on the island than abroad (Edwin Meléndez 2007). However, middle-class sectors have increasingly relocated abroad, seeking a better "quality of life," including security, tranquility, health, housing, and education. The new migrants include a substantial proportion of teachers, nurses, engineers, and physicians, among other well-qualified professionals. Journalists have sounded the alarm of a "brain drain" from the island. Paradoxically, the migrants' racial composition underrepresents both the "white" and "black" sectors of the population and overrepresents those who consider themselves "other." During the 1990s most migrants classified themselves as "some other race" (55.2 percent), while 39.8 percent described themselves as white and only 4.5 percent as black (Christenson 2001).

The current stage may be called "post-Nuyorican" because many Puerto Ricans have moved away from the New York metropolitan area, especially to Central and South Florida. As the diaspora has become more scattered, regional differences have intensified. For instance, Puerto Rican communities in the Southeast and Southwest tend to be financially better off than those in the Northeast and Midwest (Acosta-Belén and Santiago 2006). Moreover, Puerto Ricans are more likely to encounter Cubans in Miami and Mexicans in Los Angeles than either group in New York City, where they are more prone to interact with African Americans and Dominicans.

Partly in response to local conditions, stateside Puerto Ricans have developed varied cultural identities. For example, "Chicago-Ricans" embraced a pan-Latino label earlier than elsewhere, because they often mingled with Mexicans as coworkers, neighbors, and marriage partners, and mobilized politically according to their common Hispanic origins (Felix Padilla 1985). Still, Puerto Ricans and Mexicans in Chicago and elsewhere racialize each other's cultural and language practices and maintain their social distance, reinforced by distinct settlement patterns (de Genova and Ramos-Zayas

2003). I take up the issue of the intersecting identities of Puerto Ricans as Hispanics or Latinos in chapter 5.

The Dominican Exodus

The Trujillo Era

Two main periods mark Dominican migration to the United States and Puerto Rico: before and after 1961 (see table 2.4). Under the three-decade dictatorship of Rafael Leónidas Trujillo (1930–61), the Dominican government issued few passports — only 1,805 out of 19,631 applications in 1959 (de Frank Canelo 1982: 42). Trujillo's restrictive policies sought to prevent criticism of his regime and promote population growth in the Dominican Republic (Grasmuck and Pessar 1991; Ramona Hernández 2002). Hence, the number of Dominicans abroad was extremely low. Between 1930 and 1961, the United States admitted just 19,148 Dominicans. According to the census, U.S. residents of Dominican birth rose from 1,212 in 1930 to 12,044 in 1960 (figures 2.1 and 2.2). At this stage, Dominican migration consisted primarily of upper- and middle-class people, especially entrepreneurs and professionals, some of whom were exiles. Most were light-skinned and well-educated. Among them were two well-known literary scholars, the siblings Pedro and Camila Henríquez Ureña, who taught at several U.S. universities, and Juan Bosch, Trujillo's longtime nemesis.

Small Dominican settlements emerged in New York City during the first half of the twentieth century, especially on the Upper West Side of Manhattan, near the current site of Lincoln Center; in Morningside Heights, near Columbia University; and in East Harlem. At the time, many working-class Puerto Ricans, Cubans, and Spaniards lived in these neighborhoods. The first known Dominican-owned bodega (grocery store) in the city was established in 1933 on West 100th Street in Upper Manhattan (Rodríguez de León 1998: 185). During the 1950s a Dominican community developed in the Corona section of Queens, which still has a substantial Dominican population (Ricourt 2002; Ricourt and Danta 2003). Because many of the first arrivals were from the northern town of Sabana Iglesia, near Santiago de los Caballeros, they called the Corona area "Sabana Church" (Hendricks 1974). By the early 1960s Dominicans congregated on the Lower East Side of Manhattan, in the Williamsburg section of Brooklyn, and, increasingly, in the Upper Manhattan neighborhoods of Washington Heights and Inwood.

TABLE 2.4 Dominican Diaspora to the United States, 1925–2009

Years	Number of Migrants	Related Historical Events
1925–29	2,422	After eight years of occupation, U.S. marines withdraw from the Dominican Republic (1924).
1930–39	1,333	Rafael Leónidas Trujillo rules the Dominican Republic (1930–61). Trujillo's army massacres Haitians along the Dominican-Haitian border (1937). Juan Bosch is exiled (1938–61). Bosch forms the Partido Revolucionario Dominicano (PRD) in Havana (1939).
1940–49	4,099	Pedro Henríquez Ureña is a visiting professor at Harvard University (1940–41). The United States ends its customs receivership of the Dominican Republic, established since 1905 (1941). Camila Henríquez Ureña teaches at Vassar College (1941–59).
1950–59	9,915	Trujillo's secret police kidnaps and murders the Spanish exile Jesús de Galíndez (1956).
1960–69	84,065	The Mirabal sisters, who opposed Trujillo, are assassinated (1960). Trujillo is assassinated (1961). Bosch is elected president (1962). The Centro Cívico Cultural Dominicano is founded in New York City (1962). Joaquín Balaguer forms the Partido Revolucionario Social Cristiano (PRSC) in New York City (1963). A coup d'état deposes President Bosch (1963). A civil war takes place in Santo Domingo (1965). The United States invades the Dominican Republic (1965–66). The Club Juan Pablo Duarte is founded in New York City (1966). Balaguer is elected president and reelected twice (1966–78).
1970–79	141,578	The first news of undocumented Dominican migration is reported in Puerto Rico (1972). Bosch forms the Partido de la Liberación Dominicana (PLD) (1973). Antonio Guzmán is elected president (1978).
1980–89	226,853	Twenty-two Dominican stowaways suffocate in the cargo ship Regina Express (1980). The first Dominican Day Parade is held in New York City (1982).

TABLE 2.4 (*continued*)

Years	Number of Migrants	Related Historical Events
		Dominicans protest against austerity measures imposed by the International Monetary Fund (1985).
		The U.S. Immigration Reform and Control Act (IRCA) is approved (1986).
		Alianza Dominicana is founded in New York City (1987).
1990–99	365,545	Guillermo Linares is the first Dominican elected to the New York City Council (1991).
		The Dominican Congress approves dual citizenship (1994).
		Adriano Espaillat is the first Dominican elected to the New York State Assembly (1996).
		Leonel Fernández is elected president of the Dominican Republic (1996).
		The Dominican Congress approves external voting in presidential elections (1997).
		The Dominican American National Roundtable (DANR) and Dominicanos 2000 are formed (1997).
2000–2009	292,728	Overseas Dominicans vote in presidential elections (2004).
		Leonel Fernández is twice reelected president (2004, 2008).
Total	1,128,538	

Sources: Larson and Sullivan 1989; U.S. Citizenship and Immigration Services 2002–9; U.S. Department of Justice 1962–77, 1978–95, 1996–2001.

After Trujillo

THE 1960S

Large-scale migration from the Dominican Republic began shortly after Trujillo's assassination on May 30, 1961. The volume of Dominicans admitted to the United States multiplied tenfold between the 1950s and 1960s. The earliest groups to leave the Dominican Republic after 1961 were affiliated with the Trujillo regime, especially conservative political leaders, government employees, and members of the ruling class. Beginning in 1962 U.S. Ambassador John Bartlow Martin openly facilitated migration to stabilize the Dominican Republic and prevent "another Cuba." The U.S. consulate in Santo Domingo gave immigrant visas to hundreds of alleged "Castro/Communist subversive agents" (Martin 1966: 7–8). On September 25, 1963, a coup d'état deposed the recently elected President Bosch, provoking a second wave of moderate and radical expatriates. The 1965 U.S. invasion of Santo Domingo culminated a cycle of political violence that led to the deportation of more "subversives." The beginnings of Dominican mass migration thus were rooted in political turbulence.

Since the mid-1960s, the steep decline of sugar, coffee, and other traditional agricultural exports undermined the socioeconomic status of the Dominican rural population. Growing numbers of people flocked from the countryside to the cities, especially the capital, Santo Domingo, and later to San Juan and New York. Many left their villages in the Cibao Valley, such as Sabana Iglesia, Licey al Medio, Tamboril, El Rubio, and Los Ranchos (Georges 1990; González 1970; Grasmuck and Pessar 1991; Hendricks 1974). The main reason for emigration from this region was a large pool of surplus workers created by a decaying agricultural economy.

THE 1970S

A second stage began in the 1970s, as material hardship increasingly drove the Dominican exodus. By 1974 three-fourths of the Dominicans living in the United States and Puerto Rico came from urban areas, especially Santo Domingo. Most had belonged to relatively affluent social strata in the Dominican Republic, as measured by their occupational status and educational attainment (Ugalde, Bean, and Cárdenas 1979; see also Báez Evertsz and d'Oleo Ramírez 1985; and Grasmuck and Pessar 1991). The high cost of moving abroad — even illegally — prevented the poorest of the poor from leaving their country. The migrants' primary motivations were escaping unemployment and underemployment, as well as securing higher incomes and consumption levels. As many Dominicans put it, they move abroad *buscando mejor vida* — searching for a better life, meaning better jobs and higher salaries.

THE 1980S

During this phase, the crisis of the Dominican economy boosted the volume of migrants. Growing unemployment and underemployment; the rising cost of living; a chaotic transportation system; and the near-collapse in basic public services such as electricity, running water, housing, health care, and education were powerful incentives to move abroad. In addition, the Dominican economy suffered from declining prices for its major export crops (including sugar, coffee, cocoa, and tobacco); rising prices for oil, foodstuffs, and other imported commodities; an increasing deficit in the balance of payments; and a growing foreign debt. As in other Latin American countries, the 1980s were a "lost decade" for the Dominican economy. The basic incentive for the large-scale displacement of Dominicans to the United States was the wide gulf in the wage levels of the two countries — especially since 1983, with the first of many devaluations of the Dominican peso vis-à-vis the U.S. dollar. (In July 2010 the official exchange rate was thirty-seven pesos per dollar.)

As the exodus expanded, it became more representative of the sending population, including more blacks and mulattos, as well as members of the lower classes. By 1990 more than 25 percent of the Dominicans in New York City said they were black, while 24 percent considered themselves white and 50 percent described their race as "other" (Grasmuck and Pessar 1996: 285). Given U.S. restrictions on immigrant visas, many Dominicans traveled illegally on unseaworthy boats, known as *yolas*, to Puerto Rico (Hernández and López 1997; Hernández Angueira 1997; Ricourt 2007), which became the preferred entry point to the United States for undocumented Dominicans (see chapter 9).

SINCE THE 1990S

The Dominican government responded to the economic crisis of the 1980s by promoting export manufacturing (especially through *zonas francas*, or free trade zones), tourism, and nontraditional agricultural exports. Although this strategy stimulated economic growth during the 1990s, it did not improve living conditions for most Dominicans. Instead, unemployment and poverty levels have expanded considerably. Hence, emigration has become a common survival strategy for the lower and middle classes. The root causes of the sustained movement of Dominicans are the extensive labor market dislocations produced by a development strategy that privileges tourism and export industrialization but creates insufficient jobs to replace those lost in agriculture and other traditional economic sectors (Torres-Saillant and Hernández 1998: 53–60).

The exodus reached unprecedented levels during the 1990s but tapered off somewhat during the first decade of the twenty-first century. The U.S. government admitted 365,545 Dominicans between 1990 and 1999 and 292,728 between 2000 and 2009. At the same time, undocumented migration rose dramatically. Between 1990 and 2009 the U.S. Coast Guard (2009) intercepted 35,471 undocumented Dominicans at sea; many more were not caught and entered Puerto Rico clandestinely.

Dominican migrants can no longer be portrayed exclusively as either middle or lower class, urban or rural, educated or illiterate. As the Dominican American sociologist Ramona Hernández (2002: 26–27) argues, the migrants are not "a monolithic group endowed with high human capital qualities, who move in search of improving their incomes and who do not represent surplus labor in the sending society." The current migrant flow — both documented and undocumented — represents a broad cross section of the Dominican population.

Recent statistics suggest a bimodal occupational distribution among Dominicans admitted to the United States (table 2.5). On the one hand, one out of three migrants had a relatively skilled and well-paying job in the Dominican Republic, such as manager, professional, salesperson, or office worker. On the other hand, two out of three were employed in low-skilled and low-paying occupations, particularly as service, factory, and construction workers. The small proportion of agricultural workers suggests that most were not from the countryside. Thus, the contemporary Dominican diaspora draws primarily on the urban working class rather than the middle class or the peasantry.

The Hispanic Caribbean and Its Diasporas:
A Transnational History

The transnational movement of people from the Spanish-speaking countries of the Caribbean islands took on massive proportions during the second half of the twentieth century. Growing numbers of Cubans, then Puerto Ricans, and finally Dominicans have resettled in the United States. Today, few regions of the world have such a large share — nearly one-third — of their populations living abroad. Although the Cuban exodus began well before 1959, it intensified with the radical changes in Cuba's political ideology and social structure. Puerto Rico exported much of its surplus labor during the swift transition from an agricultural to an industrial economy after 1947. The Dominican exodus took off in the aftermath of the political and economic instability of the post-Trujillo era, beginning in 1961. Although historical factors specific to each sending country precipitated these population movements, they have all produced large-scale, long-term diasporas.

Transnational migration from the Spanish-speaking Caribbean has now taken place over several generations. Before World War II, leaving their countries was not a basic livelihood strategy for most Hispanic Caribbean

TABLE 2.5 Occupational Background of Dominican Immigrants Admitted to the United States, 2003–2008, and Occupational Structure of the Dominican Republic, 2007 (in Percentages)

Occupation in Country of Origin	Dominicans Admitted to U.S.	Occupational Structure of Dominican Republic
Managers and professionals	16.1	15.4
Sales and office	18.7	26.8[a]
Production, transportation, and material moving	15.8	26.1
Construction, extraction, maintenance, and repair	11.4	21.4
Service	31.5	—
Farming, fishing, and forestry	6.4	9.5
Armed forces	—	0.8

Sources: Oficina Nacional de Estadística 2009a; U.S. Citizenship and Immigration Services 2003–8.

[a]Includes service workers.

residents. But over the last five decades, diasporic communities from Puerto Rico, Cuba, and the Dominican Republic have mushroomed, especially in New York City and Miami, as well as in other cities and countries, including Puerto Rico itself. One understudied aspect of these communities is their interaction with one another (see Virginia Domínguez 1978). Another pending issue is the extent to which each group has embraced the *Latino* or *Hispanic* sobriquet in the United States (see chapters 4 and 5). Moreover, the dispersal of Cubans, Dominicans, and Puerto Ricans poses numerous questions about the intersections among national identities, legal boundaries, and cultural borders, which are addressed throughout this book. The next chapter analyzes the contemporary situation of the three diasporas in the United States.

The Contemporary Hispanic Caribbean Diasporas

A Comparative Approach

In 2009 almost 7.5 million U.S. residents were of Puerto Rican, Cuban, or Dominican ancestry (U.S. Census Bureau 2010).[1] This figure is equal to 29.8 percent of the combined populations of Puerto Rico, Cuba, and the Dominican Republic. Such large-scale population displacements have transformed daily life in the Spanish-speaking countries of the Caribbean islands — from family structure and religious practices to businesses and political ideology. They have also reshaped the physical and cultural landscape of several U.S. neighborhoods, cities, and states. Their impact is most notable in New York City and Miami, their main ports of entry. In particular, Hispanic Caribbean diasporas have contributed to eroding the conventional dichotomy between black and white people that has prevailed throughout U.S. history and continues to be important today.

This chapter assesses six aspects of the current settlements of Cubans, Dominicans, and Puerto Ricans in the United States. First, the immigrants concentrate in several northeastern and southeastern states and metropolitan areas. Second, Hispanic Caribbean communities in the United States have adopted transnational spatial practices that connect them to their home countries. Third, each diaspora has followed distinct modes of incorporation into the U.S. labor market. Fourth, remittances have become increasingly significant to the Hispanic Caribbean. Fifth, public discourses toward migration in both sending and receiving societies are extremely ambivalent and often contradictory. Sixth, the racial compositions of the three migrant groups differ greatly, according to recent U.S. census data.

TABLE 3.1 Top States for Hispanic Caribbean Residents of the United States, 2009

Cubans			Dominicans			Puerto Ricans		
State	Number	%	State	Number	%	State	Number	%
Florida	1,158,152	68.3	New York	672,145	49.6	New York	1,099,167	24.8
New Jersey	89,269	5.3	New Jersey	168,229	12.4	Florida	816,002	18.4
California	75,790	4.4	Florida	160,683	11.8	New Jersey	424,891	9.6
New York	70,870	4.2	Massachusetts	105,610	7.8	Pennsylvania	346,786	7.8
Texas	37,087	2.2	Pennsylvania	55,440	4.1	Massachusetts	250,136	5.7

Source: U.S. Census Bureau 2010.

Current Settlement Patterns

For decades, Hispanic Caribbean migrants have clustered in the northeastern and southeastern United States. According to the 2009 American Community Survey, more than two-thirds of all U.S. Cubans live in Florida, whereas half of the Dominicans and slightly less than one-fourth of the Puerto Ricans live in the state of New York (table 3.1). Puerto Ricans are thus more scattered than Cubans and Dominicans, who agglomerate in a single state. All three groups have substantial concentrations in New York, New Jersey, and Florida. Puerto Rico has also received thousands of Dominican and Cuban immigrants since the 1960s (see chapter 9).

Within their primary states of destination, Hispanic Caribbean migrants congregate in the metropolitan areas of southern New York, northeastern New Jersey, and South and Central Florida (table 3.2). For Cubans, the top five settlements are in Miami, New York, Tampa, Los Angeles, and Orlando. For Dominicans, New York, Miami, Boston, Providence, and Orlando are the leading areas. Puerto Ricans cluster in New York, Orlando, Philadelphia, Miami, and Chicago. Many of these places have more people of Hispanic Caribbean ancestry than the largest cities in the countries of origin. Miami has more Cuban residents than Santiago de Cuba, Cuba's second-largest city, while New York City has more Puerto Rican residents than San Juan, the capital of Puerto Rico, and more Dominican residents than Santiago de los Caballeros, the second-largest city in the Dominican Republic. Furthermore, southwest Miami, the South Bronx, and Washington Heights have some of the highest densities of Cuban, Puerto Rican, and Dominican residents in the world.

TABLE 3.2 Top Metropolitan Areas for Hispanic Caribbean Residents of the United States, 2009

	Cubans			Dominicans			Puerto Ricans		
	Metropolitan Area	Number	%	Metropolitan Area	Number	%	Metropolitan Area	Number	%
	Miami–Ft. Lauderdale-Pompano Beach, Fla.	931,258	56.7	New York, N.Y.–Northern New Jersey–Long Island, N.Y.	800,460	59.0	New York, N.Y.–Northern New Jersey–Long Island, N.Y.	1,241,206	28.0
	New York, N.Y.–Northern New Jersey–Long Island, N.Y.	139,193	8.4	Miami–Ft. Lauderdale–Pompano Beach, Fla.	97,286	7.1	Orlando–Kissimmee, Fla.	248,201	5.6
	Tampa–St. Petersburg–Clearwater, Fla.	80,246	4.9	Boston–Cambridge–Quincy, Mass.	89,196	6.6	Philadelphia, Pa.–Camden, N.J.–Wilmington, Del.	226,275	5.1
	Los Angeles–Long Beach–Santa Ana, Calif.	47,056	2.9	Providence, R.I.–New Bedford, Mass.–Fall River, Mass.	45,039	3.3	Miami–Ft. Lauderdale–Pompano Beach, Fla.	210,821	4.8
	Orlando–Kissimmee, Fla.	37,055	2.3	Orlando–Kissimmee, Fla.	28,663	2.1	Chicago–Naperville–Joliet, Ill.	173,264	3.9

Source: U.S. Census Bureau 2010.

Transnational Places

Migrants from the Hispanic Caribbean often remain symbolically tied to their homelands in their new places of residence. For example, they re-name streets and schools, redecorate inner and outer spaces, and organize parades to celebrate their heritage. In Washington Heights, Dominicans have rechristened public schools to honor prominent figures like Juan Pablo Duarte, Gregorio Luperón, Salomé Ureña, and Juan Bosch. In Miami, Cubans have renamed numerous streets and avenues, including Miami Sound Machine Boulevard (S.W. 10 Terrace), in honor of local heroes. In Union City, New Jersey, 43rd Street became Celia Cruz Way, after the famous Afro-Cuban singer. In Manhattan, thousands of Puerto Rican flags temporarily occupy Fifth Avenue every June for the Puerto Rican Day Parade. In Spanish Harlem, portions of East 106th Street are called Julia de Burgos Boulevard, after the best-known Puerto Rican poet, just as Jersey City has a Luis Muñoz Marín Boulevard, after the island's first elected governor. The commemora-tion of such iconic figures promotes the migrants' attachment to their coun-tries of origin.

Cubans in the United States are heavily concentrated in South Florida. With nearly 57 percent of all U.S. Cubans in 2009, the Miami metropolitan area is the hub of Cuban America. Little Havana stretches westward across four square miles from downtown Miami toward the sprawling suburban area that Cubans affectionately call La Sagüesera (the Cuban pronunciation of "Southwest"). Another sizable Cuban settlement is located in Hialeah, north of Miami. In 2000 almost 30 percent of all Cubans in Miami–Dade County lived in the central city district of Miami, while another 26 percent lived in Hialeah (U.S. Census Bureau 2009a).

In South Florida, Cuban American culture thrives through numerous Spanish-language mass media, coffee shops, bakeries, restaurants, bodegas, social clubs, private schools, churches (including Catholic, Protestant, Jew-ish, and Afro-Cuban denominations), artistic and musical activities, and the Calle Ocho Festival. The shrine to Our Lady of Charity embodies the Catho-lic identity of most Cubans in exile (Tweed 1997). In Little Havana, Cubans commonly speak Spanish at home, in businesses, and in the streets. Scores of voluntary associations — including the municipalities in exile — preserve social, cultural, and emotional ties between Cubans on and off the island. Nowhere can a Cuban American feel more at home than in Miami (see Pérez Firmat 1994).

In 2009 nearly 43 percent of all Dominicans in the United States lived in New York City (U.S. Census Bureau 2010). Washington Heights houses the single largest concentration of Dominicans outside the Dominican Republic. Dominican-owned bodegas, restaurants, bars, bakeries, beauty parlors, gypsy cabs (unregistered taxis), travel and remittance agencies, and retail stores, along with dozens of hometown clubs, create the atmosphere of "Quisqueya Heights," as many Dominican residents call their neighborhood (Quisqueya is said to be one of the indigenous names for the island of Hispaniola). Dominican popular music, especially merengue and *bachata*, is constantly played at home and in the streets. Since 1996 a local community festival has been dubbed "Quisqueya on the Hudson" (see Duany 2008b [1994]). New York City, especially Washington Heights, is so closely associated with the Dominican diaspora that scholars tend to focus on this area as a microcosm of the immigrants' experience (Aparicio 2006; Ricourt 1998, 2002; Sørensen 1994; Torres-Saillant and Hernández 1998; Weyland 1998). It is there that the transnational identity of U.S. Dominicans has taken shape most completely.

In 2009 almost 18 percent of stateside Puerto Ricans lived in New York City (U.S. Census Bureau 2010). Although the South Bronx has the largest number of Puerto Rican residents, Spanish Harlem (popularly known as El Barrio) is the historic center of the diaspora. In the 1930s about 22 percent of the city's Puerto Ricans lived in El Barrio; by 1990, about 6 percent did. According to the 2000 census, Puerto Ricans were 58 percent of the Hispanic residents of Spanish Harlem (U.S. Census Bureau 2009a). The area contains many icons of Puerto Rican culture, such as La Marqueta (the outdoor produce marketplace), restaurants and cafeterias selling *cuchifritos* (fried pig) and *mofongo* (mashed fried plantains), Pentecostal storefront churches, and *botánicas* (stores specializing in religious paraphernalia). Important artistic institutions include El Museo del Barrio, the Julia de Burgos Latino Cultural Center, and Taller Boricua.

The area is also home to many *casitas*, small, brightly colored, balloon-framed wooden houses reminiscent of Puerto Rican rural dwellings. More than five hundred *casitas* have been built in vacant lots in Spanish Harlem, the Lower East Side, and the South Bronx. Others can be found in the Puerto Rican barrios of Chicago and Boston. *Casitas* show how Puerto Ricans have appropriated urban space to revitalize their neighborhoods and recreate their memories of the island (Aponte-Parés 2000). Through such practices, Puerto Ricans in the United States invoke romanticized images of their

TABLE 3.3 Occupational Distribution of Hispanic Caribbean Workers in the United States, 2009 (in Percentages)

Occupation	Cubans	Dominicans	Puerto Ricans
Management, professional, and related	31.6	18.5	26.9
Sales and office	26.8	24.5	28.8
Production, transportation, and material moving	12.4	17.6	13.8
Construction, extraction, maintenance, and repair	10.3	7.4	7.4
Service	18.0	31.9	22.8
Farming, forestry, and fishing	0.9	0.2	0.2

Source: U.S. Census Bureau 2010.

Note: Second and third columns do not add up to 100 percent because of rounding.

homeland, even among members of the second and third generations (Toro-Morn and Alicea 2003).

Modes of Labor Incorporation

Migration from the Hispanic Caribbean has had a substantial impact on the U.S. labor market, particularly in the New York and Miami metropolitan areas. On average, Cuban workers hold better-paying jobs, such as managers and professionals, than other Hispanic Caribbean immigrants in the United States (table 3.3). Conversely, Puerto Ricans and Dominicans are more likely than Cubans to work in blue-collar and service occupations. As I document in chapter 2, Cuban refugees — especially in the early 1960s — tended to have relatively high occupational and educational levels in their home country. Their current occupational distribution in the United States largely reflects the human capital they possessed before migrating.

Hispanic Caribbean workers in the United States specialize in the service, trade, and manufacturing industries. Cubans are better represented in professional services, finance, insurance, real estate, and construction than Puerto Ricans and Dominicans (table 3.4). Meanwhile, Dominicans are more concentrated in trade, manufacturing, and transportation and warehousing than the other two groups. Puerto Ricans cluster in educational services, health care, social assistance, trade, and accommodation and food services. None of the three groups is well represented in agriculture, in-

TABLE 3.4 Industrial Distribution of Hispanic Caribbean Workers in the
United States, 2009 (in Percentages)

Industry	Cubans	Dominicans	Puerto Ricans
Agriculture, forestry, fishing and hunting, and mining	1.1	0.1	0.4
Construction	7.7	4.6	4.5
Manufacturing	8.4	9.0	8.8
Trade	15.7	17.2	16.0
Transportation and warehousing and utilities	6.5	7.3	6.1
Information	2.1	1.7	2.4
Finance, insurance, and real estate, rental, and leasing	7.9	6.3	7.5
Professional, scientific, and management and administrative and waste management services	11.4	9.4	9.7
Educational services and health care and social assistance	20.6	24.2	24.2
Arts, entertainment, and recreation and accommodation and food services	8.7	9.7	10.0
Other services (except public administration)	5.6	7.9	4.3
Public administration	4.2	2.5	6.2

Source: U.S. Census Bureau 2010.

Note: First, second, and third columns do not add up to 100 percent because of rounding.

formation, or public administration. Overall, the Hispanic Caribbean labor force concentrates in the service sector of the U.S. economy.

Other socioeconomic indicators confirm that Cubans tend to be more privileged than Puerto Ricans and Dominicans in the United States. On average, Cubans are better educated, wealthier, and more likely to be employed than other Hispanic Caribbean migrants (table 3.5). Of the three groups, Dominicans have the highest poverty rate, as well as the lowest household and per capita incomes. Although Puerto Ricans stand between Cubans and Dominicans on most counts, they are closer to Dominicans than Cubans in socioeconomic terms. The major exception to this trend is the relatively high proportion of English-speaking Puerto Ricans, largely due to the predominance of the U.S.-born. Both Puerto Ricans and Dominicans have high rates of female-headed households, closely associated with poverty and welfare dependence.

TABLE 3.5 Basic Socioeconomic Indicators of the Hispanic Caribbean Population of the United States, 2009

Indicator	Cubans	Dominicans	Puerto Ricans
Female-headed households (%)	14.0	33.6	25.9
Bachelor's degree or higher (%)	24.0	15.1	15.4
Speak English less than "very well" (%)	41.5	47.0	19.4
Unemployment rate (%)	11.3	13.3	14.8
Median household income (us$)	41,547	34,194	37,052
Per capita income (us$)	22,420	14,788	16,890
Poverty rate (%)	15.5	25.9	25.7
Owner-occupied housing units (%)	58.9	27.1	38.2

Source: U.S. Census Bureau 2010.

Explaining the Socioeconomic Differences among Hispanic Caribbean Migrants

Miami's Cuban enclave accounts for much of the exiles' legendary economic success. This mode of incorporation consists of a spatial concentration of immigrant-owned businesses in a wide range of economic activities, employing many compatriots and catering primarily to ethnic consumers (Grenier and Pérez 2003; Lisandro Pérez 2001; Portes and Bach 1985). The rise of the Cuban enclave was due to various circumstances, including Miami's strategic location between North and South America, an initial wave of exiles with substantial human capital, an infusion of federal funds for business development, and a growing Hispanic market. While most Cubans do not work within the enclave, those who do may avoid low-paying, unskilled occupations with poor working conditions and few opportunities for upward mobility. Some well-educated Cubans have secured well-paid and skilled jobs, especially as managers and professionals.

Middle- and upper-class exiles from revolutionary Cuba built Miami's enclave, especially between 1959 and 1962. However, recent Cuban and other Latin American immigrants have provided much of the cheap labor required by enclave businesses. Of all Cubans admitted to the United States between 2003 and 2008, nearly 71 percent were either blue-collar or service workers in Cuba (U.S. Citizenship and Immigration Services 2003–8). These data suggest that contemporary Cuban immigrants are not exceptionally well qualified, compared to earlier refugees or other groups from Latin America and the Caribbean. Other studies have confirmed that the average education of Cuban immigrants has declined over time (Pedraza 1996; Rodríguez Chávez 1997).

Neither Dominicans nor Puerto Ricans have developed an enclave economy to the same extent as Cubans in Miami. Although Alejandro Portes and Luis Guarnizo (1991) detected an incipient Dominican enclave in New York City, most Dominicans are blue-collar and service workers (Duany 2008b [1994]; Ramona Hernández 2002). Similarly, the Puerto Rican population in the United States shows a deprived socioeconomic profile.

Since the early twentieth century, most Puerto Ricans have been incorporated into the lower rungs of the U.S. labor market. In the 1920s and 1930s, Puerto Ricans in the United States concentrated in lower-status occupations such as laundry workers, dishwashers, porters, janitors, garment workers, waiters, and domestic employees (Chenault 1938; Sánchez Korrol 1994). During the 1940s and 1950s most Puerto Rican immigrants lacked the educational credentials, occupational experience, and English-language skills required for white-collar jobs. By 1960 Puerto Ricans in New York were predominantly unskilled workers, such as machine operators, laborers, and packers. Nowadays, Puerto Ricans in the United States are still more likely than other ethnic and racial groups to be blue-collar and service workers, except for private household workers. Conversely, Puerto Ricans have a much lower proportion of managers and professionals (26.9 percent in 2009) than most other groups. In 2007 Puerto Ricans owned less than 7 percent of all Hispanic businesses in the United States, even though they then comprised 9 percent of the Hispanic population (U.S. Census Bureau 2010).

Such figures document the continuing economic disadvantage of stateside Puerto Ricans. Their deteriorated living conditions are basically due to the deindustrialization of New York City, Philadelphia, Chicago, Boston, and other cities, as well as the increasing polarization between well-paid skilled jobs and poorly paid unskilled jobs, particularly in the service sector. The automation, computerization, suburbanization, overseas relocation, and decline of manufacturing sectors like the garment industry displaced many Puerto Rican workers, who were heavily concentrated in such sectors (Clara Rodríguez 1989). During New York City's economic restructuring in the 1970s, Puerto Ricans fared even worse than African Americans, who had a higher share of their labor force in public administration (Andrés Torres 1995).

Today, Dominicans are one of the most underprivileged groups in the United States. In 2009 Dominicans were more likely to be poor, live in female-headed households, and have lower levels of income, educational attainment, and occupational status than other major ethnic and racial groups, including African Americans and other Hispanics (table 3.5). According to Ramona Hernández (2002), Dominicans in New York City have been marginalized because of their low educational levels and limited English proficiency, as well as racial discrimination and the shift from a manufacturing to a service economy. In addition, many Dominican immigrants are undocumented and work in the informal sector.

Transnational Economic Links

Despite their relative disadvantage in earnings (even Cubans make less than the U.S. average), Hispanic Caribbean migrants play vital economic roles in their countries of origin. Their impact can be verified most clearly in the large amount of money they send back home. Most of these funds cover basic household needs such as housing, food, clothing, health care, and education. Secondarily, remittances finance small businesses and other productive activities in the home countries. Today, remittances are a major source of household income in the Dominican Republic and Cuba, and to a lesser extent in Puerto Rico. Moreover, they are the most concrete expression of continuing ties between families in and outside the Spanish-speaking Caribbean.

Since 1970 Dominican remittances have multiplied more than one hundred times (figure 3.1). In 2009 Dominicans abroad sent nearly US$2.8 billion to the Dominican Republic, exceeding the value of Dominican exports and representing the second-largest source of foreign exchange after tourism. Today, at least one in five Dominican households regularly receives remittances from relatives living abroad (Oficina Nacional de Estadística 2009b). The Dominican Republic is a prime example of a remittance economy that relies on migrants to uphold the living standards of nonmigrants (see chapter 10).

Although Cuba entered this field relatively late, it has become one of the largest recipients of remittances in the Caribbean region. As figure 3.1 shows, the value of private money transfers to Cuba rose more than twenty-five times between 1989 and 2009, from approximately US$48 million to US$1.2 billion. (Estimates of Cuban remittances were unavailable prior to 1989.) In 2002 remittances generated nearly half as much foreign exchange

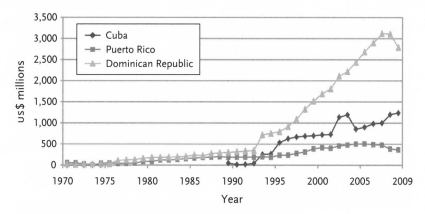

FIGURE 3.1 Remittances to the Hispanic Caribbean, 1970–2009

Sources: IADB 2010; Junta de Planificación 1970–2000, 2010; *Migration News* 2009; Orozco 2009a; Spadoni 2004.

as tourism, by then the leading sector of the Cuban economy, and represented more than half the value of all merchandise exports (Barberia 2004: 368). Journalistic sources estimate that nearly half of all Cubans receive dollars from relatives in the United States (*Migration News* 1998b). The rapid expansion of Cuba's remittance economy places it squarely within a Caribbean and Latin American mold. (For a comparative assessment of remittances in the region, including Cuba, see Orozco 2002b.)

Private transfers from the United States to Puerto Rico rose fourfold between 1970 and 2009, from nearly US$95 million to almost US$365 million (figure 3.1). In 1996 remittances represented almost four-fifths of the net income originated in tourism, the island's second industry after manufacturing (Junta de Planificación 1997). Currently, Puerto Rican remittances are much smaller than Dominican and Cuban remittances, even though the volume of Puerto Rican migrants is much larger than that of the other two groups. Furthermore, only one out of twenty households in Puerto Rico regularly receives remittances (Duany 2007). This trend is related to the economic situation of the countries of origin, as well as the migrants' age, birthplace, education, occupation, and income. Moreover, U.S. federal government transfers to Puerto Rico (almost US$12.9 billion in 2009) far outweigh private remittances (Junta de Planificación 2010). I return to this issue in chapter 10.

Stigmatizing the Diaspora

Public opinion toward emigration is surprisingly similar throughout the Spanish-speaking Caribbean. In all three societies, nonmigrants often view migrants with a mixture of fright and admiration, envy and resentment, familiarity and suspicion. For orthodox nationalists, to leave one's country is to betray the homeland. For working-class families, migration is often a survival strategy under harsh economic conditions, such as chronic unemployment. For the middle classes, it could maintain or improve their social status through higher education and better professional opportunities. For decades, members of the middle and upper class have studied abroad, with some staying while others return home after completing their education. Each sending country has developed ambivalent discourses about transnationalism.

Although the pejorative label "Nuyorican" originally referred to Puerto Ricans born or raised in New York City, it is now commonly applied on the island to all those who return as well as those who remain abroad. The Nuyorican stereotype highlights the migrants' supposed Americanization, including their way of speaking, dressing, and walking. As the Puerto Rican anthropologist Marvette Pérez (1996: 192) puts it, "Nuyoricans are discursively constructed as dangerous, hybrid, and contaminated beings, and, upon returning to Puerto Rico, a threat to contaminate Puerto Ricans." Typically, islanders deem Nuyoricans as more aggressive, disrespectful, and promiscuous than themselves. In turn, Nuyoricans perceive themselves as more cosmopolitan and sophisticated than islanders (Lorenzo-Hernández 1999). Natives of Puerto Rico often treat returnees as illegitimate strangers (as *los de afuera*, as Gina Pérez found in her 2004 study), who deviate from local standards of behavior. Return migrant students often experience a dissonance in cultural values with their teachers and peers. Many returnees are not fluent in the Spanish language, a litmus test of Puerto Ricanness on the island (Findlay 2009; Reyes 2000; Zentella 2003). Often deemed too "gringo," Nuyoricans allegedly threaten Puerto Rico's national identity.

During the past few decades, residents of the Dominican Republic coined the epithet "Dominican-York" (as well as *cadenú* and *Joe*) to describe Dominicans born or raised abroad, especially in New York City (Guarnizo 1997; Pessar 1995; Torres-Saillant 1999). Like Puerto Ricans, many Dominicans typecast return migrants as culturally alien. Since the 1980s the stereotype of the tasteless, Americanized, and pushy Dominican-York has become widespread in the Dominican Republic. Especially popular is the idea that returnees have made their fortunes in drug trafficking (hence the epithet *cadenú*, alluding to their presumed inclination to flaunt gold necklaces earned through illegal activities). Some neighborhoods, schools, and clubs in the Dominican Republic discriminate against Dominican-Yorks (Guarnizo 1995). Journalists have blamed deported and returning migrants for increasing the crime rate in the Dominican Republic. In 1999 members of the Dominican Congress proposed to officially eliminate the term *Dominican-York* and replace it with *dominicano ausente* (literally, absent Dominican) (Cámara de Diputados 2002: 102–4). Overall, the Dominican experience follows closely an earlier Puerto Rican practice of depreciating those who go back home — often with money but seldom with more prestige.

The stigmatization of émigrés is strongest in Cuba, where Castro's government branded them as *gusanos* (worms), counterrevolutionaries, reactionaries, turncoats, and unpatriotic sellouts. The name-calling became even more severe during the Mariel exodus, when government propaganda cast the émigrés as *escoria* (scum) and "lumpen" (García 1996; Masud-Piloto 1996; María de los Angeles Torres 1999). Thus, the fault lines between Cubans "here" and "there" have been drawn more sharply than among other diasporas. In 1978, however, Fidel Castro initiated a dialogue with Cuban émigrés, subsequently authorizing their visits to Cuba. More recently, the Special Period in Peacetime prompted a rapprochement between Cuban families on and off the island. Contemporary attitudes toward émigrés on the island are more favorable than before, thus moving closer to Hispanic Caribbean standards. Moreover, the neutral term *emigration* has displaced the politically charged *exile* in Cuban official statements.

Identity Discourses

The migrants themselves have often dismissed negative stereotypes and sought alternative ways of asserting their identity. Many first-generation Cubans in the United States insist that they are exiles, not migrants, but the second generation frequently prefers to be called Cuban American. Most Cuban Americans, at least in Miami, do not identify themselves primarily as Hispanics or Latinos (Lisandro Pérez 2001). One of the crucial ideological issues among U.S. Cubans is their still incomplete transformation from exiles to immigrants to ethnics. For some Cubans, the 1994 U.S. decision to return *balseros* to the island ended their exile in the United States. Another turning point was the 1999–2000 saga of the *balsero* child Elián González, who was forcibly removed from his relatives' home in Little Havana and returned to his father in Cuba. During this episode, the Cuban American community remained isolated in Miami, as well as nationally and internationally. This experience led many Cubans in the United States to perceive themselves as a minority group rather than as perpetual exiles.

Few Dominican immigrants accept the *Dominican American* label, although their descendants are slowly embracing it. During my 1993 fieldwork in Washington Heights, most informants called themselves not "Dominican-York" or "Dominican American" but simply "Dominican" (Duany 2008b [1994]). Like other Hispanic Caribbean migrants, Dominicans in the United States cling to their national origin (see de la Garza et al. 1992 for an earlier survey of Mexicans, Puerto Ricans, and Cubans in the United States). Many describe themselves as "Hispanic" or "Latino," particularly as an alternative to "black" or "African American" (Bailey 2002; Candelario 2007). This self-perception may change as the number of U.S.-born Dominicans rises. For example, some dark-skinned members of the second generation have adopted an Afro-Dominican identity.

Of the three groups, Puerto Ricans are the most adamant on a national terminology, rarely describing themselves as "Puerto Rican American." As the Puerto Rican literary critics José L. Torres-Padilla and Carmen Haydée Rivera (2008) suggest, Puerto Ricans on the island and abroad live "off the hyphen." Perhaps because "Puerto Rican American" sounds redundant or because they resist becoming another ethnic minority, stateside Puerto Ricans continue to define themselves primarily as *puertorriqueños* or *boricuas*. (The latter derives from Borinquen, the island's indigenous name.) Except for some writers, artists, and intellectuals, Puerto Ricans in the United States seldom call themselves "Nuyorican." Despite their U.S. citizenship (or precisely because of it), Puerto Ricans claim a separate identity more eagerly than either Cubans or Dominicans, who come from sovereign states. Cultural pride is stronger than popular support for Puerto Rican independence, although many stateside Puerto Rican leaders and activists prefer that option for the island (Falcón 2007).

The immigrants' reception in the United States has varied from group to group and over time. Until 1980 the U.S. mass media tended to portray Cuban exiles as hardworking, independent, law-abiding, and successful refugees from communism. But after the Mariel exodus Cubans were increasingly depicted as undesirable, economically deprived, and criminal aliens. Perhaps the most popular representation of Mariel refugees as ruthless hoodlums is Brian de Palma's 1983 remake of the gangster film *Scarface*. In 1994 the Clinton administration began to deport *balseros*, like other undocumented migrants. This decision symbolized the Caribbeanization of Cubans by the U.S. government, as well as a profound shift in U.S. public opinion toward Cuba after the Cold War.

In contrast, the dominant image of Puerto Ricans and Dominicans in the United States has been uncharitable from the start. During the 1940s and 1950s the New York press often depicted the growing influx of Puerto Ricans as a social problem — from creating housing shortages and crowding schools to increasing unemployment, crime, and welfare dependence rates. The best-known representation of stateside Puerto Ricans remains the 1957 Broadway musical and 1961 Hollywood movie *West Side Story*, focusing on teenage gangs. Within academic circles, Oscar Lewis's classic *La Vida* (1966) painted a depressing portrait of poor Puerto Rican families in San Juan and New York. According to a report by the Puerto Rican Forum (1964: 2), New York Puerto Ricans were publicly characterized as "indigent, disorganized, and lacking in civil responsibilities." Even today, they are commonly derided as ignorant, lazy, dirty, and violent.

In the 1980s Dominicans joined Puerto Ricans as one of the most stigmatized ethnic minorities in the United States. A host of popular films and television series has associated both groups with poverty, welfare abuse, urban blight, and crime. Journalistic reports routinely identify Dominicans as one of the main culprits of drug trafficking — especially the cocaine and heroin trade — along the U.S. northeastern corridor. Washington Heights is widely touted as "the crack capital" of New York City and even the United States (see Krauss and Rohter 1998; and Rohter and Krauss 1998). During my fieldwork in Washington Heights in the early 1990s, violent confrontations pitted young Dominicans against the police and firefighters. Invariably, the mainstream media portrayed New York's Dominican community as strange, disorderly, and dangerous. Like other "colored" groups from the Caribbean and Latin America, Dominicans have been criminalized in the United States, Puerto Rico, and other countries. Disparaging stereotypes about African Americans and Puerto Ricans have been extended to Dominican Americans, especially those with a dark complexion.

Crossing Racial Borders

A pressing issue for Hispanic Caribbean residents of the United States is the reconstruction of their racial identities. On the one hand, transnationalism can erode hegemonic racial discourses in both sending and receiving countries. On the other hand, the racialization of Hispanic Caribbean people in the United States — as well as Dominicans in Puerto Rico or Haitians in the Dominican Republic — can harden fundamentalist concepts of cultural difference. This last section of the chapter concentrates on the immigrants' clash with the dominant system of racial classification in the United States.

Since 1980 the U.S. Census Bureau has asked all respondents to classify themselves by race, separately from their Hispanic origin. In 2009 almost nine out of ten Cubans in the United States answered that they were white (table 3.6). In contrast, slightly more than half of the Puerto Ricans and one-third of the Dominicans considered themselves white. Less than 4 percent of the Cubans, 7 percent of the Puerto Ricans, and almost 11 percent of the Dominicans said they were black. The most striking response was the proportion of people choosing "some other race" — ranging from 6 percent among Cubans to more than 28 percent among Puerto Ricans and nearly 49 percent among Dominicans. These figures run parallel to the large proportion of U.S. Hispanics — 29.5 percent in the 2009 American Community Survey — who prefer the "some other race" category when describing their race. When asked to clarify, most respondents use the panethnic labels *Hispanic* or *Latino*, their national origins, and other folk terms for racial mixture, such as *trigueño*, *moreno*, or *indio*. (In the Dominican Republic, the third term designates people with a dark complexion, except Haitians. For an excellent discussion, see Candelario 2007, especially chapter 2.)

These statistics suggest four main patterns in the social construction of race among Hispanic Caribbean migrants. First, many of them avoid the racial binary that prevails in the United States. Rather, they continue to use a tripartite system that recognizes an intermediate stratum along the color continuum (as well as hair texture and facial features). Second, many people employ "some other race" as equivalent to "brown," "tan," or *trigueño* (literally, wheat-colored; figuratively, dark-skinned). To this extent, Latinos have become a "middle race" between whites and blacks in the United States (Virginia Domínguez 1973). Third, the Census Bureau — even though it purports to distinguish between race and ethnicity — tends to collapse the two categories, as it regularly compares Hispanics to "racial" groups such as non-

TABLE 3.6 Self-Reported Race of Hispanic Caribbean Residents of the United States, 2009 (in Percentages)

Race	Cubans	Dominicans	Puerto Ricans
White	87.4	34.5	56.3
Black or African American	3.8	10.7	7.0
American Indian or Alaska Native	0.1	0.5	0.6
Asian	0.1	0.1	0.2
Native Hawaiian and other Pacific Islander	0.1	0.1	0.3
Some other race	6.0	48.5	28.2
Two or more races	2.4	5.4	7.4

Source: Ruggles et al. 2010.

Note: First column does not add up to 100 percent because of rounding.

Hispanic whites and blacks, American Indians, and Asians. Finally, Hispanic Caribbean immigrants are artificially separated from Afro-Caribbean immigrants, such as Haitians and Panamanians of Jamaican origin, with whom they share much history and culture. Instead, they are lumped together with other immigrants of Latin American origin under the terms *Hispanic*, *Latino*, or *Spanish*.

The Transnationalization of the Hispanic Caribbean Population

This chapter has surveyed the current geographic and social locations of Hispanic Caribbean residents of the United States. Most of the immigrants have settled in the Northeast and Southeast of the United States, especially in New York, New Jersey, and Florida. Within these states, they cluster in the metropolitan areas of New York City, Miami–Ft. Lauderdale, and Orlando-Kissimmee. A larger proportion of Cubans than Puerto Ricans and Dominicans has joined the upper and middle sectors of the U.S. labor market. In industrial terms, all three groups concentrate in services and trade. Overall, Cubans have better socioeconomic indicators than the other two groups. In addition, Cubans in the United States are more likely to consider themselves white than either Puerto Ricans or Dominicans.

Over the past three decades, migrants have sent millions of dollars to the Hispanic Caribbean. Remittances are one of the clearest signs of expatriates' enduring attachments to their nations of origin. But such ties are not universally welcome in the region. The migrants' ambivalent image in the Hispanic Caribbean suggests a tortuous relation between diasporas and their homelands. Even more problematic is that Dominicans, Puerto Ricans, and to a lesser extent Cubans are racialized as nonwhite in the United States, often against their will and using categories that differ greatly from their own. In each case, the massive displacement of people has raised difficult questions about how national membership is defined and who can claim citizenship rights in the home country. The next chapters delve deeper into these questions and the range of responses they have provoked in the Spanish-speaking countries of the Caribbean islands. I begin with the historical origins of the Puerto Rican diaspora, the largest Hispanic Caribbean group in the United States after World War II.

A Transnational Colonial Migration

Puerto Rico's Farm Labor Program

4

Puerto Ricans in the United States have been dubbed "colonial immigrants," as U.S. citizens who can travel freely to the mainland but are not fully protected by the U.S. Constitution on the island.[1] Colonial immigrants tend to move abroad primarily for economic reasons, live in segregated quarters, work in low-status jobs, and attend inferior schools in their metropolitan countries (Clara Rodríguez 1989: 19). As Ramón Grosfoguel (2004) has argued, Puerto Rico has much in common with other Caribbean dependencies that have sent large numbers of people to their European "mother countries." In particular, Puerto Ricans in the United States and Antilleans in France and the Netherlands share subordinate positions within their metropolitan societies, largely as a consequence of colonial racism, despite conditions of legal equality. Although colonial immigrants hold metropolitan passports and are entitled to metropolitan subsidies, they often experience discrimination because of their physical and cultural characteristics (see also Cervantes-Rodríguez, Grosfoguel, and Mielants 2009; Clegg and Pantojas-García 2009; de Jong 2005; Giraud 2002; Milia-Marie-Luce 2002, 2007; and Oostindie and Klinkers 2003).

For some analysts, Puerto Rico resembles a "postcolonial colony," combining elements of classical colonial rule with political autonomy, a relatively high standard of living, and a strong national culture (Duany 2002; Flores 2000, 2008). The island's political status is largely based on majority will rather than sheer external imposition. Puerto Rican voters (some 95 percent) are now split between supporting the Commonwealth and the island's annexation as the fifty-first state of the U.S. union, with less than

5 percent favoring independence. Most value their U.S. citizenship, the freedom of movement that it entails, and "permanent union" with the United States. Even the president of the Partido Independentista Puertorriqueño (PIP), or Puerto Rican Independence Party, Rubén Berríos, has advocated the unrestricted entry of Puerto Ricans into the United States, should the island become a sovereign republic (Magdalys Rodríguez 1997). At the same time, Puerto Ricans of all political ideologies, not just independence supporters, assert their identities in nationalistic terms. At any rate, Puerto Rico occupies a marginal space within the U.S. academy and particularly within postcolonial and transnational studies, partly because it is officially recognized neither as a colony nor as a nation in its own right. Yet, as I argue below, the island's government was one of the first modern states, colonial or postcolonial, to organize migration transnationally.

Scholars have recently revisited Puerto Rico's colonial history, national identity, and diaspora from various viewpoints, including transnational, postcolonial, postmodern, gender, queer, and cultural studies (see Aranda 2007; Duany 2002; Flores 2008; Grosfoguel 2003; La Fountain–Stokes 2009; Martínez–San Miguel 2003; Negrón-Muntaner 2004, 2007; Pabón 2002; Gina Pérez 2004; and Ramos-Zayas 2003). Most scholars no longer question whether Puerto Rico is a colony of the United States (but see Soto-Crespo 2009). They often discuss, sometimes angrily, the precise form of U.S. colonialism on the island, the extent to which it has acquired "postcolonial" traits such as linguistic and cultural autonomy, and the possibility of waging an effective decolonization process. Puerto Rico's national identity is contested as fiercely as ever. What distinguishes current academic discussions is that many intellectuals, especially those who align themselves with postmodernism, are highly critical of nationalist discourses.

Other debates focus on population movements between the island and the U.S. mainland. Some outside observers deem Puerto Rican migration as internal or domestic to the United States, while others, including myself, refer to it as transnational or diasporic. Much of this controversy hinges on the significance of geographic, cultural, linguistic, and even racial borders between the island and the U.S. mainland, as opposed to legal boundaries. As I show below, Puerto Rico occupies a liminal status between a state of the U.S. union and a separate country. From the standpoint of international law, the island's inhabitants are subject to U.S. sovereignty; within the United States, they are often treated as "legal aliens."

In this chapter, I approach the Puerto Rican diaspora as a transnational colonial migration. In so doing, I define Puerto Rico as a nation, an imagined community with its own territory, history, language, and culture. At the same time, the island lacks a sovereign state, an independent government that represents the population of that territory. This unsovereign state has long sponsored population displacements from Puerto Rico to the United States. During the first half of the twentieth century, colonial officials embraced migration as a safety valve for the island's overpopulation. During the 1950s and 1960s the Commonwealth government spurred the "Great Migration" to the U.S. mainland. In particular, the Farm Labor Program, overseen by the Migration Division of Puerto Rico's Department of Labor, illustrates the complicated negotiations required by a transnational colonial state. In many ways, Puerto Rico's postwar migration policies anticipated those of contemporary transnational nation-states, such as the Dominican Republic.

Following Migrant Citizens to "Ethnologically Alien Environments"

Soon after the U.S. occupation of Puerto Rico, the colonial government encouraged migration to the United States (Lapp 1990). This public policy was based on the widespread perception that Puerto Rico was a small, poor, and overcrowded country with few natural resources. According to the first civilian U.S. governor, Charles Allen (1902: 75), "Porto Rico has plenty of laborers and poor people generally. What the island needs is men with capital, energy, and enterprise."[2] Governor Arthur Yager (1912: 147) held that "the only really effective remedy [to the problem of overpopulation] is the transfer of large numbers of Porto Ricans to another region." In 1917 General Frank McIntyre (1982 [1917]: 104), chief of the Bureau of Insular Affairs, favored "the colonizing of several hundred thousand of the Porto Rican people in Santo Domingo." A 1919 report for the U.S. Department of Labor pondered migration to the Dominican Republic and Cuba but concluded that "it falls short of its purpose when submitted to careful analysis" (Joseph Marcus 1919: 49). Instead, the report recommended establishing an office of the U.S. Employment Service in Puerto Rico to facilitate the relocation of Puerto Ricans to the United States. Three decades later the Committee on Insular Affairs (1945: 25) of the U.S. House of Representatives endorsed "a wise and prudent program of emigration" to alleviate the island's "lack of natural resources" and "congestion of population."

The earliest recruitment of labor on the island under U.S. rule (especially between 1900 and 1930) was geared toward the sugar plantations of Hawaii, the Dominican Republic, Cuba, and the U.S. Virgin Islands, particularly St. Croix. Smaller groups of Puerto Ricans built railroads in Ecuador, cut cane in Mexico, grew coffee in Colombia, and worked in a clothing factory in Venezuela. A few thousand picked cotton in Arizona during the 1920s (History Task Force 1979; Maldonado 1979; Mustelier Ayala 2006; Rosario Natal 1983; Senior 1947; Whalen 2005). The Puerto Rican exodus picked up momentum during the 1940s, when it was largely reoriented toward the U.S. mainland. After World War II, thousands of Puerto Ricans found jobs in seasonal agriculture, manufacturing, domestic service, and other service industries in the United States.

Notwithstanding its lack of sovereignty, Puerto Rico's government acted as a "transnational" intermediary for its migrant citizens for most of the twentieth century (Edgardo Meléndez 1997). The island's government set up several agencies in the United States under different guises: the Bureau of Employment and Identification (1930–48), the Office of Information for Puerto Rico (1945–49), the Employment and Migration Bureau (1947–51), the Migration Division of the Department of Labor (1951–89), and the Department of Puerto Rican Community Affairs in the United States (1989–93). Among other initiatives, these agencies issued identification cards for Puerto Ricans as U.S. citizens; promoted employment opportunities for Puerto Ricans abroad; oversaw the recruitment of workers; negotiated cheap airfares between the island and the U.S. mainland; registered thousands of Puerto Rican voters in the United States; helped organize overseas Puerto Rican communities; and fostered Puerto Rican culture on the mainland (Duany 2002; García-Colón 2008; Lapp 1990; Pagán de Colón 1956; Stinson Fernández 1996). To my knowledge, no modern state, colonial or otherwise, has engaged in more extensive and long-standing activities concerning its expatriates than the Puerto Rican government.[3]

U.S. sociologist Clarence Senior, who later directed the Migration Division (1951–60), first elaborated the project of organizing and supervising Puerto Rican migration. In an influential monograph, Senior (1947) proposed an emigration office attached to the governor's executive staff and working closely with the island's Department of Labor. The main function of this office would be to facilitate the recruitment of workers to the United States and Latin America, especially Venezuela. The agency would provide migrants with information about job openings, training, transportation, settlement, and insurance, as well as promote further emigration from the island. Although the plan to relocate Puerto Ricans in Latin America proved too expensive, the idea of finding jobs for them in the United States later crystallized in the Migration Division. As Senior (1947: 119) surmised, "Migration to the continental United States seems to offer the best immediate opportunities."

Luis Muñoz Marín, then president of the Senate (1941–48) and later governor (1949–64) of Puerto Rico, accepted Senior's blueprint for planned emigration. Muñoz Marín (1946: 3) agreed that it was "necessary to resort to emigration as a measure for the immediate relief to the problem posed by our surplus population, while we seek permanent solutions in the long run." The chief economist of the Office of Puerto Rico in Washington, D.C., Donald J. O'Connor, also urged the resettlement of Puerto Ricans in the United States and other countries such as Venezuela and the Dominican Republic. According to O'Connor (1948: 2), "Migration can accomplish what economic programs on the island cannot do quickly" — that is, create jobs and sources of income, while reducing population growth. In particular, O'Connor (1947) advocated the annual migration of thirteen to fifteen thousand young women to the United States, especially to work as domestic employees in Chicago. High-ranking members of the ruling Partido Popular Democrático (PPD), or Popular Democratic Party, such as Antonio Fernós-Isern, Teodoro Moscoso, Rafael Picó, and Salvador Tió, concurred with O'Connor's optimistic assessment. Thus began a state-supported project of emigration as a safety valve for Puerto Rico's socioeconomic problems.

On December 5, 1947, the island's legislature passed Law 25, establishing Puerto Rico's migration policy and creating the Employment and Migration Bureau. According to this law, "The Government of Puerto Rico neither encourages nor discourages the migration of Puerto Rican workmen [sic] to the United States or any foreign country; but it considers its duty . . . to provide the proper guidance with respect to opportunities for employment and the problems of adjustment usually encountered in environments which are ethnologically alien" (Asamblea Legislativa 1947a: 386). From its inception, the bureau (and its heirs, the Migration Division and the Department of Puerto Rican Community Affairs in the United States) sought "to follow its migrant citizens to facilitate their adjustment and adaptation in the communities in which they chose to live" (Administration 1972–73: 2). The policy of "following migrant citizens," while officially "neither encourag[ing] nor discourag[ing]" their departure, paid off in the short run. The growth of the island's labor force slowed down as living standards rose substantially between the 1940s and 1960s. Population control was a key tenet of the PPD's development strategy throughout this period (Pantojas-García 1990).

In charge of the island's government between 1941 and 1968, the PPD crafted the Migration Division as an informal "consulate" in the United States. For decades, the agency's basic mission was "*giving voice* [emphasis in the original] to the thousands of Puerto Ricans who come to reside in the cities and towns of the United States" (Administration 1961–62: 182). Throughout the 1950s the division attempted to articulate the interests of Puerto Rican migrants to the U.S. public and government officials. As Law 25 stated, "the efforts of the Government of Puerto Rico in this connection should constitute a liaison at all times and under all circumstances between the Puerto Ricans who are going to reside in the city of New York and other cities of the United States, and the governments of such cities, states, and the United States" (Asamblea Legislativa 1947a: 388). In turn, U.S. public authorities often relied on the agency as the official mouthpiece of the overseas Puerto Rican population. Michael Lapp (1990) has criticized the division's attempt to co-opt the diaspora to further the interests of the Commonwealth government. Representatives of mainland Puerto Rican communities did not participate in formulating the agency's policies, which depended exclusively on the PPD during the period under consideration.

Muñoz Marín (1960: 9) thus summarized his party's migration policy:

> The government of Puerto Rico is the first that establishes offices here [in the United States], outside its own territory, to help its compatriots. The offices of our Department of Labor in New York, and in ten other cities, are devoted to this purpose of helping our fellow citizens adapt themselves to life in the new places of residence they have chosen, as quickly as possible. We constantly strive to combat the lack of information, the prejudices that, unfortunately, always tend to accompany the reception of the newly arrived, from all countries, regardless of what country they come from.

Representatives of the prolonged PPD administration explicitly connected economic development to sponsored migration. As a division report stated bluntly, "It is obvious that migration, although voluntary, is an integral part of the program of economic and social development that is being carried on by the Commonwealth of Puerto Rico. It is so because migration helps to maintain the population index at a more or less stable level with the corresponding effects on employment and unemployment, education, housing, health, and all the other factors that affect the development of Puerto Rico's government programs" (Administration 1966–67: 8–9). According to Joseph Monserrat (1991: 27), who headed the Migration Division between 1960 and 1968, "Operation Bootstrap and Fomento's programs [promoting the island's industrialization] have always had a senior silent partner — the Puerto Rican migration to the United States. This migration, of which migrant agricultural workers formed an important segment, is and has been an intrinsic part and a basic factor in the economic growth and development of the island." Another report asserted: "The Office of Services to Migrant Agricultural Workers has contributed greatly to the mobility of Puerto Rico's population, thus providing a powerful escape valve to our great problem of overpopulation and high chronic unemployment" (Reports 1974–75: 1). The metaphor of migration as an "escape valve" recurs frequently in the official discourse of the period.

When the pro-statehood Partido Nuevo Progresista (PNP), or New Progressive Party, gained power in 1969 and again in 1977 and 1985, it restructured the Migration Division to advance the island's annexation into the United States. Apparently, the PNP did not advocate the same migration policies as the PPD, particularly the Farm Labor Program. In 1969 the agency's staff was downsized, together with its orientation and educational programs for seasonal farmworkers (Reports 1972–73). In 1979 PNP Governor Carlos Romero Barceló eliminated the division's Cultural Affairs Program, which would be reinstated by PPD Governor Rafael Hernández Colón in 1985. Finally, in 1993, PNP Governor Pedro Rosselló and other pro-statehood leaders, then a majority in the island's legislature, abolished the Department of Puerto Rican Community Affairs in the United States. They believed that the agency represented an unwarranted instance of applying public policy in another jurisdiction. Still, the Commonwealth government retains a formal presence on the mainland through the Puerto Rico Federal Affairs Administration (PRFAA). Nowadays, this agency has greatly reduced its budget and influence over the diaspora.

"Surplus Hands":
The Rise and Fall of the Farm Labor Program

Postwar Puerto Rican migration has ebbed and flowed according to various stages of Operation Bootstrap (*Manos a la Obra* in Spanish), the island's program of "industrialization by invitation" (largely of U.S. manufacturing

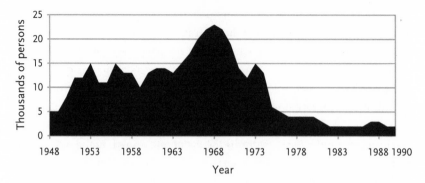

FIGURE 4.1 Number of Puerto Ricans Referred by the Farm Labor Program in the United States

Sources: Monserrat 1991; Reports 1956–92.

capital), as well as to the changing demands of the U.S. economy, particularly in the large urban centers of the Northeast (Rivera-Batiz and Santiago 1996; Clara Rodríguez 1989; Whalen 2001). Although Operation Bootstrap created thousands of factory jobs, it could not absorb many more thousands of unskilled workers displaced by a swift agricultural decline. In 1940 agriculture employed 44.9 percent of the island's labor force; by 1970 that sector only employed 9.9 percent (Junta de Planificación 1983). During this period, Puerto Rico's development strategy expelled a large share of its rural population, both on and off the island. As the Puerto Rican sociologist Frank Bonilla (1994) once quipped, *Manos a la Obra* (literally, "[putting] hands to work") could be renamed *Manos que Sobran* ("surplus hands").

The Farm Labor Program provides a fascinating case study of how Commonwealth officials navigated the "colonial" and "transnational" intricacies of Puerto Rico's political status. Between 1948 and 1990, the program recruited 421,238 Puerto Ricans to work on the U.S. mainland (see figure 4.1). This was the second-largest organized movement of temporary laborers in the United States, after the Mexican *bracero* program (1942–64) in the Southwest. Indeed, Senior (1947: 52) regarded the negotiations between the Mexican and U.S. governments as a model for the Migration Division. These agreements included recruitment, transportation, housing, wages, food, working conditions, hours, savings funds, and repatriation of agricultural laborers.

Although Puerto Rican farmworkers traveled to many states, they concentrated in the Northeast, especially in New Jersey, Connecticut, New York, Delaware, Massachusetts, and Pennsylvania (see figure 4.2). The vast

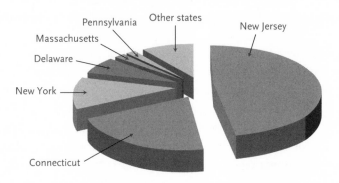

FIGURE 4.2 Destination of Puerto Rican Farmworkers in the United States, 1963–1987

Source: Reports 1956–92.

majority were young men with little schooling and proficiency in the English language. Most had been landless rural laborers in the sugar, coffee, and tobacco industries on the island (Bonilla-Santiago 1988; Cruz 1998; García-Colón 2008; History Task Force 1979; Whalen 2001). They were popularly known as *los tomateros* (the tomato pickers), because that was one of the main crops they harvested. Puerto Ricans also planted and cut shade tobacco in the Connecticut River Valley; picked corn, blueberries, asparagus, broccoli, and onions in the Delaware River Valley; strawberries, cabbages, and carrots in New York; apples in New England and Washington; potatoes in Maine; peaches in South Carolina; avocadoes and lettuce in South Florida; and other crops like cranberries, oranges, and mushrooms in various places.

On May 9, 1947, the Puerto Rican government created the Farm Labor Program through Law 89. The main purpose of this law was to regulate the recruitment of workers in Puerto Rico and to make the island's Commissioner of Labor responsible for this process (Asamblea Legislativa 1947b). In 1948 nearly five thousand Puerto Ricans traveled to the U.S. mainland under the Farm Labor Program. In 1951 the Wagner-Peyser Act, which established the Bureau of Employment Security within the U.S. Department of Labor, was extended to Puerto Rico. Thereafter, the federal government recognized the island as part of the domestic labor supply in the United States (Monserrat 1991). In effect, U.S. officials treated Puerto Rico as a state of the union concerning seasonal agricultural workers. Henceforth, the island's Farm Labor Program processed thousands of interstate clearance orders from mainland employers requesting farmworkers through the U.S. Department of Labor.

The arrangement between the Commonwealth and federal governments worked reasonably well between the 1950s and 1970s. It produced the peculiar situation of a "colonial" state "giving voice" to its "migrant citizens" within a complex metropolitan legal structure and labor market. According to a lawsuit against the Migration Division, "The operation of the Department of Labor of Puerto Rico relating to migrant farmworkers is completely integrated in, and interdependent with, a comprehensive federal scheme established by the Wagner-Peyser Act" (PRLDEF, February 18, 1975). Thus, Commonwealth representatives insisted that Puerto Ricans were legally "domestic" in the United States.

However, according to Petroamérica Pagán de Colón, who directed the Employment and Migration Bureau, "within official circles in Washington and in all states, the Puerto Rican worker was considered a foreigner who was going to displace other workers from their jobs" (Pagán de Colón 1956: 13). Because most of the workers could not speak English, U.S. employers and journalists often referred to them as "aliens" and "semi-foreigners" (Apple Harvest File 1959–81: August 13, 1976; Growers Association Files 1955–82: September 11, 1965). Commonwealth officials admitted that "cultural differences . . . represented some of the problems faced by Puerto Ricans in the United States, which make their adjustment to the new environment difficult" (Administration 1964–65: 2). In a strange twist of the legal doctrine, Puerto Rican farmworkers were "foreign in a domestic sense."

The Migration Division developed into a formidable bureaucratic structure. By 1958 it had a staff of 130 people and a budget of US$1 million (Continuations Committee 1959: 27). At its peak in 1968 the agency had thirteen offices throughout the U.S. mainland. Many of its resources were geared toward seasonal agricultural workers. The director of the Farm Labor Program supervised field operations near rural areas where the workers clustered, including Camden and Keyport, New Jersey; Newburgh and Rochester, New York; Middletown, Delaware; Hamburg, Pennsylvania; Hartford, Connecticut; Boston; and Cleveland. The division signed contracts with numerous agricultural employers, especially the Glassboro Service Association in New Jersey, the Curtis Burns Corporation and the Apple Growers Association in New York, and the Shade Tobacco Growers Association in Connecticut.

The Farm Labor Program sought to meet the cyclical demand for workers to weed, plant, fertilize, pick, pack, load, and unload fruits and vegetables.

Employers usually covered the cost of air transportation between Puerto Rico and the United States, to be repaid by the workers in weekly installments. Housing was provided at no cost to the workers. Working hours were typically from seven in the morning to six in the evening. Hourly wages ranged from eighty cents to one dollar in 1960 and from US$2.61 to three dollars in the late 1970s. The period of employment lasted from several weeks to three months, often coinciding with the dead season of the island's sugar harvest (from May through August). The program extended Puerto Rico's labor market to the U.S. mainland, just as the island was transformed from an agricultural to an industrial economy (Monserrat 1991: 27).

The field representatives of Puerto Rico's Farm Labor Program had multiple duties. First, they oversaw the workers' transportation from the island and often welcomed them at U.S. airports. Second, they oriented the migrants about their rights as U.S. citizens. Third, they inspected housing and eating arrangements at labor camps to ensure their compliance with the Commonwealth's contract with employers. Fourth, they investigated health, accident, salary, and unemployment claims by disgruntled workers (and they were many). Fifth, they mediated disputes between workers and employers, usually organized through growers' associations. Finally, they coordinated the services offered by state, federal, and private agencies, including insurance, health care, English-language classes, and recreational activities. A fictional character in a promotional film commissioned by Puerto Rico's Department of Labor, *Los beneficiarios* (*The Beneficiaries*, Viguié Films, n.d.), quips that the field representative of the Migration Division played the roles of "father confessor, nurse, psychologist, chauffeur, translator, teacher, defense lawyer — and everything for the worker." Another character adds, "He's a friend of the worker. Someone who fixes everything [*arréglalotodo*]."

Puerto Rico's Farm Labor Program waned during the 1970s and practically faded away during the 1990s (see figure 4.1). Several factors caused this decline. First, the demand for seasonal agricultural workers in the U.S. Northeast decreased because of crop mechanization and increasing availability of local labor. In addition, the growing number of unauthorized immigrants from Mexico and Central America diminished the need for Puerto Rican agricultural labor. Furthermore, as U.S. citizens, Puerto Ricans usually earned higher wages and had better working and living conditions than temporary foreign laborers, such as Jamaicans or Mexicans. Puerto Rican farmworkers also organized labor unions to defend their collective rights, a role formerly played by the Migration Division (Bonilla-Santiago 1988). In 1968 the election of a PNP government on the island weakened the motivation to recruit migrant workers. By this time, Puerto Rico itself had become largely urbanized and fewer Puerto Ricans sought agricultural work. Most migrants drifted toward cities, where wages tended to be higher than in rural areas. Lastly, two legal controversies undermined the division's capacity to recruit farm labor.

During the 1970s Puerto Rico's secretary of labor complained that U.S. apple growers preferred to hire West Indians rather than Puerto Ricans. In 1979 a class-action suit, *Rios v. Marshall*, contended that temporary foreign laborers, especially Jamaicans, were recruited for the New York apple harvest, without first guaranteeing jobs for Puerto Ricans and other "domestic" workers. The U.S. secretary of labor at the time had certified that "no domestic workers were available" because Law 89 eliminated Puerto Ricans from the labor supply. As the under secretary of labor, Robert Aders (1976), wrote to the chairman of the Subcommittee on Agricultural Labor of the U.S. House of Representatives, "It is our hope that the regulations under Puerto Rican Public Law 89 can be adjusted to make these workers more effectively available for employment on the mainland." In 1978 Law 89 was amended to allow exceptions to the Commonwealth's contract, which many mainland growers disliked, particularly the jurisdiction of Puerto Rican courts over labor disputes. This amendment hampered the island's bargaining position vis-à-vis U.S. agricultural employers.

Perhaps more damaging to the Farm Labor Program was the protracted litigation surrounding *Vazquez v. Ferre* [sic] (1973). This lawsuit accused former PNP Governor Luis Ferré, Secretary of Labor Julia Rivera de Vincenty, National Director of the Migration Division Nick Lugo, and other public authorities of allowing unsafe, unsanitary, and unhealthy conditions in the agricultural labor camps. The main plaintiff, David Vázquez, was a twenty-five-year-old Puerto Rican farmworker from Arecibo employed by the Glassboro Service Association in New Jersey in 1972. Among other grievances, Vázquez alleged that the camp where he toiled had inadequate living quarters, unhygienic cooking facilities, no heating, insufficient sleeping space, and unclean bathing and toilet facilities. Attorneys employed by the Puerto Rican Legal Defense and Education Fund (PRLDEF), which filed the suit on behalf of Vázquez and other migrant workers, charged that the farm's housing conditions violated the Wagner-Peyser Act, Commonwealth laws and regulations, and the contract with the Glassboro Service Association. After years of negotiations, the Commonwealth government settled the case in

1977, agreeing to inspect farms before assigning them workers (PRLDEF various dates). By then U.S. farms had recruited fewer than forty-two hundred island workers (figure 4.1).

Documenting Transnationalism from Below

Most of the extant documents on Puerto Rico's Farm Labor Program, deposited at the Centro de Estudios Puertorriqueños at Hunter College in New York, voice the perspectives of Commonwealth officials. Nonetheless, the archives sometimes provide glimpses into the mundane concerns, practices, and social relations of the migrant workers and their families. These primary sources, including unpublished correspondence, annual and monthly reports, memoranda, and newspaper clippings, help reconstruct the everyday experiences of transnationalism from below (Smith and Guarnizo 1998), from the standpoint of the migrants themselves.[4] (When translating the Spanish texts, I retain their original punctuation and syntax.)

To begin with, Puerto Rican farmworkers faced difficult working conditions. By far their most common grievance was the breach of contracts by employers. Many workers claimed that employers treated them unfairly, including withholding their wages until the end of their contracts and not giving them enough work. A letter signed by "Federico Gaspal. Alcadio Serafín" was addressed to the migration specialist in Hamburg, Pennsylvania:

> Dear Mr. Mendosa [sic].
> The present [purpose] of these short line [sic] is to let you know that you could come here because at this time this farmer during the week he gives us two or three days of work during the week and we turn to you also five weeks have passed and they haven't changed the bed linen and we'd like you to come see where we take baths which is a ranch where there are bulls ducks hens etsetera [sic] these is [un]hygienic for our health. And we've carried out our work also look we haven't been able to send much [money] to P.R. [Puerto Rico]. Because these people are really bad. Look I'd still like you to see where we live, in a shack [chiho?] where things barely fit. Look I'd also like you to see the kitchenware. Look here there were some emigrant people and they fled, I think it was because of the bad service they give here and they don't agree with what the law requires. (Reports 1956–92: October 8, 1959)

Ten years later Puerto Ricans employed by Comstock-Greenwood Foods in New York denounced similar working conditions:

> My very esteemed Jorge Colón: the Present [purpose] of this [letter] is to [offer] new information we'd like not to bother you again But it's our duty to let you know that at Curtis Burns they still [treat] us with cruelty us Puerto Ricans and I'll tell you that we expected that when the corn [season] came we'd do something and time is growing shorter and we suffer the same scarcity of work this company adds blacks [*moyetos*] and Americans to work and many of us are still look-ing at each other's faces and we complain to you Because you're the man called to solve our Problem We Pay for our meals and those from here don't pay anything and besides you told us that if anything hap-pened we should let you know so we're sincere We hope you'll visit us if it's agreeable to you and you can and we can be corresponded, by duty these people should share with everyone and if they want us to come later to work for them. We hope you'll answer and visit us.
>
> Yours truly,
>
> Workers at Curtis Burns
>
> (Growers Association Files 1955–82: September 19, 1969)

The above letter suggests that many migrants indeed perceived the field rep-resentative as a Mr. Fixit.

In addition to work-related issues, migrants complained about daily dis-turbances at the camps:

> So we want to inform you that most of these laborers [in Windsor, Connecticut] are young men who go to these camps to smoke mari-juana and sniff coke and other drugs, and then when they're under the drug's effects they start to laugh, tell jokes, and turn on the radio, and [listen to] Rdio Picat all night, and if you tell them you want to sleep because you have to work the next day to fulfill your contract duties.
>
> They respond that you were in Puerto Rico before if you don't like it move back, and if you took [the job], you have to put up with it now, and there are also many individuals who take loose women [*mujeres de la vida alegre*] to these camps to sell them to the workers and then many of them get sick putting at risk the others' health, and also these same women together with those who bring them coax many of the workers, hitting and assaulting them. (Growers Association Files 1955–82: July 5, 1974)

Health problems were commonplace. In Chester County, Pennsylvania, Puerto Ricans were susceptible to a respiratory disease caused by a substance used in growing mushrooms (Regional and Field Office Farm Labor Files 1959). In Massachusetts, the division tried to inform Bernardo Avilés Ramos's relatives that he had been hospitalized at Northampton State Hospital for ten days because of "mental disturbances" (Reports 1956–92: June 11, 1971). In Hartford, a few months later, Jesús Aponte Figueroa wrote:

> Mr. Rafael Muñoz
> Amidst the disturbance in which I find myself I take the pen to notify you of my state of health. And my working conditions, I Jesús Aponte Figueroa write this letter to request your help and that of other collaborators of the labor office because here where I'm at what you find is an injustice toward agricultural workers mainly Puerto Rican I should manifest now, this is mycase [*sic*]. Which may seem of no importance if it's declared by Mr. [Gilberto] Camacho [the field representative], I Jesús am a worker at the Imperial Nurseries, where many of us risk our necks that weed makes fun of us because we don't speak English. It's been two weeks since I was working when unfortunately some dirt fell on my right eye which I got when I went to put down a tree in a brook. . . .
>
> I wish you can help me get a ticket back to PR since I don't think I'll work any more because I feel bad from the heart and from an eye I've almost lost which I know that not even my island has a cure and my sickness appears to be internal. (Reports 1956–92: September 23, 1971)

On visiting the camps, field representatives frequently found substandard housing conditions. Their inspection report included an assessment of sleeping quarters, sanitary conditions, kitchen and laundry facilities, and recreational grounds. A Commonwealth official in Hartford wrote about "a family of 9 living in a cottage without hot water, toilet, showers, and without proper ventilation. Another group of 5 men living in a dirty small barrack not big enough for 1 person." The owner of the apple orchard declared that "the Puerto Ricans do not deserve any better" (Apple Harvest File 1959–81: July 15, 1965). Puerto Rican workers often described the camps as filthy (in one case, calling them *un corral de puercos*, a pigs' pen). Some compared them to "concentration camps" because "the worker cannot go out unless he has a special permission from the guards . . . and where the guards carry clubs and use them fearlessly" (Regional and Field Office Farm Labor Files 1958–83: January 27, 1960).

Aside from the camps' overcrowded, unkempt, and Spartan conditions, many Puerto Ricans were dissatisfied with the food they ate there. Although the Commonwealth contract stipulated that employers should provide three hot meals per day, this requirement was rarely met. A field representative in Camden was told that "we Puerto Ricans do not eat soup that way [in thermoses brought to the labor camps] and much less beans for lunch" (Growers Association Files 1955–82: n.d.). At a Windsor camp, "the men showed a desire for more variety [in their lunches]. . . . They feel that the fish and chicken cooked for the evening meals are not highly seasoned enough" (Regional and Field Office Farm Labor Files 1958–83: June 22, 1972). Similarly, workers criticized the menu at the Green Giant Company in Middletown, Delaware: "breakfast a loaf of bread and (two small slices) of bread and coffee and milk that tasted like a rusty nail. For lunch they gave us a sticky rice, *marota* [?], always beans and chickpeas that looked like stones. For seven days rice and beans and chickpeas. In the afternoons they gave us the same food" (Growers Association Files 1955–82: n.d.).

Another report from Hartford dwelt on the cultural differences between Puerto Ricans and Americans regarding food:

> The problem lies in that what "*solid food*" [emphasis in the original] [means] for the Shade [Tobacco Growers Association] are soups for the worker. Soups for Americans are broth; soups for Puerto Ricans are boiled rice with chicken, much softer than solid. They allege that's not solid food. Because of the enormous quantity prepared at Shade, it can't be tasty.
>
> Most of them don't eat chili con carne, which comes in a one-gallon container.
>
> They don't like the various types of spaghetti and macaroni, also heated from gallon containers.
>
> All of the food for lunch, except for sandwiches, is semi-solid or semi-liquid. The workers expected a solid lunch with rice and beans. (Growers Association Files 1955–82: March 27, 1971)

The Migration Division's representatives constantly pleaded with the employers to offer meals that better reflected the workers' cultural tastes.

In one documented case, an enterprising Puerto Rican named Carlos Arroyo established a clandestine food retailing business at the Curtis Burns camp. According to a field representative, Arroyo had smuggled numerous groceries into his barracks, including ten boxes of pig's tripe (*mondongo criollo*); ten boxes of Corona Malt beverage; twenty-two boxes of guava, orange, soursop (*guanábana*), pear, peach, and apricot juice; two boxes of sausages; two boxes of rice and chicken soup (*asopado*); and fourteen boxes of Rico cookies (Growers Association Files 1955–82: December 12, 1967).

Traveling to "*Las Américas*":
The Dilemmas of Emotional Transnationalism

In this section, I focus on the subjective impact of uprooting farmworkers from their home communities. I build on Elizabeth Aranda's (2007) work on emotional transnationalism, highlighting how migrants sustain affective attachment to their places of origin. Aranda calls attention to the personal challenges posed by physical separation, "the empty spaces of migration," and cultural alienation. The Migration Division recognized the emotional dimensions of migration, using the nationalistic rhetoric typical of the 1970s: "The Puerto Rican people are composed of two parts: almost halves, divided between those who reside in the island-motherland and those who live in the continental United States; . . . both communities maintain affective and material ties, which are constant: they worry about each other; they share joys and tragedies; they feel affected by the political and social currents on both sides of the sea. In sum, they feel like a single people, a single identity, Puerto Ricans all" (Administration 1975–76: 2–3).

Several letters written by farmworkers and their families in Puerto Rico articulate the emotional strains on separated couples and households. Inquiries about relatives in the United States were common. Lidia Esther Berríos, a resident of Villa Palmeras in Santurce, was concerned about Rafael López Berríos, a worker for the Glassboro Growers Association in New Jersey: "The writer of this letter is his mother, who wants to find out why they treat him so badly over there. . . . His employer has something against him, he treats him like a slave they treat him like a thief and like a nobody" (Growers Association Files 1955–82: July 7, 1969).

One letter reflects family tensions over the decision to migrate. Daniel Medina Cruz was a sixteen-year-old migrant worker in New Jersey: "I came to work on my own with a contract with the Labor Department of Puerto Rico. My dad and mom called to ask me to go back to P.R. I won't go back to P.R. because I want to work and fulfill my contract and make money this is my decision and nobody has forced me to do it" (Regional and Field Office Farm Labor Files 1958–83: September 30, 1971).

Some migrants lost touch with their loved ones. As part of its many duties, the Migration Division served as a transnational liaison between farmworkers and their families in Puerto Rico. During the 1970s the agency even advertised in New York's newspaper *El Diario/La Prensa*, relaying messages to migrants from their relatives. Several letters attempted to reestablish communication with departed workers, such as one penned by Edna Luz Arriaga, from Cataño, which began: "Baby: The present [purpose] of this little letter is to know about you and how it's going over there I as for me and your son I'll tell you that we're both down with a cold" (Growers Association Files 1955–82: October 11, 1973).

Other correspondents reported serious illnesses and deaths in the family:

> Mr. Daniel Torres
> Brother this letter has the goal of greeting you and at the same time give you some bad news from our mother on the 15th of this month she died which was yesterday. Agustín Paco Chee and Rafi are already in Puerto Rico today Toña Pedro arrives. So if you want to see Picto well I think when you receive this letter and it's too late you won't be able to see her. With no other news your sister Yuly who loves you and take it easy don't do anything silly.
> Your sister Yuly
> Oh and Pito is also gravely ill he's in the hospital he was throwing up blood through his nose and mouth. (Growers Association Files 1955–82: April 16, 1974)

The most heartbreaking messages involved abandoned wives and children. Lydia Acosta Estrada, from Gurabo, was searching for her husband, Iluminado Acosta Jiménez:

> My painted lips
> My dearest husband:
> I wrote this [letter] without receiving any [response]. where I'll tell you that your children they're fine in health. Thank God and I wish the same to you together with your fellow workers. As to myself I'll tell you that I've been nervous and [in]tranquil because I haven't heard from you. Look daddy you know I suffer a lot because of you because I don't know [about your life?] I'm your wife I want to know

about you since I don't know your whereabouts tell me what's happened to you since I received a single letter from you and I haven't received anything else from you. . . . When you come back you'll find me losing weight and thinking about your trip I hope you won't make me suffer anymore my sweetheart you know that I'm crazy about you and I please you in every way My beautiful sweetheart I think I'm the only woman who has understood you. . . . Look I went to the State Fund and they had the address of the owners of the farms and I got this one from over there so that's why I wrote to this director of the farm who's trying to look for this gentleman who works in the state of Indiana, named Iluminado Acosta Jimenez. . . . I look for you everywhere. That's so you know that I love you, kisses and hugs, from your children my kisses and hugs from your wife Lydia who loves you forever. Who won't ever forget you Answer soon by all means I await your response. (Growers Association Files 1955–82: September 12, 1975)

The Commonwealth office located the husband at the Curtis Burns camp in Rochester, New York.

The Migration Division even acted as a bilingual social service agency. In one instance, a migration specialist served as translator for four Puerto Rican workers accused of molesting three girls in Moorestown, New Jersey. The judge dismissed the charges after hearing the girls' testimony. The Commonwealth official commented: "Not every person who speaks Spanish and English can act as interpreter in court in the best interest of our workers. It takes a person with a thorough knowledge of both languages plus a full understanding of how our workers thinks [sic], act and react" (Growers Association Files 1955–82: September 15, 1969).

Another case involved a dysfunctional family, referred to the division by Catholic Charities in Reading, Pennsylvania. According to the migration specialist in Hamburg, Eugenia Galán threatened to "sleep in the street with my six children rather than keep on living with this old man [the husband]. Last night he was about to strangle himself with a string of rope tied to the bed, with a tight knot around the neck, and I think that someone who dares to do that, is capable of killing anyone. When the son cut the string, he said he was going to buy a revolver to kill me. I want to leave here right away." The woman insisted on going back to Puerto Rico, because "I don't like *las Américas.*" The Commonwealth official took her to the Salvation Army Women's

Lodge (Reports 1956–92: March 2, 1959). Galán later changed her mind about returning to the island.

One of the most poignant examples of the human toll of transnational migration is the case of Carlos Torres, who worked in a tomato farm in Greshville, Pennsylvania. On August 20, 1959, Luis Rivera Hernández, another Puerto Rican worker, shot and killed Torres after arguing over a prostitute in their barracks. The migration specialist in Hamburg served as interpreter for the accused. Rivera Hernández pleaded guilty to voluntary manslaughter and was sentenced to six to twelve years in prison. The deceased man's sister, Georgina Hernández, claimed the body and his meager personal belongings:

A jacket
A shirt
A black suit
A pair of brown shoes
A red hat
A belt
A can of hair ointment
A box of cigarettes
An old wallet
A can of shoe polish
A tie
(Reports 1956–92: August 25, 1959)

Comparing Transnational Colonial States and Transnational Nation-States

The postwar Puerto Rican experience of government-sponsored migration prefigured what are now known as "transnational nation-states." Such states have institutionalized their interests in the populations residing outside their original territories, "claiming that [their] emigrants and their descendants remain an integral and intimate part of their ancestral homeland, even if they are legal citizens of another state" (Fouron and Glick Schiller 2001: 19). As Luis Guarnizo (1998) has shown, many contemporary migrant-sending states, including the Dominican Republic and Mexico, have redefined the meaning of citizenship and nationality to integrate diasporas into their countries of origin (see also Itzigsohn and Villacrés 2008). Among other measures, transnational nation-states have restructured their ministerial and consular bureaucracies, recognized dual citizenship, extended the right to vote abroad, permitted candidates to run for public office from overseas, provided state services to nationals living abroad, and reinforced expatriates' sense of membership in the sending countries. Peggy Levitt and Rafael de la Dehesa (2003) argue that transnational-nation states follow such policies because of the growing significance of remittances as well as changing norms of governance across state boundaries. In addition, migrants often organize themselves to participate in homeland politics and press for the sending state's recognition of their citizenship rights.

After World War II the Puerto Rican government adopted several transnational migration policies, though it did not grant voting rights to Puerto Ricans in the United States. (As I have noted, Puerto Ricans on and off the island share U.S. citizenship, albeit with different rights and obligations.) Beginning in 1947 the island's bureaucracy "followed its migrant citizens" to the U.S. mainland and promoted their adjustment to an "ethnologically alien" setting. In particular, the Farm Labor Program walked a tightrope between defining Puerto Ricans as "domestic labor" and preserving their "foreign" culture and language in the United States.

After 1952 the Commonwealth government expanded its "transnational" reach, from promoting job opportunities and enforcing labor contracts to providing legal defense and health insurance, as well as translation and education services. As the Puerto Rican anthropologist Ismael García-Colón (2008: 285) observes, the Migration Division "acted contradictorily as a labor organization and, at the same time, as a hindrance to independent labor organizing efforts." Moreover, the agency had a vested interest in maintaining a regular labor flow to the mainland because of its economic benefits for the island. Between 1947 and 1959, when remittances were not as carefully monitored as they are today, farmworkers sent US$291.7 million to the island (Monserrat 1961: 35). Finally, the Migration Division operated as a liaison between the Puerto Rican government and city, state, and federal agencies in the United States.

Compared to transnational nation-states such as the Dominican Republic, the Commonwealth government has not fully incorporated its émigrés into homeland politics. Perhaps the most controversial issue is how the diaspora can contribute to solving Puerto Rico's "colonial" status. Until now, all local elections, referenda, and plebiscites have been restricted to U.S. citizens who reside on the island. Nonetheless, Puerto Ricans in the United States have reiterated their wish to participate in defining the island's political future (Delgado 2008; Falcón 1993, 2007). On April 29, 2010, the U.S. House of Representatives approved a bill to hold a new plebiscite on Puerto Rico's status. The Puerto Rico Democracy Act of 2009 (H.R. 2499), sponsored by Resident Commissioner Pedro Pierluisi, would grant the right to vote in the plebiscite to all U.S. citizens born in Puerto Rico, regardless of their current residence. If approved by the Senate, this proposal would allow stateside Puerto Ricans to formally take part for the first time in the status debate. As of October 2010, however, the U.S. Senate's Committee on Energy and Natural Resources had virtually paralyzed the bill.

"Foreign in a Domestic Sense": The Rise of a Transnational Colonial State

After the Spanish-Cuban-American War of 1898, Puerto Rico became an un-incorporated territory of the United States. This legal status determined the island's equivocal condition as neither a state of the U.S. union nor an independent country. Although Puerto Ricans did not become U.S. citizens until 1917, the Supreme Court recognized their right of abode in the continental United States in 1904. After Congress conferred on them U.S. citizenship, Puerto Ricans could be fully protected by the U.S. Constitution if they moved to the U.S. mainland. This territorially grounded distinction in citizenship rights remains a defining characteristic of U.S. Colonialism on the island.

The Estado Libre Asociado did not end Puerto Rico's colonial dependence on the United States, although it did provide greater local autonomy. On the one hand, Commonwealth status allowed — perhaps even required — the island's public authorities to intervene on behalf of migrants to the mainland. On the other hand, the Puerto Rican government must comply with all applicable federal laws and regulations. The Farm Labor Program best exemplifies the island's "transnational" migration policies, which facilitated the transfer of "surplus hands" to the mainland after World War II. The large-scale displacement of agricultural workers established the earliest settlement patterns of Puerto Ricans in the U.S. Northeast as well as the circulation of labor that persists today.

To promote the recruitment of Puerto Rican farmworkers, Common-wealth officials argued that they should be given preference over foreigners in the United States. Still, many U.S. employers considered Puerto Ricans "alien workers," especially because they spoke little English and practiced a "foreign" culture, including their eating habits. According to a Commonwealth official in Hamburg, "the language barrier" was "the number one problem" for Puerto Rico's migrant workers (Reports 1956–92: October 13, 1959).

In sum, Puerto Ricans illustrate one of the main dilemmas of colonial subjects in their metropolitan countries: although legally domestic, they are often viewed as culturally foreign. Thus, the Puerto Rican diaspora is both transnational, because it involves crossing the cultural borders between the island and the U.S. mainland, and colonial, because it does not entail traveling across the legal boundaries between independent states. This ambiguity is the long-term consequence of the oxymoronic legal doctrine that Puerto Rico "belongs to but is not a part of the United States." Such a doctrine, established at the beginning of the twentieth century, laid the groundwork for a massive transnational colonial migration during the second half of the century.

The next chapter shifts methodological and chronological gears to examine the recent exodus of middle-class Puerto Ricans to Orlando, the fastest growing metropolitan area for Puerto Ricans in the United States in the 1990s. In so doing, I move from archival sources to ethnographic fieldwork, but I retain a focus on the transnational ties of contemporary Puerto Rican migrants, especially on the reconstruction of their cultural identities. Even though most Puerto Ricans in the United States are no longer farmworkers, they preserve strong emotional and cultural attachments to their homeland.

The Orlando Ricans

Overlapping Identity Discourses among
Middle-Class Puerto Rican Immigrants

5

Since the 1980s Latin American migration to the United States has become increasingly diverse in its national origins and settlement patterns.[1] Cities formerly dominated by a single group of Hispanics or Latinos[2] — such as Puerto Ricans in New York, Cubans in Miami, or Mexicans in Los Angeles — have received a large influx of people from other countries, such as the Dominican Republic, Nicaragua, and El Salvador. At the same time, Mexicans have moved en masse to New York and other nontraditional destinations like North Carolina and Georgia; many Puerto Ricans have resettled in Florida; and Dominicans have dispersed even more widely to Puerto Rico, Spain, Venezuela, and elsewhere.

Scholars have analyzed the growing Latinization of such urban spaces as El Barrio (also known as Spanish Harlem), the traditionally Puerto Rican neighborhood in Manhattan; Corona, Queens, with one of the most diverse Hispanic populations in the United States, including Colombians, Dominicans, and Cubans; Humboldt Park, the core of Chicago's Puerto Rican community; and Little Havana, the heart of Miami's Cuban enclave (see Dávila 2004; Laó-Montes and Dávila 2001; Price 2007; Ramos-Zayas 2003; Ricourt and Danta 2003; and Stepick et al. 2003). In each of these neighborhoods, immigration from various Latin American countries (especially Mexico and the Dominican Republic in El Barrio, and Nicaragua and Colombia in Little Havana) has reconfigured ethnic, panethnic, national, and transnational identities. A crucial issue is whether the immigrants will forge broader alliances with other Hispanics; assert their national origins and transnational connections to their home countries; or combine the two strategies. Histori-

TABLE 5.1 Selected Characteristics of Puerto Ricans in the United States, New York City, and the Orlando-Kissimmee Metropolitan Area, 2009

Characteristic	United States	New York City	Orlando-Kissimmee
Bachelor's degree (%)	10.6	8.4	11.7
Graduate or professional degree (%)	4.8	3.7	3.6
Unemployed (%)	14.8	15.7	14.7
Managers and professionals (%)	26.9	26.8	22.3
Service workers (%)	22.8	26.6	23.8
Self-employed workers (%)	3.0	2.9	3.2
Median household income (us$)	37,502	29,536	37,561
Poverty rate (%)	25.7	32.0	17.3
Owner-occupied housing units (%)	38.2	16.4	51.0

Source: U.S. Census Bureau 2010.

cally, most groups have favored a nationally based identification, but little is known about people of mixed Latino heritage, such as Puerto Rican Dominican, Mexican Guatemalan, and Ecuadorian Colombian, or the second generation born in the United States. Rethinking the Puerto Rican diaspora in its larger Latin American and Caribbean context offers a unique opportunity to examine the extent to which the Hispanic or Latino label is grounded in the immigrants' experiences.

Regrettably, researchers have not scrutinized emergent collective affiliations in new Latino destinations such as Orlando, Florida. Between 1990 and 2009 the Hispanic population of Orange County — the heart of the Orlando metropolitan area — quadrupled, from 64,946 to 259,240 people. Of the latter, nearly half (122,414) were of Puerto Rican origin (more than half of whom were born on the island, with the rest born in the fifty United States). The remainder was primarily of Mexican, Cuban, Colombian, Dominican, and Venezuelan ancestry (U.S. Census Bureau 2010). During the past three decades, the Hispanic, and particularly the Puerto Rican, population in the Orlando metropolitan area had one of the fastest growth rates in the United States. According to Angelo Falcón (2004: 6), Orlando experienced the largest increase (142 percent) in the number of Puerto Ricans stateside between 1990 and 2000. As Susan Eichenberger (2004: 6) remarks, "Puerto Ricans have transformed the landscape of the area so much so that they often feel that . . . [it] is an extension of the Island." She presumably means that Puerto Ricans have reshaped the Orlando metropolitan area in demographic, cul-

TABLE 5.2 Race of Puerto Ricans in Central Florida, New York City, the United States, and Puerto Rico, according to the 2000 Census (in Percentages)

Race	Central Florida	New York City	United States	Puerto Rico
White	63.0	43.6	51.9	80.5
Black or African American	3.0	7.9	6.4	8.0
American Indian or Alaska Native	0.3	0.7	0.7	0.4
Asian	0.2	0.2	0.5	0.3
Native Hawaiian and other Pacific Islander	0.1	0.0	0.3	0.0
Some other race	27.1	41.5	38.2	6.8
Two or more races	6.2	6.1	7.6	4.2

Source: Duany and Matos-Rodríguez 2006, based on census data.

tural, linguistic, and even religious terms. This chapter inquires whether, how, and to what extent Puerto Rican migrants to Orlando have adopted panethnic identities, based on the amalgamation of several national origins.

In 2006 Félix V. Matos-Rodríguez and I predicted that Puerto Ricans in Central Florida could follow a different path from that of other Puerto Rican communities in the diaspora. On several counts, the socioeconomic profile of Puerto Ricans in the Orlando metropolitan area is more favorable than in the United States as a whole and particularly in New York City (see table 5.1). A distinctive feature of the recent Puerto Rican settlement in Orlando is the relatively large proportion of well-educated professionals and managers, most of whom define themselves as white (see table 5.2). This group has had a significant impact on Puerto Ricans' settlement patterns, as well as on their reception by established residents of Central Florida. For instance, Puerto Ricans in Orlando are more likely to own their houses and live in suburban neighborhoods than in New York City. In Orlando, the locations of Puerto Rican residents differ greatly from the poor inner-city barrios of the U.S. Northeast and the Midwest (Concepción Torres 2008; Duany 2006a; Villarrubia-Mendoza 2007, 2010). Despite moderate degrees of residential segregation, Puerto Ricans in Central Florida are not as isolated from non-Hispanic whites as elsewhere (Vargas-Ramos 2006).

This chapter analyzes in-depth interviews with Puerto Rican business, civic, political, educational, and religious leaders in Orlando. I concentrate on how this privileged group represents itself as part of the Spanish-speaking population of Central Florida. A recurring theme in our conversations was Puerto Ricans' contested relations with other Latinos, including Cubans,

Venezuelans, Mexicans, and Colombians. Many of the interviewees insisted on preserving and promoting Puerto Rican culture, especially through community organizations, festivals, businesses, and other institutions. Furthermore, the interviews generated a wealth of qualitative data on how middle-class members of Orlando's Puerto Rican community — primarily those born and raised on the island — maintained transnational connections, especially kinship ties. This research complements earlier work based largely on census statistics (de Jesús and Vasquez 2007; Duany and Matos-Rodríguez 2006; Villarrubia-Mendoza 2007), by providing new insights into the immigrants' motivations, decisions, attitudes, and experiences. Most of all, the results shed light on how middle-class Puerto Ricans in Orlando construct their identities.[3]

Why Study Puerto Ricans in Orlando?

First, the Puerto Rican population in Florida is significant, demographically as well as economically. The U.S. Census Bureau (2009a) found that the number of Puerto Ricans residing in the state nearly doubled during the 1990s. According to the 2009 American Community Survey, Florida had the second-largest concentration of stateside Puerto Ricans (816,002), after New York. The Orlando-Kissimmee metropolitan area had 248,201 Puerto Rican residents, or 50.2 percent of the area's Hispanic population. Furthermore, Puerto Ricans cluster in several counties, such as Orange and Osceola, and in specific localities, such as the middle-class neighborhoods of Meadow Woods and Buena Ventura Lakes, or the more economically disadvantaged district of Kissimmee. Moreover, Puerto Ricans have established numerous enterprises in Florida, mostly in services, retail trade, transportation, and construction. In 2007 Puerto Ricans owned 42,418 businesses in the state, including 6,738 in the Orlando-Kissimmee metropolitan area (U.S. Census Bureau 2010). Compared with Puerto Ricans in New York City, those residing in Orlando have higher income, occupational, and educational levels (Duany and Matos-Rodríguez 2006).

In addition, the Puerto Rican electorate in Florida could influence local, state, and even presidential elections. The mass media have paid much attention to the expansion of the Democratic Party in Central Florida, largely due to the backing of Puerto Ricans and other Hispanics, in contrast to the predominantly Republican Cubans in South Florida (see, e.g., Glanton 2000; Lizza 2000; and Milligan 2000). More than 70 percent of Puerto

Rican voters in Florida supported the Democratic candidate, Al Gore, in the 2000 presidential elections. In 2004 59 percent of Florida's Puerto Ricans favored Senator John Kerry, while 39 percent supported the reelection of President George W. Bush. That year nearly two hundred thousand Puerto Ricans were eligible to vote in Florida, the second largest number after New York's almost three hundred thousand Puerto Ricans (Delgado 2001, 2008; Friedman 2004). In 2008 Puerto Ricans and other Hispanics helped elect President Barack Obama. Yet the political activities of Puerto Ricans in Florida have not been well documented from a social scientific standpoint (see Cruz 2010 for an exception). This lack of information is intriguing because Puerto Ricans are the second-largest Latino group in the United States (after Mexicans) and Florida (after Cubans), and the largest in Orlando, one of the main gateways for new Latin American immigrants (along with Miami).

Studying the Puerto Rican experience in Florida can contribute substantially to the literature on the Puerto Rican diaspora, which has focused on the older communities in New York City, Chicago, and Philadelphia (see Haslip-Viera, Falcón, and Matos-Rodríguez 2004; Gina Pérez 2004; Ramos-Zayas 2003; and Whalen 2001). Studies of Florida Puerto Ricans have been conducted only recently (see Aranda 2009; Aranda, Chang, and Sabogal 2009; Concepción Torres 2008; Duany and Silver 2010; Eichenberger 2004; Hernández Cruz 2002; María Pérez 2008; and Luis Sánchez 2009).[4] Most social research on contemporary Hispanic immigration in Florida has dwelt on Miami's Cuban enclave, while historical research has concentrated on Cubans in the Tampa area in the late nineteenth century (see Greenbaum 2002; Grenier and Pérez 2003; Louis Pérez 1978; Portes and Stepick 1993; and Poyo 1989). Consequently, such pressing issues as Puerto Ricans' changing settlement patterns, diverse class composition, relations with other Hispanics, or adoption of a Latino identity are not well understood.

Finally, exploring the Puerto Rican diaspora in Florida can advance current knowledge of transnationalism. As I pointed out in chapter 1, most of the academic literature has neglected the Puerto Rican situation as an example of the lasting links between people of the same national origin across great distances (for exceptions to this trend, see Alicea 1997; Aranda 2007; Duany 2002; Gina Pérez 2004; and Toro-Morn and Alicea 2003). This is an unfortunate omission, because Puerto Rico is a classic case of the large-scale circulation of people and the first airborne migration (see Alicea 1990; Hernández Álvarez 1967; Hernández Cruz 1994; and Edwin Meléndez 1993). Furthermore, the Puerto Rican government was one of the earliest states, sovereign or not, to sponsor transnational migration in the 1940s (chapter 4).[5]

How Puerto Ricans, who are U.S. citizens by birth, compare to other migrants, such as Dominicans or Cubans, most of whom are not U.S. citizens, merits further investigation. So does the question of how Puerto Ricans cross the cultural border with the United States, which is technically not an international boundary because Puerto Rico is a territory that "belongs to but is not part" of the United States. And yet the geographic, linguistic, religious, and racial contrasts between the island and the mainland are sufficiently large to conceive them as transnational. Among other differences, Puerto Ricans acquire the full rights of U.S. citizenship — such as voting for the president or members of Congress — as well as its responsibilities — such as paying federal income taxes — only when they move to one of the fifty United States.

Colonial Transnationalism, Panethnicity, and Racialization

As I mentioned in chapter 1, much of the relevant literature takes for granted that transnationalism occurs between sovereign countries (see the classic statements by Basch, Glick Schiller, and Szanton Blanc 1994; and Glick Schiller, Basch, and Blanc-Szanton 1992). However, every year, tens of thousands of Puerto Ricans move to the United States, just as other Caribbean peoples relocate to their European metropoles, such as the United Kingdom, France, and the Netherlands. As citizens of their metropoles, colonial subjects may circulate more frequently between their places of origin and destination than those who lack legal access to migration. At the same time, the dominant Euro-American imaginary racializes colonial subjects as criminal, lazy, dumb, dirty, and uncivilized. Hence, colonial migrants face strong barriers to incorporation into their "mother countries."

The term *colonial transnationalism* may be applied to migrants from colonial peripheries to metropolitan centers. Colonial migrants can be deemed transnational because they transgress the geographic, cultural, linguistic, and racial borders between peripheral and core countries, even though they do not cross the legal boundaries between nation-states. As I argued in the introduction, it is necessary to analytically decouple the nation from the state by differentiating a boundary (a juridical and administrative division between independent countries) from a border (a geographic and cultural contact zone, such as the one between the island and the U.S. mainland) (see Kearney 1991).[6]

How people define themselves across borders and boundaries remains poorly documented. Even less understood is how transnational migrants forge new identities, based exclusively neither on their home countries nor on the dominant groups in the host society but on panethnic allegiances such as those often pursued by Latinos or Asians in the United States. Much of this process of identity construction responds to ethnic and racial categories imposed by public officials, media executives, and intellectuals (see Cobas, Duany, and Feagin 2009; Dávila 2001; Flores 2000; and Oboler 1995). But a panethnic consciousness may also arise from the daily interaction (*convivencia diaria*) among various Latin American immigrant groups (Ricourt and Danta 2003). A grassroots discourse of *Hispanidad* can be traced to the late-nineteenth-century settlements of Cubans, Puerto Ricans, and Spaniards in New York City (Laó-Montes and Dávila 2001).

Nowadays, self-classification as Latino or Hispanic may also be a way to evade the polar extremes of the U.S. racial stratification system. For example, Dominicans in New York City and Providence, Rhode Island, usually adopt the *Hispanic* or *Latino* moniker as an intermediate category between white and black (Bailey 2002; Itzigsohn 2006; Itzigsohn and Dore-Cabral 2000). Similarly, Afro-Cubans in Austin and Albuquerque negotiate their identities as both black and Hispanic, in a context where "Cuban" has little resonance (Newby and Dowling 2007). Puerto Ricans in the United States may define themselves as a "racial," ethnic, national, panethnic, or transnational group, according to various political projects, social and geographic locations, and historical moments (see Duany 2002; Negrón-Muntaner and Grosfoguel 1997; and Felix Padilla 1985).

Panethnic labels typically collapse people who look or sound the same to the dominant majority into a single group based on physical appearance, language, or geographic origin. As Suzanne Oboler (1995: 2) has argued, a catchall term such as *Hispanic* or *Latino* (or *Asian* or *Oriental*) often "homogenizes class experiences and neglects many different linguistic, racial, and ethnic groups within the different nationalities themselves." For instance, the U.S. government, media, and public opinion commonly assume that all Hispanics or Latinos are racially mixed. In the United States, the "Latin look" usually features olive or brown skin and dark, straight hair (Dávila 2001; Mendible 2007). This body type is ambiguously located between prevailing Anglo-American images of whiteness and blackness.

Despite little comparative work on the subject (see de Genova 2006), the racialization of Latinos and Asians in the United States follows a similar logic: neither group is deemed white or black. Consequently, the federal government has created separate ethnoracial categories for each minority. In 1980 the Census Bureau asked all residents of the United States if they were of Spanish or Hispanic origin, including Mexicans, Puerto Ricans, Cubans, Central and South Americans, and Spaniards (Clara Rodríguez 2000). Since then, the census has also lumped together several groups under the Asian and Pacific Islander heading, including Asian Indian, Chinese, Filipino, Japanese, Korean, and Vietnamese, as well as Hawaiian, Guamanian, Samoan, and other native peoples of the Pacific islands (Reeves and Bennett 2003).

A lively academic and public debate has emerged about the overlapping of Puerto Rican, Hispanic, and Latino identities in the United States. For some authors, Puerto Ricans are Hispanic or Latino by default, because they can trace their origin to a Spanish-speaking country. Furthermore, Puerto Ricans, together with Mexicans, constitute the prototypes of the Hispanic category popularized since the 1970s. For others, Latinidad or Hispanidad refers to the idea that, despite their differences, the peoples originating in Latin America share a geographic, historical, cultural, and linguistic background (Diaz McConnell and Delgado-Romero 2004; Ricourt and Danta 2003). According to its critics, the Hispanic/Latino classification glosses over a wide variety of immigrant histories, colonial legacies, racial and ethnic groups, social classes, cultural traditions, languages, and dialects (Dávila 2001, 2008; de Genova and Ramos-Zayas 2003; Flores 2000; Oboler 1995). Thus, some argue, Puerto Ricans should not be pigeonholed with other populations of Latin American ancestry. This chapter addresses whether middle-class Puerto Ricans in Orlando identify themselves primarily as members of an ethnic, national, or panethnic group.

Researching Orlando Ricans

I interviewed sixteen members of the Puerto Rican community in the Orlando metropolitan area for this study. I chose the participants because of their reputation or referral by other well-known Puerto Ricans. I sought representatives from various business, civic, political, educational, and religious sectors of the population. The two main criteria for selection were (1) Puerto Rican birth or origin and (2) recognition as a leader of Orlando's Puerto Rican community.

The interviewees included a similar proportion of men and women between twenty-seven and sixty-nine years of age, and most were born and
raised on the island. All had completed at least a college degree, worked as
managers or professionals, and spoke both Spanish and English (although
English was the second language for most). At the time of the interview, the
respondents had lived an average of twenty-four years in the United States.
Table 5.3 details the main characteristics of the sample. As expected, the
interviewees represent the well-educated and upper-status occupational
sectors of the Puerto Rican population in the Orlando-Kissimmee metropolitan area.[7]

With Elizabeth Aranda's permission, I adapted her semistructured interview guide to study migration between Puerto Rico and the United States.
The guide included twenty-eight open-ended questions about the informants' socioeconomic profile, migration history, participation in voluntary
associations, kinship and friendship networks, and identity. I also inquired
about the participants' relations with Cubans and other Hispanics, as well
as their personal, economic, and business links with the island. A crucial
part of the interviews was querying the informants' definition of themselves
as Puerto Rican, Hispanic, Latino, or some other ethnic category. Finally, I
explored the cultural differences between Puerto Ricans born on the island
and those born on the mainland. On average, each interview lasted about
an hour and a half. Although I gave my informants the choice of speaking
Spanish or English, only one conducted the entire interview in English.

I first drew up a list of Puerto Rican voluntary associations in the Orlando
metropolitan area. Then I identified the leaders of these associations, with
the help of a prominent member of the Puerto Rican community. The next
step was to telephone them and set up an appointment in a place of their
choice, usually their office or a public location, such as a coffee house or
fast-food restaurant. I explained the basic purpose of my study and assured
participants that the results would be confidential. During the interview,
I took extensive notes while the informants answered my questions. I decided not to tape record the interviews to maximize the informal nature
of the conversation and make participants more comfortable. At the end of
the interview, I asked the informants to recommend other persons whom I
should contact for this project. Eventually, many names on my list began to
repeat themselves. In the following pages, I use pseudonyms to protect the
respondents' identities.

TABLE 5.3 Characteristics of the Orlando Interview Sample

Pseudonym	Sex	Age	Birthplace	Place Where Person Was Raised	Education
Sandra	Female	58	Mayagüez, P.R.	Puerto Rico	PhD
Raúl	Male	39	San Juan, P.R.	Puerto Rico and United States	MA
María	Female	49	Brooklyn, N.Y.	United States and Puerto Rico	MA
Clarita	Female	55	Cayey, P.R.	Puerto Rico	PhD
Raymond	Male	35	Caguas, P.R.	Puerto Rico	MA
Alberto	Male	64	Santurce, P.R.	Puerto Rico	BA
Miriam	Female	69	Mayagüez, P.R.	Puerto Rico and United States	BA
Ernesto	Male	40	San Juan, P.R.	Puerto Rico	BA
Ángel	Male	46	Youngstown, Ohio	United States and Puerto Rico	BA
Diana	Female	54	Río Piedras, P.R.	Puerto Rico	BA
Luisa	Female	51	Raleigh, N.C.	Puerto Rico	MA
Manuel	Male	47	Hato Rey, P.R.	Puerto Rico	BA
Margarita	Female	37	San Juan, P.R.	Puerto Rico	PhD
Jorge	Male	43	San Juan, P.R.	Puerto Rico	MS
Raquel	Female	61	San Juan, P.R.	Puerto Rico	BA
Rosa	Female	27	Ponce, P.R.	Puerto Rico	BA

[a]In the informant's estimation.

[b]In the case of informants born in the United States, year refers to year of their first return trip from the island to the mainland.

Current Occupation and Industry	Fluency in Spanish[a]	Fluency in English[a]	Year of First Trip to United States[b]
Manager, public administration	Native	Fluent	1973
Professional, professional services	Native	"As good as my Spanish"	1979
Manager, public administration	Fluent	Native	1979
Manager, public administration	Native	Fluent	1976
Manager, public administration	Native	Fluent	1993
Retired (formerly sales manager, information)	Native	Fluent	1978
Retired (formerly manager, retail trade)	"Primary"	Fluent	1945
Private contractor, construction	Native	"Medium"	1987
Manager, public administration	"Primary"	Fluent	1985
Manager, communication	Native	Fluent	1981
Manager, communication	Native	Fluent	2005
Professional, communication	Native	"Second language"	1977
Professional, education	Native	Fluent	1989
Manager, communication	Fluent	"Primary"	1981
Manager, public administration	Native	Fluent	1993
Professional, communication	Native	Fluent	2005

Migration Histories

The First Generation

Most of my informants migrated as adults from Puerto Rico to the United States. Many had lived elsewhere on the mainland before relocating to Orlando, including New York, New Jersey, Texas, Georgia, Ohio, and North Carolina. For example, Sandra moved from the island in 1973 to pursue her PhD at a northeastern university. After completing her degree, she "couldn't stand the cold any more," so in 1998 she moved to Orlando. "We used to come here often on vacations," she remembered, and she and her husband liked the area's Hispanic environment, economic development, and job opportunities. Moreover, "coming to Orlando allowed me to reconnect with the Puerto Rican community. . . . Now you can even find many products from Puerto Rico in local supermarkets." Although she traveled to the island every two years, she did not plan to live there, because her children and grandchildren were living in Orlando.

Margarita also received her graduate education in the United States. In 1989 she began studying for her master's degree in New York and continued in Europe. She returned to Puerto Rico for a year and eventually obtained her doctorate in the United States. In 1996 Margarita settled down in Orlando, where she found work in her professional specialization. She had visited the island many times since then (almost twice a year), especially to see her parents, who still owned a house there. When asked if she would return to live there permanently, Margarita responded: "Return? I don't know. I'm always changing. I won't say I won't, I won't say I will. My parents and family are in Puerto Rico. I feel more integrated to the United States and South America. My plans are here."

Upon graduating from high school in Puerto Rico in 1981, Jorge enrolled at the University of Central Florida (located in Orlando). After a year and a half, he transferred to a Texas college. When he graduated, he started working and married there. For thirteen years, Jorge lived in a largely Mexican American town, where he felt isolated because he was the only one with his surname. In 1996 he moved back to Orlando and has lived there since. He felt "more comfortable here" because of the area's climate, exciting city life, nearness to the island, and acceptance of the Puerto Rican community. "It's good to know others like you," Jorge added.

Looking for a "better quality of life," Raquel took an early retirement from her job as a marketing executive in Puerto Rico. After divorcing her husband, she decided to move to the mainland with her three children. Although her first choice was Atlanta, she moved to Orlando in 1993. One of her sons had already traveled to Florida when he was in high school. All were completely bilingual because they had attended a good private school in San Juan. This academic background helped them integrate into their new peer groups in Orlando. For her sixth-grade daughter, the family's change of residence was "very traumatic." In the beginning, Raquel experienced discrimination in Orlando because of her Spanish surname. After two or three years of adjustment, she felt at home there.

"I never imagined I'd live here," Diana admitted. "But I came for my honeymoon and liked the place, its climate, and its friendly people." In 1981 she and her husband moved to Orlando, primarily because one of their three children was allergic and needed a change of environment. At the time of the interview, Diana had been living in the area for twenty-six years. A recent widow, she headed a local media company. She did not intend to return to live on the island.

Alberto's migration history was complicated. Because he objected to joining the U.S. Army in 1968, he suffered political persecution on the island. In 1978 he first moved with his mother to Texas, where he worked in three different cities for several years. His employer, an information processing company, later transferred him to Atlanta. He finally retired in Orlando in 2000 with his family of five. Although Alberto felt closer to Puerto Rico in Orlando and liked its weather, he planned to move back to the island, where he owned a house. Only his commitment to a local voluntary association held him down for now.

Among the interviewees, Rosa was the most recent arrival from Puerto Rico. When I met her, she had lived in Orlando for less than a year (although she had spent a few months there before). She moved with her husband, while the rest of her family stayed on the island. Employment opportunities, public schools, climate, quality of life, the Hispanic population, and tranquility drew her to Orlando. "I don't think I'll go back," Rosa said of Puerto Rico. "The economy is bad, the environment is unfavorable, and there's no safety." Despite the U.S. recession, life seemed better in Orlando than in San Juan.

Although the motivations of first-generation immigrants from Puerto Rico ranged widely, economic considerations did not figure prominently among them. My informants mentioned educational opportunities, profes-

sional advancement, "quality of life," climate, and health concerns more frequently than finding a job or earning a higher salary in Orlando. As Jorge
summed it up, "We didn't come for economic reasons." This is a major difference between middle-class and lower-class migrants, who are primarily
motivated by the search for employment abroad. Compared to earlier movements to New York or Chicago, recent Puerto Rican migration to Orlando
is more strongly associated with efforts to maintain or achieve middle-class
status.

The 1.5 Generation

Although Miriam was born in Mayagüez, she and her parents moved to New
York in 1945 aboard the famous steamship the *Marine Tiger*. She was only
eight years old then. Starting in 1959 she visited the island once a year. Her
parents eventually moved back to Puerto Rico, where she learned to speak
Spanish well. She later migrated again to the mainland, only to return to
Puerto Rico in 1980. After divorcing her husband, Miriam relocated to the
United States seven years later, because her daughter was sick and could not
be treated on the island. She settled in Central Florida, where she became
active in the Puerto Rican community. "The same thing happened here as
when I came on the *Marine Tiger*. . . . They discriminated against me in New
York. They also discriminated against me in Puerto Rico."

Manuel's family moved from San Juan to Miami when he was eleven years
old. He is typical of the 1.5 generation of immigrants, who left their country
of birth as youngsters. In 1979 a major airline company transferred Manuel's
father to Miami, but he soon lost his job there. Because his older brother was
living in Orlando, the entire family moved north. Manuel still had close relatives in Miami as well as in Tampa. Whether he returned to live permanently
on the island depended on his employer.

Similarly, Raúl first arrived in Orlando as a teenager. "We left Puerto Rico
for security reasons. They broke into our house twice in the 1970s, even
though we lived in gated communities." In 1977 his father started a small
business in South Florida, while his sister studied in the Midwest. Because
the firm did not do well, the family moved farther north in Florida. After
graduating from high school, Raúl attended the University of Central Florida
and later found work in Orlando. "There were very few [*éramos cuatro gatos*]
of us [Puerto Ricans] here in 1985," he recalled. Although he traveled to the

island once or twice a year, he did not anticipate resettling there: "My wife isn't Puerto Rican and my daughters were born here. I don't see myself there, but I don't say I never will [*no digo de esa agua no beberé*]."

As expected, members of the 1.5 generation moved to Orlando as a result of their parents' decisions. Most of them eventually settled in the area, but others were not completely rooted there. Some expressed feeling "in-between" the United States and Puerto Rico, not quite at home in either country. Their plans to return to Puerto Rico or stay in Florida were more tentative than those of the first or second generation. Most followed a typically middle-class mode of incorporation into the Orlando metropolitan area.

The Second Generation

Circular migration has been a way of life for Ángel, who was born in Ohio but moved with his family to New York in 1969, when he was eight years old. They later returned to Bayamón, Puerto Rico. "Both languages were spoken at home," he recalled. "They used to make fun of you in elementary school because of your accent in Spanish." He attended college in the United States and went back to the island after earning his BA. In 1985 Ángel moved to Orlando because his parents and other relatives were living there. "It was a safe place for the family and to raise children," he said. "Now it's not so safe as before." Ángel and his wife kept a summer home in Puerto Rico, where they spent their vacations. "We love it [*nos fascina*] there," he said. "The link to the island can't be broken."

Although Luisa was born in North Carolina, her parents took her to Puerto Rico when she was only three months old. She grew up and spent most of her life on the island. In 2005 she accepted a professional job offer in Orlando. "In the beginning," she recalled, "I thought it was going to be very difficult to adapt to this environment. I felt like a fish out of water." But eventually she felt better. "Everyone speaks Spanish here." She traveled to Puerto Rico every three months and hoped to retire there, "to grow old with my people." Sometime after the interview, Luisa returned to the island when the company she worked for closed down its Orlando operations.

Of all my informants, only María was born and raised on the U.S. mainland, specifically in New York City. Even she experienced a return to the island. María moved to Puerto Rico with her family when she was ten years old, left the island again when she was sixteen, completed her university education in the United States, and had not traveled to Puerto Rico in fourteen years. She was the only one in the sample who did not visit the island regularly. However, she intended to do research there for her doctoral dissertation.

The few second-generation immigrants interviewed for this study did not differ greatly from other participants, at least concerning their migration histories. They were as mobile as the other informants, including multiple changes of residence between the United States and Puerto Rico. Their emotional connections to the island appeared as strong as the connections of those who were born and raised there. More research is needed to unveil the differences between first- and second-generation Puerto Ricans in Orlando.

The informants' migration histories displayed various motivations, including studying, working, retiring, seeking medical treatment and a safer environment, and following their relatives. A critical event in the life cycle, such as a divorce or a relative's illness, often triggered the move abroad. Economic opportunities, a growing Hispanic population, and a relatively mild climate attracted Puerto Ricans to Central Florida. Many of my informants had visited the area as tourists before relocating there. Some of them had already lived in the United States. As I elaborate below, informal social contacts — such as kinship and friendship ties — also put Orlando in the migrants' mental map.

Kinship and Friendship Networks

Many participants in this study were emotionally connected to both the island and the United States. Some were still focused on Puerto Rico, but most had reoriented their family life toward the U.S. mainland. All had numerous contacts in both places. The quantity, density, and frequency of kinship and friendship networks shaped the informants' identity, as well as their plans to remain in Orlando or return to the island. Many could be classified as transnational in that they remained tied to their home country.

Retaining a Primary Island Focus

Some respondents expressed a stronger emotional attachment to the homeland than others. Most of Clarita's relatives, including her mother, lived in Puerto Rico. They often visited her in Orlando and she traveled back home every year. "I'm very proud of my roots," she asserted. She arrived in Orlando in 1976 with her five-year-old son, after divorcing her husband. Clarita's mother owned a house in Puerto Rico as well as in Orlando.

Similarly, most of Ángel's family was still in Puerto Rico, including his cousins, uncles, aunts, nephews, and nieces. "They're spread all over the island," he noted. His mother-in-law also stayed in Puerto Rico. Ángel communicated with his relatives by telephone, mail, and visits. These two cases illustrate tightly knit transnational families between Central Florida and Puerto Rico.

Maintaining Bifocality

Other informants juggled their ties to the island and the mainland. Ernesto's extended family was split between Puerto Rico and Florida. His parents moved to Orlando and his uncles and aunts also retired there, whereas his cousins still lived on the island. He kept in touch with them by telephone and by traveling two or three times a year to the island, for business-related activities. However, he did not remain in contact with his friends there. "Each one goes on with his life," Ernesto explained. "I'm not interested in attending high school reunions."

When Raquel first moved to Orlando, she dearly missed her "very select circle of friends" in Puerto Rico. In the beginning, "it was very difficult to connect with a group of friends" in Orlando. So she joined several voluntary associations, made a difficult work transition, and found a better job. "Being by yourself and having the responsibility of advancing your family [echar la familia pa'lante]" were very stressful, especially raising three children. She would not go back to live on the island, because she felt "very well adapted and involved here." "All of my children are here," she asserted. "We sold everything over there." But she and her children visited the island at least once a year. "I still have fabulous friends over there," Raquel explained. "I don't relate to [the rest of] my family in Puerto Rico."

Alberto's family was widely dispersed. His sister and niece lived in Orlando, but his brother, son, and granddaughters lived in Puerto Rico. He also had relatives in Michigan and Texas. He contacted them regularly by e-mail, sending and receiving jokes, comments, and greetings. He also telephoned his six siblings frequently. Once a year, the family got together in Puerto Rico. These periodic visits rekindled emotional connections to the island, as Aranda (2007) has documented. They helped immigrants "keep one foot here and one foot there," as the popular expression goes.

Reorienting Social Ties toward the United States

The majority of the respondents had friends and relatives in the Orlando area. Most of Sandra's friends were Puerto Rican, although they included other Hispanics, such as Cubans, Colombians, and Venezuelans, as well as Anglos. She separated from her Puerto Rican husband years ago, before coming to Orlando. Her children and grandchildren grew up there, while the rest of her family remained in Mayagüez. She telephoned her relatives on the island every week. Sandra often hosted relatives and friends, especially when they visited Disney World and other recreational theme parks. She doubted that she could grow accustomed to living on the island again, after so many years abroad.

Raúl's closest relatives, including his parents and daughters, lived in Orlando. His sister was in Atlanta and his father in Wisconsin, but his mother and her family remained in San Juan. They used to visit him every year. But their main contact was an aunt who died recently. So they did not call each other as often as before. Raúl still communicated with some of his high school friends, who had just organized a class reunion in Puerto Rico. "I haven't seen most of them" since they graduated twenty-five years ago.

When I asked Jorge where his family lived, he took a quick inventory: one brother in Miami, another in Puerto Rico, one sister in California, another sister and his father in Orlando. They all gathered in Orlando and in Puerto Rico whenever they could. Jorge maintained contact with his relatives on the island, usually by e-mail and occasionally by telephone. Most of his friends, both Anglo and Hispanic, lived in the United States.

Manuel kept in touch with relatives and friends in Miami, Tampa, and San Juan by telephone. Most of his immediate family lived in Florida. They often got together, usually in Tampa, to celebrate birthdays, Christmas, and New Year's Eve. Every year Manuel visited the island, where he still had cousins and friends.

Diana's five children lived in Orlando, as well as her parents and grandchildren. She also had relatives in South Florida and Kentucky. Nevertheless, the extended family got together in Puerto Rico every five years. She still kept an apartment in San Juan, near the beach. "I had to see the sea," she explained. Diana's situation illustrates the maintenance of "dual home bases" in the United States and Puerto Rico (Alicea 1990), even though she had reoriented her kinship networks toward the mainland.

Although she did not visit her siblings in Puerto Rico, Miriam kept family contacts in New York, especially by telephone. Only one brother visited her frequently in Orlando. Her father's children were "all over [*regados*]" and several cousins lived on the island, especially in Arecibo. Some time ago, she organized a large family gathering in Puerto Rico. Until recently, she owned a house on the island, which she rented out, as well as some land and a car. Eventually, she sold everything and moved to Orlando. Like the other interviewees mentioned in this section, Miriam's most significant social networks are in the United States.

To varying degrees, my informants' kinship and friendship ties bridged Puerto Rico and the United States. Most had shifted their immediate social connections to Orlando and other mainland cities. Some remained anchored in the island. Like the participants in Marixsa Alicea's (1990) and Elizabeth Aranda's (2007) studies, many of my interviewees were part of extended transnational families that sustained contact through telephone calls, correspondence, and visits. Most were still connected to the island through close friends, business associates, and other social networks. Their financial resources allowed them to travel frequently to the island. Their sense of identity was embedded in long-distance relations, not just in their current geographic locations.

Identity in Question

Puerto Rican

Toward the end of the interview, I asked my informants: "How would you define yourself, as Puerto Rican, Hispanic, Latino, or something else?" The overwhelming response — for fourteen out of sixteen interviewees — was simply Puerto Rican. Sandra felt "100 percent Puerto Rican," an identity she also ascribed to her children. For her, the island is "the fatherland I love, even though it's far away. . . . When I moved here, I renewed my ties [to the island] and my identity has never changed." She further explained: "Many [Puerto Ricans] live with one leg here and another in Puerto Rico. We never forget about over there. There's an underlying connection. You hear the news on TV, on the radio, and on the computer. There's communication with Puerto Rico through Wapa América, Univisión, and Telemundo [television stations]." According to Sandra, "Puerto Rican culture is very rich" and should be upheld abroad. She referred specifically to Three Kings Day, *aguinaldos* (Christmas carols), folk arts, painting, and music.

Like Sandra, Ángel responded that he was "100 percent Puerto Rican," but he added that you have to be part of the "Hispanic umbrella." In his office, he displayed the flags of Puerto Rico, the United States, Murcia (Spain), the Canary Islands, Italy, Florida, and Ohio. For him, "being Puerto Rican is something different. There's a passion, a love for the island." He talked about a "clash of mentality" between Puerto Ricans, who preferred to speak Spanish, and third- and fourth-generation Cubans, who were supposedly more "assimilated" to U.S. culture. "If I'm talking with other Hispanics," Ángel said, "there's always the pride of being Puerto Rican. Still, I have very cordial relations with Cubans. We support each other." He also pointed out that Colombians have become well integrated with Puerto Ricans in the Catholic Church, to which he belonged. Ángel has witnessed the growth of Orlando's Hispanic Catholic community, which he believed had "a more profound spirituality" than Anglo-Americans, as expressed in more "excited music and devotions."

"I'm Puerto Rican above all," concurred Luisa. "But I'd like Puerto Ricans to be more tolerant toward other Hispanics, such as Mexicans, Colombians, and Venezuelans." In Orlando, she said, Puerto Ricans and Cubans do not interact as frequently as in other Florida cities like Tampa. "It's as if this [Orlando] were our property." This comment echoes Eichenberger's (2004) observation that many Puerto Ricans see Central Florida as a symbolic extension of the island's culture. This sense of proprietorship sometimes leads them to neglect other Hispanic contributions to the area. According to Luisa, "We're not making a common front" of Puerto Ricans and other Hispanics in Orlando.

Miriam quipped: "When they ask me if I'm Hispanic or Latino, I put down Puerto Rican. I don't feel Hispanic. Not all Hispanics go to war. Mine do." She was presumably referring to the fact that all Puerto Ricans are U.S. citizens by birth. Serving in the U.S. armed forces, then, emblematizes civic loyalty, patriotism, and legitimacy. Miriam's opinion resonates with the distinction made by some Latinos in Miami and Chicago between "deserving" and "undeserving" immigrants (Aranda, Chang, and Sabogal 2009; de Genova and Ramos-Zayas 2003). For her, the legal rights and duties associated with U.S. citizenship set Puerto Ricans apart from other Latin Americans. Miriam's comment is typical of middle-class, legal residents, who often look down on lower-class, undocumented residents.

When Margarita first arrived in Orlando, she "wasn't connected with the Latino community." "This is the only place where I have faced racism," she noted. At work, she was told that she "wasn't too bad for a Puerto Rican. . . . They take us too casually. There's no appreciation of our achievements. . . . There were insults. They looked at us in a strange way. It hasn't been easy." In response, Margarita joined several social, professional, and business groups founded by Puerto Ricans. She defined herself as Puerto Rican and always introduced herself that way in her professional activities. "I have relations with other groups and have been to all the countries of South America," she clarified. "There are clashes, but they have to do more with personality than with philosophy." For Margarita, being Puerto Rican meant appreciating the island's art, painting, music, food, and drinks. Toward the end of the interview, she proclaimed that "I have no identity problem" because "Puerto Rico lives in me" — echoing an often-quoted line from the poem "Ode to the Diasporican" by María Teresa Fernández ("Mariposa") (2000).

Although Raúl's parents were European, he was born in Puerto Rico. He stated emphatically: "I always define myself as Puerto Rican." He has never thought of himself as "Puerto Rican American." "I feel very, very Puerto Rican," Raúl reiterated. "When I go to Puerto Rico, I feel at home. . . . Here I feel like in a limbo, as if I were borrowed [como prestado]." He had never felt discriminated against, because he looks "like a gringo." Raúl's two daughters often asked him, "What am I?" Because his wife was Venezuelan, he told them that they were "boricua-Venezuelan-American." As to other Hispanics, Raúl believed that "each one goes their own way [cada cual jala pa' su lao]. . . . They cut each other's heads [se tumban la cabeza]." In Raúl's experience, Colombians were "groupies" who "stick together," and Cubans' relations with Puerto Ricans showed some tension ("tirantez"). In Orlando, Cubans and Puerto Ricans have separate social clubs. In addition, "other Latin Americans criticize us because of the way we talk." At work, Raúl strived to maintain a "neutral" accent in Spanish.

Similarly, Raymond's father was a Euro-American, while his mother was born in New York of Puerto Rican origin. Raymond was born and raised on the island, spoke Spanish as his native language, and defined himself as Puerto Rican. Because of his light complexion, he has often heard the phrase "You don't look Puerto Rican," as if all Puerto Ricans had the same physical type. Several light-skinned interviewees commented that they deviated from the "Latin look" and thereby avoided racial discrimination in the United States.

"I'm Puerto Rican," asserted Raquel, "and I also feel Hispanic. I use them as synonyms. But not Latina. I'm not Brazilian," a group that could be included under the Latino heading. Raquel's children, born in Puerto Rico but raised in Orlando, felt the same way. When they grew up, they all dated other Hispanics, especially Cubans. In Raquel's view, the greatest challenge in relations between Puerto Ricans and other Hispanics was that "we're [U.S.] citizens and other groups resent that, such as Venezuelans. . . . We can vote and they can't. It takes them time. [Yet] we as Puerto Ricans fail. We don't vote." On the other hand, "the Cuban has had to struggle so much. . . . They have assimilated better. They have gained more positions [of power] than we have." In contrast, "we [Puerto Ricans] continue our traditions, our roots, such as Three Kings Day. We speak Spanish." Raquel articulated the common perception that island-born Puerto Ricans are more attached to their Hispanic and Catholic "roots" than other Latin American immigrants.

Ernesto argued that the "Hispanic or Latino" idea is "totally American, it doesn't exist in Puerto Rico. It's a sociopolitical concept used for their [Americans'] benefit and to distribute funds." He preferred not to answer Hispanic/Latino on census forms, because people from Latin America have different cultures, dialects, and "races." "We're not colored. . . . We're multicolored," he insisted. Moreover, Ernesto resented that Cubans "control the economy and politics" in Florida because many came from "moneyed families." Lately, "many Venezuelans are arriving with a lot of money." In his experience, both Cubans and Venezuelans often disparage Puerto Ricans ("*les tiran a los puertorriqueños*"). In his words, Cubans "took over" the Hispanic Chamber of Commerce in Orlando, so Puerto Ricans had to form their own chamber. (At the time of my interviews, the president of the Hispanic Chamber was Venezuelan.) Ernesto had suffered racism, both by "Anglos" and "other Hispanics," because of his dark skin color, although he identified himself as white in the census.

Hispanic or Latino

For some respondents, like Diana, being Hispanic, Latino, and Puerto Rican "represents the same thing." Still, Diana felt Hispanic (not Latina) and "above all Puerto Rican." Although Alberto's primary identity was Puerto Rican, being Latino or Hispanic was "OK" with him. Puerto Rico is "a beautiful little island in the Caribbean," he added. "The term *Latino* unites us [*nos hermana*] with other Spanish-speaking people, such as Cubans, Colombians, and Dominicans."

Given the choice between *Latino* and *Puerto Rican*, most of my informants preferred the latter. The supranational sense of *Latinidad* was much weaker than their attachment to *puertorriqueñidad*. Contrary to other parts of the United States, Puerto Ricans in Orlando rarely use the term *Latino*. *Hispanic* is more common but lacked a strong emotional appeal for most participants in this study. Perhaps this is because they recognized the cultural differences as well as similarities among Latin American immigrant groups. According to a Venezuelan businessman in Orlando, "One of our main challenges as Hispanics is the integration of different cultural traditions."

Only one respondent felt more Latino than Puerto Rican. "I was born there [on the island]," said Manuel, "and I'm very proud of it. But when I'm defining myself, I emphasize the Latino root." When he moved as a child to the United States, first to Miami and then to Orlando, Manuel experienced an "identity crisis" because of the "clash" with other Hispanic students, such as Cubans and Colombians. He had always felt an affinity with Cubans, even before leaving San Juan, where many of his teachers and fellow students were Cuban. He often went to Casa Cuba, a social club in Isla Verde, with his Cuban friends. "The Cubans from here [Orlando] have made me an adoptive son of Cuba," he stated. He kept in touch with Cuban and Colombian friends in Miami.

For Manuel, a devout Catholic, the Church must be aware of cultural differences, such as food preferences and popular devotions, among Hispanic parishioners. He has observed some tensions among Hispanics, notably "Cuban resistance" to mingling with other groups. By and large, however, Orlando's Hispanics have experienced a "contagion of identity," including Puerto Ricans, Colombians, and Venezuelans. According to Manuel, they all sought to "maintain their [Hispanic] roots." In his view, the Catholic Church plays a "very important role" in recreating a "community of faith" among Hispanics (see Eichenberger 2004).

According to María, who was born and raised in New York, one's identity does not come "from where you were born, but from the blood you have inside." As a girl she returned to the island with her family. Because she did not speak Spanish then, they would tell her "gringa, go home." Her parents eventually returned to the United States, specifically to Tampa. There she was told to "go back to Puerto Rico." So she faced ignorance and prejudice, on both the island and the mainland. "There's discrimination [against Hispanics] and there always will be," she acknowledged. But "we haven't let discrimination stop us" from advancing in the United States. Throughout our conversation, María often referred to herself and others as "Hispanic" rather than "Latino." She never called herself "Puerto Rican American" because she thought it was redundant. No other respondents chose this compound to describe themselves.

American

Only one of my informants, Jorge, identified himself as "American first." But he also felt Puerto Rican by culture and Hispanic by language. He considered himself "a white Hispanic with an Anglo personality." By the latter, Jorge meant a more easygoing attitude, adaptation to stateside experiences, and English-language fluency. Compared to Orlando, Puerto Rico has "a more hectic lifestyle, is more crowded and busy." Jorge was also the only one who preferred to conduct the interview in English. He grew up in a military base near San Juan, because his father was in the U.S. Army, and he had many Anglo friends. As a child he spoke Spanish at home and English in school.

After moving to the mainland, Jorge married a "tenth-generation" Mexican American and became increasingly "bicultural." At home they celebrated both Anglo-American and Hispanic traditions, such as during Christmas (but not Three Kings Day, he remarked). Jorge had "never [witnessed] any rift" in relations between Puerto Ricans and other Latinos. But he acknowledged that "traditionally, there has been a butting of heads" among Hispanics and that Puerto Ricans often told "jokes about Cubans. Some Cubans have a chip on their shoulder. They don't have a country to go back to." He had never suffered discrimination as a Hispanic because he did not "look the part."

According to my respondents, some of their children, who had grown up in the United States, felt American. Many did not speak Spanish well and had never been to Puerto Rico. Some had married Americans. But others felt Puerto Rican, like Clarita's granddaughter, who kept in contact with her cousins on the island. A few second-generation Puerto Ricans belong to Hispanic gangs in Orlando, Ángel noted. But most do not consider themselves either black or white, according to U.S. racial terminology. This in-between status of second- and third-generation Puerto Ricans has been examined elsewhere (see Gina Pérez 2004; Toro-Morn and Alicea 2003; and Zentella 2003).

Nuyorican

None of the interviewees defined themselves as Nuyoricans, the epithet applied by island-born Puerto Ricans to all U.S.-born residents of Puerto Rican ancestry, regardless of their place of residence. The term usually evokes an ill-mannered youth who speaks Spanish poorly, dresses inappropriately, and does not respect customary rules of conduct on the island. This label stigmatizes return migrants and their children as more Americanized and less "authentic" Puerto Ricans than those who were raised on the island. The perceived divisions between island-born Puerto Ricans and the so-called Nuyoricans have been well documented, in both Puerto Rico and the United States (Findlay 2009; Lorenzo-Hernández 1999; Gina Pérez 2004; Ramos-Zayas 2003; Luis Sánchez 2009; Zentella 2003). Moreover, middle-class Puerto Ricans often express negative attitudes toward Nuyoricans, whom they usually view as less educated and skilled than themselves. Even Miriam, who spent much of her childhood in New York, did not describe herself as a Nuyorican. When that term came up in our conversations, it always alluded to others, not to the respondents' self-classification.

During the interviews, island-born Puerto Ricans were at pains to distinguish themselves from Nuyoricans. Sandra noted the basic linguistic contrast between Puerto Ricans raised "here and there." By and large, second-generation Puerto Ricans prefer to speak English, while islanders favor Spanish. The dichotomy between Spanish and English overlaps with other social, economic, and cultural differences. According to Raúl, islanders "talk in derogatory terms about them [Nuyoricans]. They speak differently from us [Puerto Ricans from the island]." Still, Diana pointed out that "they speak English, but they think like Puerto Ricans. They eat rice and beans and dance salsa." Manuel's mother, who was raised in New York, traveled back to the island when she was seventeen years old and "fell in love with Puerto Rico." But her father shunned her as a Nuyorican.

Most of my informants would disagree with Alberto's view that "there's no conflict with Nuyoricans" in Orlando. For Jorge, Nuyoricans were more "brass" and "assimilated" than those who came directly from Puerto Rico. "It's a very different community . . . though we share the same culture, language, and experience." According to Raquel, "They behave differently, they have a different way of dressing, they're aggressive in the way they speak." For Ernesto also, Nuyoricans were "more aggressive" than Puerto Ricans from the island; they often acted "in your face." In his view, "Puerto Ricans in New York already had their struggle [to survive] . . . and they didn't triumph." With Puerto Ricans from Chicago, "you have to be careful." Ernesto implied that they were somehow more "dangerous" and prone to crime than those from the island. "They have a certain idiosyncrasy," according to Clarita. "There are clashes" with island-born immigrants. Raquel summed up the main point: "For Anglo-Saxons, all Puerto Ricans are the same [as Nuyoricans]. Those from here [the United States] don't get along well with those from there [Puerto Rico]."

Most of my informants, then, identified primarily as Puerto Rican and secondarily as Hispanic. For many, relations with other Latin Americans were conflict-ridden, although some had Cuban, Venezuelan, Mexican, and Argentinean friends and spouses. Middle-class Puerto Ricans in Orlando resisted being assimilated into mainstream U.S. culture as well as being bracketed as a racial minority with other people of Latin American ancestry. They insisted on calling themselves Puerto Rican, rather than Nuyorican, Puerto Rican American, or any other compound expression. They tended to view *Hispanic* and *Latino* as externally imposed, problematic, and psychologically distant terms of reference. Their self-perception was still largely anchored in an island-centered culture, not on the U.S. mainland. As the Puerto Rican anthropologist Ana Yolanda Ramos-Zayas (2003: 145) found in Chicago, "The Island invariably remained a geographical referent of cultural authenticity and a driving force in nostalgic narratives and imagery."

Plotting the Intersections among National, Transnational, and Panethnic Identities

In this chapter I have probed how some middle-class Puerto Ricans in Orlando articulate the overlapping discourses of Puerto Rican, Hispanic, and Latino identities. As transnational colonial migrants who appreciate the benefits of U.S. citizenship and consider themselves to be white, most of my interviewees detached themselves from other Latin Americans. They tended to mistrust the catchall categories of *Latinidad* and *Hispanidad*, which treat people from Latin America as a single collectivity. Instead, many were committed to long-distance nationalism (to borrow Benedict Anderson's [2001] expression), that is, "a nationalism that no longer depends as it once did on territorial location in a home country." This sense of loyalty relies primarily on cultural, familial, and emotional connections across the borders (though not always the boundaries) between countries. Because most respondents were born and raised on the island, they spoke Spanish and practiced Puerto Rican customs at home. They belonged to Puerto Rican and Hispanic associations and cultivated kinship and friendship ties to the island. Many traveled regularly between Orlando and San Juan. Some still owned property in Puerto Rico. A few hoped to retire there.

Compared to lower-class, dark-skinned residents of the United States, most of my informants suffered less prejudice, discrimination, and segregation because of their middle-class backgrounds and light skin color. The respondents' higher education, occupational status, and residential patterns often exposed them to Anglos on an equal footing in their business, political, recreational, and social lives. A recurring theme in the interviews was not conforming to the "Latin look" and avoiding negative stereotypes based on physical appearance. Only three of the sixteen respondents had experienced racial discrimination in Orlando. In turn, most resisted being racialized as Hispanics or Latinos.

This study has found little evidence for the "downward assimilation" (Portes and Rumbaut 2006) of middle-class Puerto Ricans in Orlando, who typically do not regard themselves as Latinos, Hispanics, or "people of color." Instead, my interviews documented a tightly knit transnational community that holds onto its values and customs while enjoying substantial upward social mobility. Still, many of my informants recognized the cultural, religious, and linguistic affinities between Puerto Ricans and other Hispanics.

The demographic and cultural predominance of Puerto Ricans in Central Florida has encouraged their mobilization primarily around national origin, not multiethnic coalitions. Occasionally, Puerto Ricans make common cause with Cubans, Venezuelans, Mexicans, and other Latin Americans, such as electing a candidate for public office or supporting bilingual education. Some belong to voluntary associations that promote the welfare of the Hispanic community — but in practice most of these groups' members and leaders are of Puerto Rican origin. By and large, Orlando's prominent Puerto Ricans cling to their national origin, cultural traditions, and transnational connections. They often cultivate long-distance social networks with the island.

How do representatives of the Puerto Rican middle class in Orlando define their identity? Their main criteria are birthplace, family background, language, religion, and other cultural practices such as cuisine, music, and folk arts, especially those related to Christmas festivities. (My informants frequently singled out Three Kings Day as a key symbol of Puerto Ricanness.)

This relatively privileged group was predominantly born and raised on the island, had many relatives there, spoke Spanish at home, attended a Catholic church, and cherished their homeland. Its members usually measured the cultural "authenticity" of Puerto Rican identity by how well one spoke the island's vernacular, played dominoes, or danced salsa. Another common token of *puertorriqueñidad* was eating traditional foods like *arroz con gandules* (rice and pigeon peas), green plantains, and fried pork. Although this form of symbolic ethnicity may seem trivial, it nurtures immigrants' sense of home away from their homeland.

An often implicit but crucial series of group boundaries is built around class and race. Together with their middle-class status, most interviewees were white in physical appearance — although some might not "pass" as such according to U.S. racial categories. The selective class and racial background of recent Puerto Rican immigrants in Orlando might put them at odds with their less fortunate compatriots, especially those from other parts of the U.S. mainland, who tend to be poorer and darker-skinned than those arriving from the island. Second-generation immigrants usually speak English more fluently than Spanish and may know little about Puerto Rican culture on the island. The growing gap between islanders and the so-called Nuyoricans deserves more systematic research, especially in connection with class and race fissures. The question of who can legitimately claim to be Puerto Rican hangs in the balance.

In the United States, the physical appearance and cultural practices of Latinos have been racialized. The dominant image of a "Latin look" draws on age-old stereotypes of swarthy people of mongrel races. Carving a motley category out of different national and ethnic groups is based on the lingering belief that Spanish-speaking people are racially mixed and culturally inferior to Anglo-Saxons. Moreover, the Spanish language, Catholic religion, and extended family are often taken as essential markers of *Latinidad*. Although the Census Bureau officially recognizes that "Hispanics can be of any race," it tends to treat them apart from non-Hispanic whites and blacks. Similarly, the U.S. mass media, the police, schools, universities, and other institutions reproduce the popular notion that Hispanics are distinct from other "races," such as African Americans, Native Americans, and Asian Americans.

Allegiance to *Latinidad*, beyond national and ethnic identities, is still emergent, uneven, disputed, and regionally specific. Some people of Latin American origin have embraced a broader category to advance their collective plight as a racialized minority in the United States. Others, like the middle-class Puerto Ricans in Orlando who participated in this study, usually reject the panethnic label. At this point, a generic Latino or Hispanic affiliation rarely overrides specific national identities such as Puerto Rican. A similar trend prevails among Cuban and Dominican immigrants, to whom I turn in the next chapters.

Revisiting the Exception

The Cuban Diaspora from a Transnational Perspective

In the foreword to the book that established the dominant model of transnational migration (Glick Schiller, Basch, and Blanc-Szanton 1992), Lambros Comitas acknowledged the Cuban anthropologist Fernando Ortiz, and his *Cuban Counterpoint: Tobacco and Sugar* (1947), as an intellectual precursor of the new paradigm.[1] In particular, Ortiz's neologism, *transculturation*, anticipated key elements of contemporary transnationalism. Among them, Ortiz underlined the emergence of hybrid cultures through successive migrant waves. However, the rest of the volume edited by Nina Glick Schiller and her colleagues overlooked the parallels between transculturation and transnationalism. Furthermore, none of the book's chapters considered Cuba a current exemplar of transnationalism, although several authors focused on Mexico, the Dominican Republic, Haiti, and other Caribbean countries. This theoretical and empirical absence of the Cuban diaspora is repeated in later works (see Basch, Glick Schiller, and Szanton Blanc 1994; Portes, Guarnizo, and Landolt 1999; Portes, Haller, and Guarnizo 2002; and Michael Smith and Guarnizo 1998), where Cubans appear as the exception to the rule in contemporary population movements.

Most studies have portrayed the postrevolutionary Cuban exodus as a unique experience with few historical or contemporary counterparts, even in the Spanish-speaking Caribbean.[2] An example of this academic trend is Guillermo Grenier and Lisandro Pérez's excellent book, *The Legacy of Exile: Cubans in the United States* (2003), which reiterates several of the dominant themes in Cuban American studies. Like many scholars, Grenier and Pérez emphasize the special legal condition of refugees from the Cuban Revolution, as well the unusual programs for economic assistance established by the U.S. government in the early 1960s. Furthermore, they argue that "even Cuba's emigration is marked by exceptionalism. . . . Emigration has maintained an exile ethos, created a powerful ethnic enclave, and exhibits relatively high levels of economic and political influence at both the local and national levels" (34). The authors insist on the singular elements of Cuban history, such as the decimation of the indigenous population, the long history of Spanish colonialism, and the island's strategic position between the Old and New Worlds. (Actually, these factors apply in some measure to Puerto Rico and the Dominican Republic as well.) Writing about Cuba's republican period between 1902 and 1958, Grenier and Pérez grant that "Cubans had every reason to believe they occupied a unique and privileged position in the world order, reinforcing a sense of singularity and self-importance in relation to [their country's] Latin American and Caribbean neighbors" (33).[3]

The recurring problem with Cuban exceptionalism, in migration studies as well as in other academic specializations, is that it tends to isolate the object of analysis from its broader context. However, the contemporary Cuban exodus is part of regional and global trends. Despite the U.S. embargo of Cuba since 1962, people, ideas, practices, and money have traveled, albeit irregularly, between Havana and Miami, especially after 1979, when refugees were first allowed to visit Cuba. During the 1990s kinship networks between Cuba and its diaspora were reinvigorated and remittances to the island increased steadily. One illustration of the complex and often conflictive political interaction between the Cuban American community and the Cuban government was the controversy over the *balsero* child Elián González in 2000, when many of the same discourses about family life were mirrored on both sides of the Straits of Florida. Ethnographic fieldwork has documented the connections between practitioners of Afro-Cuban religions in the United States and Cuba (see Burke 2002; Knauer 2001, 2003; and Mahler and Hansing 2005a). Such experiences suggest that the contemporary Cuban diaspora deserves to be reexamined from a transnational perspective and that considering the Cuban case can strengthen this perspective.[4]

The purpose of this chapter, then, is to revisit the putative Cuban exception in transnational migration. I argue that the Cuban diaspora constitutes a special (but not unique) case of transnationalism. The Cuban exodus is peculiar in its deep hostility toward the sending state (and vice versa). Still, family ties between Cubans on and off the island have persevered, particularly through remittances, visits, and telephone calls. Cubans in the

United States display transnational attitudes and practices, although less frequently than Dominicans and Puerto Ricans. In short, Cuba is no exception to current trends in transnational migration; on the contrary, the island is experiencing many of the same forces as transnational nation-states like the Dominican Republic and transnational colonial states like Puerto Rico. Admittedly, the Cuban government has responded to these forces from a socialist and nationalist perspective.

Thinking about Cuba Transnationally

Rethinking the Cuban diaspora transnationally entails identifying common denominators between Cubans and other immigrants, especially Dominicans and Puerto Ricans. It also requires sorting out the main themes of the transnational literature from a comparative perspective, such as the multiple identities resulting from transnational migration; the increasing significance of transnational economic networks; the links (or lack thereof) among states, territories, citizens, and communities; the challenges of diasporic discourses to the image of the nation as a homogenous and well-bounded entity; the efforts of transplanted groups to maintain the homeland's culture and language; and the role of émigré communities in the future of their countries of origin. These dilemmas are not unique to Cubans but are shared by diasporic peoples everywhere.

Cubans in the United States are better understood from a transnational standpoint that recognizes their basic similarities with other immigrants. Otherwise, one runs the risk of reproducing the myth of "the unique and privileged position" of Cuban Americans. A broader framework would help explain the historical roots of the Cuban diaspora, its modes of incorporation into U.S. society, transformation of cultural identities, and impact on both home and host countries. As the Cuban American political scientist María de los Angeles Torres (1999: 20) writes, "The burden of 'Cuban exceptionalism' [is] somehow lessened by understanding that there are comparable situations faced by all Latino groups — including their ambivalent relationship to homeland."

For some time, the Cuban exodus has not been as extraordinary as some scholars would have it. The most recent migrant wave from Cuba (roughly since 1989, with the beginning of the economic crisis officially known as the Special Period in Peacetime) resembles other Caribbean population movements. The similarities include the migrants' legal status (many of them undocumented), motivations (increasingly economic), and social composition (mostly working class), as well as the use of migration as a safety valve by the Cuban government. This wave fits into a well-established regional migrant profile of relatively young and urban sectors of the working classes, with intermediate schooling, seeking better wages and jobs abroad and willing to leave their country by legal or clandestine means (Aja Díaz 1999, 2009; Castro 2002; Martín Fernández, Perera, and Díaz Pérez 2001; Pedraza 2000, 2007; Rodríguez Chávez 1997). The material difficulties of daily life have led many Cubans to regard emigration as one of the few avenues for upward social mobility. In 1994, the height of the *balsero* crisis, the U.S. government began to return undocumented immigrants to Cuba, just as it had deported Haitian and Dominican boat people for decades. Moreover, since the 1990s, thousands of Cuban émigrés visited the island, like Puerto Ricans and Dominicans have done before. As Lisa Maya Knauer (2001: 22) writes, "Although Cubans do not experience the same ease and frequency of movement between 'here' and 'there' as many New York Puerto Ricans and Dominicans, in most cases immigration to the United States has not meant a radical rupture with family and community ties."

An Idiosyncratic Transnationalism

On several counts, Cubans differ from other cases of contemporary transnationalism. Above all, the long-standing antipathy between the Cuban and U.S. governments, as well as between the Cuban government and its diaspora, has tinged relations between Cubans on and off the island. "The main difference between Cubans and other [transnational] groups," writes the Cuban American sociologist Yolanda Prieto (2009: 150), "is that Cubans cannot participate in their homeland's political process." Since the 1959 Revolution, many Cubans living abroad have developed an antagonistic relation with the island's government. As Roger Waldinger and David Fitzgerald (2004: 1185) argue, in states "where emigration is tantamount to betrayal, the regular and sustained contacts between source and destination societies that supposedly distinguish transnationals from immigrants are not just out of the question, but imperil sending-country residents whom the transnationals try to contact or help." In this regard, Cuban exiles have much in common with other refugees who left their country fearing persecution, imprisonment, torture, and even death, and therefore do not intend to return to their homeland (Pedraza 2007: 26–27).

A distinctive characteristic of the Cuban case is the deeply rooted animosity between the Cuban revolutionary government and its diaspora. Since the early 1960s, the Cuban government has regarded exiles as traitors to the homeland and resorted to emigration to expel its dissidents. In turn, the U.S. government encouraged Cuban immigration as a symbolic resource during the Cold War, when many U.S. officials claimed that refugees "voted with their feet" against communism (Masud-Piloto 1996; Pedraza-Bailey 1985). Such public policies militated against close ties between Cubans on and off the island. On the contrary, travel, mail, and telephone service between the two countries became sporadic, costly, and cumbersome. "During the Cold War," notes Susan Eckstein (2009: 126), "the two governments blocked cross-border bonding among Cubans united by blood and a shared culture."

Several features of the Cuban diaspora derive from its historic tensions with the Cuban Revolution. Since 1961 the Cuban state has equated leaving the island with "abandoning" the country once and for all (Aja Díaz 2009: 122, 129; María de los Angeles Torres 1999: 53). Under the legal category of "permanent departure," émigrés forfeited their civil, political, and social rights, including the right to own property in Cuba. Until recently, they also lost their jobs when they announced their decision to move abroad. Many were ostracized from their workplaces and neighborhoods before leaving the island. Most were not allowed to return to Cuba, except for short visits. Hence, the postrevolutionary Cuban diaspora has been primarily a one-way flow, unlike the Puerto Rican and Dominican diasporas.

Until the 1990s Cuba curtailed emigration by age, gender, and occupation. But the island's prolonged economic crisis promoted a relaxation of travel requirements (see Rafael Hernández 1995; Martín Fernández and Pérez 1998; and Rodríguez Chávez 1997). Nowadays, some Cubans may live abroad temporarily without losing the right to return to Cuba. Between 1996 and 2000 the Cuban government issued about ten thousand *permisos de residencia en el exterior* (PRE), or permits to reside abroad, allowing their holders to exit and enter the country freely (Aja Díaz 1999: 11; Casaña Mata 2002a). Such permits are usually extended to Cubans living in Europe and Latin America, rarely to those in the United States. Still, Cubans are required to apply for an exit permit from the Cuban government, as well as an entry permit when they reside abroad. Those who left after 1971 must carry a valid Cuban passport to return to the island, regardless of whether they have become citizens of another country.

Although Fidel and Raúl Castro's government has made some overtures toward the Cuban community abroad, it has yet to develop a coherent stance on such issues as repatriation, retirement, and investment opportunities for exiles. As the Cuban historian Jesús Arboleya (1996: 41) acknowledges, "The rights and duties of émigrés and their descendants with regard to the Cuban nation haven't been clarified adequately." Until now, the Cuban government has not authorized émigrés to set up businesses or buy property in Cuba, while allowing citizens of Spain, Canada, and other countries to do so. Entry visas for Cuban Americans continue to be much more expensive than for foreign tourists. Travel to and from Cuba is restricted to a small fraction of Cubans on and off the island. Technically, anyone born on the island remains a Cuban citizen even if he or she acquires U.S., Spanish, or other passports. For those living abroad, retaining a Cuban passport offers few practical advantages; for some purposes, such as when traveling abroad, it is a great handicap, because most countries require a visa from Cubans.

A final peculiarity of the postrevolutionary Cuban exodus has been its public reception in the United States. During the 1960s and 1970s, the U.S. mass media consistently praised Cubans as enterprising and patriotic refugees from communism (Pedraza-Bailey 1985). Popular magazines such as *Time, Life, National Geographic*, and *U.S. News and World Report* retold the story of "those amazing Cuban émigrés," to quote the title of a 1966 *Fortune* article. As a result, many Americans initially viewed Cuban refugees more favorably than Puerto Ricans and Dominicans. But after 1980 the media increasingly portrayed Cuban émigrés as dangerous, unruly, and problematic aliens (García 1996; Masud-Piloto 1996; Pedraza 1996). The Mariel boatlift stigmatized all Cuban Americans and biased U.S. public opinion against Cuban immigration. Several thousand Marielitos were imprisoned in the United States for crimes committed in Cuba. In 1994 the Clinton administration ended the open-door policy toward Cubans detained at sea. Most Americans no longer deem Cuban exiles exceptional, if they ever did, compared to other Latin American and Caribbean immigrants.

Toward a Less Disinterested and Denouncing State

U.S.-Cuban hostilities are largely based on Havana's continuing adherence to socialism and Washington's reluctance to lift the embargo, as well as on pressure from Miami's exile hardliners. For those found in the midst of such tensions, allegiance to the United States or Cuba is usually posed in an exclusive manner. Ordinary émigrés are caught between the opposing interests of the two governments. "Dual loyalty becomes a particularly intense issue when belligerency develops between host and sending countries," write Waldinger and Fitzgerald (2004: 1178–79). For most of the period since 1959, such belligerence has dominated U.S.-Cuban relations.

During Jimmy Carter's presidency (1977–80), however, the United States began a policy of détente with Cuba. In 1977 the U.S. and Cuban governments opened "interests sections" in Havana and Washington, a first step toward reestablishing diplomatic ties. In this political climate, Fidel Castro's government approached moderate elements of the Cuban American community. In November and December 1978 Castro invited 140 émigrés to discuss issues of common concern, including traveling back to Cuba. As a result of El Diálogo (The Dialogue), the Cuban government released thirty-six hundred political prisoners, and some 150,000 exiles visited the country between 1979 and 1982. Castro began referring to the exiles as "the Cuban community abroad" rather than as gusanos (worms). In Cuban colloquial speech, the gusanos were transformed into mariposas (butterflies); even more ironically, the traidores (traitors) became traedólares ("dollar bringers"). According to one estimate, exiles transferred between US$300 million and $US1 billion annually to Cuba during the 1980s (Ackerman and Clark 1995: 34). Exiles were also allowed to bring household goods such as television sets, stereo equipment, and other electrical appliances on their return trips to Cuba (Barberia 2004: 362).

Relations between the Cuban government and the diaspora became strained after the Mariel boatlift (Eckstein and Barberia 2001; Masud-Piloto 1996; María de los Angeles Torres 1999). As I noted in chapter 3, Cuban officials were extremely hostile toward the Marielitos and mounted an intense propaganda campaign to discredit them. Ironically, the U.S. mass media echoed the public image of Mariel entrants as "scum" and "lumpen." "The immediate effect of this ideological campaign," writes María de los Angeles Torres (1999: 109), "was to reduce the number of visits allowed to Cuban exiles." In May 1985 the Cuban government prohibited émigré visits and suspended its migration accords with the United States, in response to the broadcasting of anti-Castro Radio Martí. In 1986 the Cuban government authorized visits by Cuban émigrés once again.

After 1989 the fall of socialism in Eastern Europe and the eventual collapse of the Soviet Union left Cuba with few trading partners (see chapter 7). The Cuban government turned to tourism as its primary strategy of reincorporation into the world market and secondarily to its diaspora as a source of foreign currency. Consequently, Havana's socialist regime renewed its efforts to "normalize" its contacts with the diaspora. As Eckstein (2003: 19) points out, "Cuba followed a growing trend among Third World governments, including those of the Dominican Republic and El Salvador, to reclaim their emigrant population." Migration and remittances have become two of the most common survival strategies of the Cuban people since the onset of the economic crisis.[5]

While the Cuban government encouraged Cuban American contacts with the island after 1989, the U.S. government tended to discourage them. Between 2004 and 2008 President George W. Bush imposed draconian restrictions on Cuban American visits and remittances. The election of President Barack Obama in November 2008 promised to ease contacts between Cubans on and off the island. In March 2009 the Obama administration eliminated most U.S. restrictions to traveling and sending money to Cuba by Cuban Americans. However, in September 2009, the president extended the decades-old ban on travel to Cuba by U.S. citizens of non-Cuban origin.

Like many migrant-sending countries, the Cuban government reformed its bureaucracy to address the diaspora's concerns. In 1994 Cuba's Ministry of Foreign Affairs established a Division for the Affairs of the Cuban Community Residing Abroad, later renamed the Division of Consular Affairs and Cubans Residing Abroad. In 1995 the ministry launched a glossy magazine called *Correo de Cuba*, subtitled "The Journal of Cuban Emigration," to publicize its activities. In June of the same year, the Cuban Union of Writers and Artists and the University of Havana cosponsored a symposium on national culture and identity attended by twenty Cuban intellectuals living abroad (Unión de Escritores y Artistas Cubanos and Universidad de La Habana 1995).

Since the 1990s the Cuban government has hosted three meetings on "The Nation and Emigration." The first conference was held in Havana in April 1994, attracting approximately 220 members of the Cuban community abroad. In November 1995 the second meeting drew together 357 representatives of the diaspora living in thirty-seven countries. A third conference held in May 2004 gathered 520 émigrés from forty-nine countries (see Aja Díaz 1999: 12; and Ministerio de Relaciones Exteriores 2008). Among the most frequent topics of discussion was traveling to Cuba from the United States.

Eckstein (2009: 135) summarizes the initiatives of Cuban officials to encourage Cuban American visits during the post-Soviet era:

They removed the caps on the number of Cuban Americans permitted to visit annually, they extended the length of time of permissible visits, and they made travel more affordable by ceasing to require visiting émigrés to stay in state-run hotels. . . . Cuban authorities also reduced bureaucratic hurdles. To make visits more likely, they introduced multiple entry permits. And they retracted an earlier requirement that Cubans who emigrated illegally . . . wait five years before being allowed to visit.

Nonetheless, efforts to expand the "dialogue" between Cubans on and off the island have proven feeble so far. For five decades, a politics of open confrontation and mutual isolation has prevailed, with two brief respites in the late 1970s and mid-1990s. Many Cuban officials still perceive the exiles as enemies and refer to Miami Cubans as "the Cuban American mafia."[6] In turn, most exiles consider the Castro government a ruthless dictatorship. It is probably necessary for the U.S. and Cuban governments to renew diplomatic relations before the émigrés can coexist peacefully with the current regime on the island. Still, official tensions have not entirely suppressed unofficial bonds between Cuba and its diaspora.[7] As Pedraza (2006: 46) has observed, many Cuban Americans stay in touch with their relatives and friends on the island, despite impediments by both the U.S. and Cuban governments.

The Tenacity of Kinship Networks between Cuba and the United States

Family ties between Cuba and the United States are much more restricted and irregular than those of Puerto Ricans and Dominicans with their countries of origin (Orozco et al. 2005; Pedraza 2007; Waldinger 2007). Nevertheless, the persistence of social and economic connections between the island and the diaspora resonates with other cases of transnationalism. Reflecting on the Cuban exodus might help broaden the concept of transnationalism by including the informal bridges between two quarreling nation-states.

Far from weakening, the desire to preserve personal ties with Cuba has strengthened among Cuban Americans. The vast majority — nearly 77 percent — of Miami Cubans still have close relatives on the island (Institute for Public Opinion Research 2007). Not surprisingly, many émigrés wish to communicate with their families back home and help them financially. Contacts between the Cuban population and the émigrés intensified during the 1990s, as a consequence of the economic crisis accelerated by the disappearance of the Soviet Union, Cuba's principal commercial partner before 1989. According to Eckstein (2009), recent immigrants are more sensitive than earlier ones to the economic needs of ordinary people in post-Soviet Cuba. However, Sarah Blue (2005) found that those who left Cuba before 1980 were the most likely to send remittances and visit their relatives. In any case, the closest links between Cuban Americans and island residents concentrate in Havana, the main source of the diaspora (Fresneda Camacho 2006; Martín Fernández and Pérez 1998).

One factor that facilitated family reunification was a greater tolerance of emigration by Cuban officials as a survival strategy during the economic crisis. Undoubtedly, this position is linked with the government's interest in attracting foreign currency through remittances and family visits. In Cuba, it is no longer taboo to cultivate ties with relatives abroad; such ties have become crucial for the economic well-being of many families on the island (Rafael Hernández 1995; Martín Fernández and Pérez 1998; Martínez et al. 1996; Rodríguez Chávez 1997). According to a popular joke in Cuba, one must have *fe* (which literally means faith in Spanish but is also an abbreviation of *familiares en el exterior*, or relatives abroad) to make ends meet.

Ethnographic fieldwork has documented the everyday difficulties of the Special Period, including chronic food shortages, long lines waiting for rationed goods, a deteriorating housing stock, the collapse of public transportation, and constant power outages (Holgado Fernández 2000; Rosenthal 1997; Taylor 2009). Social inequality has grown in tandem with the economic reforms introduced by the Cuban government, especially the legalization of the U.S. dollar in 1993. As Susan Eckstein and Lorena Barberia (2002: 826) write, "Cubans have come to cultivate relations with relatives in the United States they previously rejected on political grounds once they became dependent on dollars for subsistence and other needs and wants." Together with the expanding tourist industry, remittances dollarized the Cuban economy and expanded contacts with the Cuban community abroad.

How can the strength of kinship networks between Cubans on and off the island be gauged? The first measure is telephone calls, "the social glue of migrant transnationalism," as Steven Vertovec (2009: 54) describes them, because they enable everyday communication between relatives living across great distances. During the 1990s an improved communication infrastructure facilitated long-distance calls from the United States to Cuba. Telephone traffic proliferated with fewer government restrictions and

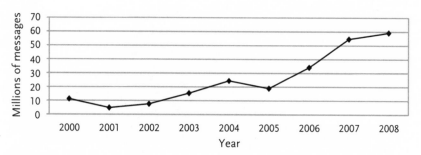

FIGURE 6.1 Telephone Calls from the United States to Cuba, 2000–2008

Source: Federal Communications Commission 2010.

cheaper telecommunications during the second half of the decade. In 1998 16.7 million telephone messages (or 14 million minutes) were billed between the United States and Cuba. Two-thirds of the calls involved U.S. residents of Cuban origin and their relatives on the island (U.S.-Cuba Trade and Economic Council 1999, 2000). The volume of telephone messages from the United States to Cuba rose more than fivefold, from 11.2 million in 2000 to 59.2 million in 2008 (see figure 6.1). Still, telephone service between the two countries is relatively expensive. In 2009 a landline call from the United States began at 70 cents per minute, while a cellular call from Cuba could cost as much as US$2.70 per minute.

Second, many migrants still use postal mail to communicate with their relatives on the island. Because mail service between Cuba and the United States was suspended in 1963, it is channeled through other countries such as Mexico or Canada. (On September 17, 2009, the U.S. and Cuban governments discussed resuming direct mail service, but this objective had still not been attained by July 2010.) A letter sent from the United States can take up to three months to reach Cuba, if it arrives at all. Many émigrés therefore send letters, photographs, video recordings, and other documents by alternate means — such as individuals who bring packages on visits to Cuba for family or professional reasons, sometimes charging for the service. Access to e-mail is still rare in Cuba, given the high cost of a personal computer and connecting to an electronic network. In 2010 only 14 percent of the Cuban population had Internet access (Internet World Stats 2010).

Third, family visits represent a constant exchange of people between Cuba and the United States. In 1979 more than one hundred thousand émigrés traveled to Cuba for the first time in two decades. Since the early 1990s

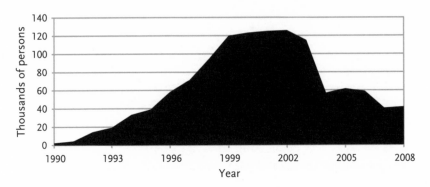

FIGURE 6.2 Cuban American Visits to Cuba, 1990–2008

Sources: Eckstein and Barberia 2001; Oficina Nacional de Estadísticas 2009; Spadoni 2004.

an even larger number of Cuban Americans have visited the island (see figure 6.2). In 1999 about 124,000 U.S. residents of Cuban origin traveled to
Cuba, while 160,000 residents of Cuba traveled to the United States (Eckstein and Barberia 2001; U.S.-Cuba Trade and Economic Council 2000). In
2002 approximately 126,000 Cuban Americans visited Cuba. The number
plummeted by nearly 50 percent in 2004, when President Bush restricted
travel to those with immediate relatives on the island. Nevertheless, many
Cuban Americans travel through countries such as Mexico, Canada, Panama, or the Dominican Republic to fly into Cuba without U.S. government
authorization. In 2007 one out of three Cubans in Miami had been back to
the island (Institute for Public Opinion Research 2007). Cuban American
visits to Cuba resurged after the easing of travel restrictions by the Obama
administration in March 2009.[8] In September 2010 one of the terminals
of José Martí International Airport in Havana was being remodeled to ac-
commodate the growing number of charter flights from "the community" in
Miami.

The fourth index of increased interaction between Cubans on and off the
island is the delivery of packages (*paqueticos*) with food, vitamins, medicines,
medical supplies, clothes, shoes, eyeglasses, and other essential articles. By
2002 more than fifty thousand parcels were sent monthly from the United
States to the island (Barberia 2004: 397). In 2009 twenty-three companies
based in the United States — fourteen of them in Florida — provided courier
services to Cuba (U.S. Department of the Treasury 2009). Many businesses
devoted to this task have flourished in Miami's Cuban community. One of
the largest of these companies anticipated earning between US$300,000 and

US$400,000 in the year 2000. At the time, the cost of sending a parcel to Cuba was US$10 per pound (U.S.-Cuba Trade and Economic Council 2000). Shipping packages to Cuba is thus a profitable business but quite expensive for customers. This is one example of how the U.S. embargo benefits certain commercial interests within the Cuban American community.

The fifth and final measure of growing Cuban transnationalism, but hardly the least significant, is remittances. In 1999 Western Union began to transfer funds electronically from Florida to Cuba. By 2009 the company had 153 offices in Havana and other cities on the island. In 2001 nearly one-third of Cuban Americans used Western Union to send remittances; in 2009 all those polled in Miami did so (Orozco 2003, 2009b). By 2009 the U.S. government had authorized seventy-two agents — fifty-seven of them in Florida — to transfer money to Cuba (U.S. Department of the Treasury 2009). A large portion of the remittances, however, moves within an informal system of couriers known as *mulas*, who travel regularly to Cuba and charge for taking money to their customers' relatives (Bendixen and Associates 2005; Orozco 2003). U.S. regulations in place as of 2010 allow residents of Cuban origin to send as much as they want to Cuba.

The Significance of Cuban American Remittances

During the Special Period, Cuba deepened its reliance on the diaspora as a source of dollars to supplement, and sometimes replace, local wages in pesos. Most of these funds cover basic households needs, such as food, clothing, shoes, and housing repairs (Bendixen and Associates 2005; Eckstein 2003; Fresneda Camacho 2006; Orozco 2009a). Compared to other countries, Cuban remittances are oriented more toward the daily subsistence of the receiving households. As in other countries, however, remittances also help finance economic activities. A small fraction of the funds is invested in small-scale private businesses, particularly those related to self-employment, such as guesthouses, *paladares* (family restaurants), *bicitaxis* (bicycle taxis), and *timbiriches* (small shops) (see Cervantes-Rodríguez 2010; Duany 2001; Henken 2002; Núñez Moreno 1997; and Benjamin Smith 1999).

One of the main problems in tracking Cuban remittances is the dearth of reliable statistics. Because U.S. dollars did not circulate legally in Cuba until 1993, it was very difficult to estimate private money transfers to the island. Moreover, the Cuban government has never published official data about remittances. Hence, recent estimates have ranged widely, from US$500 million to US$1.2 billion per year (see Barberia 2004; Monreal 1999; Orozco 2009a; Pérez-López and Díaz-Briquets 2005; and Spadoni 2004). In any case, remittances became Cuba's third-largest source of foreign exchange at the beginning of the twenty-first century. Only the export of professional services (mostly health care) and tourism generated more hard currency.

Like many migrant-sending governments, the Cuban government has sought to channel remittances through official means by charging a large commission on monetary transfers and fostering the use of state-run stores that only accept foreign or convertible currency. In 2009 the cost of sending money to Cuba was the highest in Latin America and the Caribbean, about 13 cents for every U.S. dollar remitted (Orozco 2009b: 13). Furthermore, Cubans were forced to exchange dollars to the local convertible currency at rates highly unfavorable to dollars, including a 10 percent tax. Still, remittances — along with other transactions related to migration, such as family visits — have injected millions of dollars into the Cuban economy during the Special Period. Ironically, Cuban Americans have buttressed the modest recovery of the island's economy since the early 1990s, even though most of them oppose the socialist regime. A 2004 poll conducted by Florida International University (FIU) found that 53.6 percent of Cubans in South Florida sent money to Cuba. On average, each Cuban American family remitted US$387 per year (Institute for Public Opinion Research 2004). During the Special Period, remittances reinforced the networks of solidarity between Cuba and its diaspora.

Eckstein (2009) has argued persuasively that the dollarization of the Cuban economy has promoted the "breakdown of the moral order" based on the principle of equality among classes, races, and regions. Light-skinned Cubans with relatives abroad, belonging to the upper and middle ranks of society, and those living in Havana and other major cities, receive the bulk of remittances. According to Eckstein, "transnational ties infused new materialist norms in Cuba, decreased islander economic dependence on the state, eroded Cuban state control of the economy and society, introduced new income inequities, and undermined the socialist basis of stratification premised on performance in the state-run economy" (232). However, growing transnationalism has not led to a post-Castro transition in Cuba, as many exiles had hoped. When Fidel Castro became ill and retired from public office in July 2006, he transferred power to his brother Raúl in a remarkably stable fashion. At the time of this writing, in October 2010, the one-party system and central planning of the economy seem entrenched in Cuba.

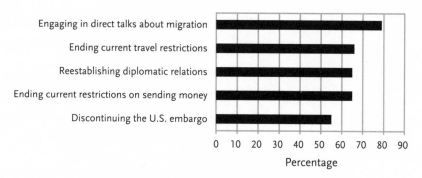

FIGURE 6.3 Measures toward Cuba Favored by Cubans in Miami, 2008
Source: Institute for Public Opinion Research 2008.

Transnational Attitudes and Practices of Cubans in the United States

Since the 1990s, Cuban Americans have become more supportive of increasing contacts with their country of origin. Figure 6.3 summarizes the responses to the 2008 FIU poll of Cuban American public opinion (Institute for Public Opinion Research 2008). According to this source, more than half of Miami's Cubans no longer back the U.S. embargo of Cuba. Furthermore, two-thirds of the interviewees favored ending U.S. restrictions on travel and remittances to Cuba, as well as reestablishing diplomatic relations between Washington and Havana. These findings suggest a substantial change in Cuban Americans' attitudes toward their country of origin, particularly among recent and younger immigrants. The poll confirmed the emergence of a new cohort of Cubans in the United States — especially those who arrived after 1980 — who are willing to negotiate with the island's government.

The 2008 FIU Cuba Poll revealed marked generational differences in Cuban American attitudes toward Cuba. Respondents between eighteen and forty-four years old were more likely to favor ending restrictions on sending money and traveling to Cuba than those aged forty-five and over. Younger Cubans also backed direct talks about migration between the U.S. and Cuban governments more often than older Cubans. Finally, younger Cubans supported reestablishing diplomatic relations between Cuba and the United States by a wider margin than older ones. Other research confirms that U.S.-born Cubans are more open to contact with Cuba than those born on the island (Eckstein 2009).

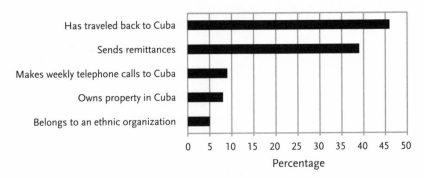

FIGURE 6.4 Transnational Practices of Cubans in the United States, 2006
Source: Waldinger 2007.

Figure 6.4 corroborates that traveling and sending money are the most common transnational practices among Cuban Americans. Both activities persisted despite U.S. government restrictions at the time of the survey. Less frequent are making telephone calls, belonging to an ethnic organization, or owning property in Cuba. Undoubtedly, transnational ties among Cubans face more legal, political, and economic barriers than among other Latinos in the United States. For instance, traveling, sending money, or making telephone calls to Cuba is much more expensive than to other Latin American and Caribbean countries. As a result, Cuban Americans have a low level of transnational engagement compared to other Latinos, such as Dominicans (Orozco et al. 2005; Waldinger 2007). Nonetheless, the cultural, familial, and emotional bridges between Cubans on and off the island have consolidated over the past two decades, especially during the profound economic recession between 1989 and 1994 (Blue 2005; Eckstein 2004a; Mahler and Hansing 2005a). Such links benefited from relaxed travel restrictions by the Cuban and U.S. governments, except for the period between 2004 and 2009.

A significant phenomenon, although difficult to quantify, is the expansion of religious ties between Cuba and the United States. Many Catholic parishes in South Florida engage in transnational activities, such as establishing "sister parishes" in Cuba and collecting donations for their brethren on the island. Several faiths — including Catholics, Protestants, Jews, and Afro-Cuban religions such as Santería — have intensified their transnational links. This spiritual revival culminated with the visit of Pope John Paul II to Cuba in January 1998, when the Pope exhorted, "May Cuba open itself up to the world and may the world open itself to Cuba" (see Mahler and Hansing 2005b: 135–40; Pedraza 2007: 250–55; and Prieto 2009: 104–12). Cubans on both shores have increased their participation in a transnational ritual economy through visits, telephone calls, letters, and e-mail, fostering the circulation of numerous religious beliefs and customs (Burke 2002; Knauer 2003; Mahler and Hansing 2005a). For example, many Cuban Americans travel to the island to become initiated in the cult of the *orichas* (Yoruba gods) under the tutelage of *babalawos*, the priests of the Regla de Ocha (as Santería is also known). Similarly, objects of spiritual value such as offerings, amulets, shrines, images, books, and herbs constantly move between Cuba and the United States. Relatives, friends, and followers of the same faith also exchange more mundane artifacts such as photographs, video and audio recordings, and packages.

Beyond the Exception:
Cuba's Unofficial Transnationalism

Informal family ties between Cuba and the United States have persevered despite the belligerence between the two governments. Cubans have developed a distinctive brand of transnationalism, characterized by their largely unofficial political, economic, and cultural interactions with the United States. After 1959 the Cuban government adopted a stance toward the diaspora of disinterest and denunciation. For decades, Havana's socialist regime excluded the émigrés from its discourse about citizenship and nationality, primarily for political reasons. From the standpoint of the Cuban Revolution, exiles — dubbed "worms" — were traitors to the homeland. Consequently, the Cuban government considered that those who left the island "abandoned" it permanently.

As refugees banned from returning to their homeland, Cubans abroad developed a more adversarial relation to their sending state than either Dominicans or Puerto Ricans. As émigrés from a country embargoed by the U.S. government, Cubans' contact with their home country cannot be as habitual as that of other transnational migrants. Still, many make telephone calls; send letters, photographs, video recordings, money, and packages; and visit relatives on the island. Cubans increasingly leave their country for economic reasons, similar to other migrant workers, even though political motivations still loom large. Transnational households and kinship networks, ambivalent attachments to home and host countries, hybrid cultural practices, and multiple identities characterize the Cuban diaspora as they do the Puerto Rican and Dominican diasporas.

Since the 1990s Cuban American remittances have contributed to the survival of thousands of households on the island. Today, the Cuban economy could not function without the massive influx of U.S. dollars. The long-term effects of such funds on the island's productive structure, as well as their ideological and cultural repercussions, should be examined more systematically. During the Special Period, the flow of ideas, values, practices, and experiences between Cubans on and off the island intensified. Still, political tensions between the Cuban and U.S. governments strain such social and economic ties. I hope that someday Cubans here and there might resume normal relations, regardless of where they live, what political ideology they profess, or whether they earn a living in pesos, dollars, or euros.

Do Cubans, then, occupy a unique and privileged position in contemporary transnational migration? I have argued throughout this chapter that they do not. Like those from the rest of the Caribbean region, the most recent migrant wave from Cuba draws on relatively young, urban members of the working class seeking higher wages and living standards, through both legal and clandestine means. After the end of the Cold War, Cubans no longer enjoy a privileged status in U.S. immigration policy, although the Cuban Adjustment Act (1966) still allows undocumented Cubans to stay if they reach U.S. soil. In turn, the Cuban government has become less disinterested and denunciatory of its diaspora, partly because of the economic significance of Cuban American remittances and visits.

Most important is that Cubans, like other Hispanic Caribbean migrants, have spun a dense web of social, economic, political, cultural, and even religious ties with their homeland. Like Puerto Ricans and Dominicans, many Cubans abroad aspire to sustain a meaningful connection to their country of origin, even if they disagree with the Castro regime. This effort bodes well for any future attempts at reconciliation between Cubans on and off the island. For myself, I find comfort in the belief that sharing the immigrant experience with fellow travelers can lighten the burden of Cuban exceptionalism. Fortunately, we are not alone in our journeys back and forth. The next chapter analyzes the most recent phase of the Cuban exodus, which best illustrates the transnational ties I have already discussed.

Beyond the Rafters

Recent Trends and Projections in Cuban Migration

In chapter 6, I argued that the contemporary Cuban diaspora is best understood from a transnational perspective. Here I focus on the Cuban exodus since the 1990s because it exemplifies many recurring themes in transnationalism, including the migrants' efforts to remain in touch with their relatives back home through remittances, family visits, and telephone calls.[1] Furthermore, more Cubans have come to the United States since 1989 than during any other period since the 1959 revolution. It is therefore instructive to trace the basic contours of this wave and forecast its probable course in the second decade of the twenty-first century.

In 1989 Cuba entered its worst economic crisis in contemporary history. During the 1990s the island's annual average economic growth rate was –1.9 percent. Between 1989 and 1993 Cuba's gross domestic product (GDP) plunged by 39.4 percent. Between 1994 and 1999 the island's economy recovered modestly (growing at an annual average of 3.4 percent). During the first decade of the twenty-first century, the Cuban government reported an average growth of 5.6 percent per year (after changing the calculation method to include subsidized social services such as health care and education). By these measures it took fifteen years for the Cuban economy to return to its 1989 levels (González-Corso 2007; Mesa-Lago 2007). In 2009 the government estimated that the island's economy grew by merely 1.4 percent (Weissert 2009).

During this time Cuba lost its preferential commercial relations with the former Soviet Union and the socialist countries of Eastern Europe, organized around the Council for Mutual Economic Assistance (COMECON), which represented about 85 percent of Cuba's foreign trade in 1989. Nonetheless, the Cuban economy would probably have undergone a crisis even without the dismantling of the Soviet Union and COMECON. The Cuban economy faced serious structural problems since the mid-1980s, such as a growing external debt, lack of export diversification, reliance on imported oil, inefficiency of state enterprises, and low productivity. (For analyses of recent economic trends in Cuba, see Brundenius 2009; Domínguez, Pérez Villanueva, and Barberia 2004; González Núñez 2002; Mesa-Lago 2007; Monreal and Carranza Valdés 2000; Pérez López 2006; Vidal Alejandro 2009.)

The Special Period in Peacetime (as Fidel Castro officially branded the crisis in 1990) has hampered the well-being of the Cuban population. Among the consequences of the crisis were the severe deterioration of nutrition, transportation, and housing; the declining value of wages (particularly in Cuban pesos); and the rising cost of living (increasingly dependent on access to U.S. dollars). Between 1989 and 1993 per capita caloric intake fell from 3,052 to 2,099 calories per day. During this time, adult Cubans lost an average of twenty pounds, and 19 percent of the population remained undernourished in 1998 (Office of Global Analysis 2008: 16; Uriarte 2002: 21). Moreover, the unemployment rate reached a high of 7.9 percent in 1995; many public services (especially health care and education) were curtailed; social inequality (by class, race, and region) intensified; the informal sector (particularly self-employed workers) expanded; and the disjuncture between scarce jobs and a highly skilled labor force produced an enormous waste of human capital (Brundenius 2000).

In addition, the U.S. embargo or blockade[2] worsened Cuba's economic situation. In 1996 the U.S. Congress approved the Cuban Liberty and Democratic Solidarity (LIBERTAD) Act, or Helms-Burton Act, which threatened to sanction foreign companies trading with Cuba. On the one hand, essential articles, especially foodstuffs, medical supplies, and fuel, became scarcer on the island. Many of these products, such as cereals and fertilizers, could be imported from the United States at lower costs than from other countries. On the other hand, the disappearance of the protected Soviet market, together with diminished international prices for sugar, contracted Cuba's exporting capacity. The U.S. embargo has made it difficult for Cuba to find new outlets for its traditional products, such as sugar, tobacco, nickel, and citrus fruits. During the 1990s Venezuela and China only partially compensated for the loss of Cuba's trading partners. The Cuban government estimates that the blockade cost US$236.2 billion between 1962 and 2008 (Ministerio de Relaciones Exteriores 2009).

This chapter assesses the impact of the lingering economic crisis and the U.S. embargo on contemporary Cuban migration to the United States. During the Special Period the Cuban exodus has increased substantially and diversified its destinations. In the short and medium term emigration will probably continue because of Cuba's economic difficulties and the strength of transnational kinship networks. A new wave of mass migration from Cuba to the United States is the most likely scenario for the near future, although not the most desirable one.

The Contemporary Cuban Exodus

The combination of the economic crisis and the U.S. embargo accelerated the Cuban diaspora since 1989. Cuban scholars have found that material deprivation and family reunification became the primary motives for leaving the country during the Special Period (Aja Díaz 2009; Hernández et al. 2002; Rodríguez Chávez 2000). Scholars based in the United States have insisted that economic scarcity aggravated political dissatisfaction with the Cuban government (Ackerman 1997; Ackerman and Clark 1995; Pedraza 2000, 2007). The material and ideological motives of the diaspora became practically inseparable. During the Special Period the number of migrants reached a level comparable to the 1980 Mariel exodus. Cuba's economic slump created a large pool of surplus labor and increased social and economic inequality.

On August 5, 1994, for the first time in three decades, hundreds of Cubans protested publicly against the government in the streets of Centro Habana, in what became known as the *maleconazo* (from El Malecón, Havana's seafront boulevard). On August 12, Fidel Castro announced that his government would let those who wanted to leave the country do so in any way they could. For the third time after Camarioca and Mariel, the Castro regime encouraged a sudden, chaotic, and mass migration to the United States. Thousands took to the sea in small boats, homemade rafts, inner tubes, refurbished vehicles, and anything that floated. The ensuing *balsero* crisis dramatized mounting social pressures due to worsening living conditions in Cuba.

TABLE 7.1 Occupational Background of Cuban Immigrants Admitted to the United States, 2003–2008, and Cuba's Occupational Structure, 2008 (in Percentages)

Occupation	Cuban Immigrants Admitted to U.S.	Cuba's Occupational Structure
Managers and professionals	14.4	7.7
Technicians	—	28.3
Sales and office	13.8	5.2
Operatives	—	35.8
Production, transportation, and material moving	30.3	—
Construction, extraction, maintenance, and repair	20.1	—
Service	20.3	23.0
Farming, fishing, and forestry	1.2	—

Sources: Oficina Nacional de Estadísticas 2009; U.S. Citizenship and Immigration Services 2003–8.

Table 7.1 shows the occupational distribution of recent Cuban migrants to the United States. Compared to earlier migrant waves, the current wave is much more representative of the island's occupational structure. During the first decade of the twenty-first century, the diaspora drew primarily on the lower and middle rungs of the island's labor force, especially unskilled and semiskilled labor (particularly service workers and "operatives," as they are classified in Cuba). At the same time, the recent exodus includes relatively high proportions of professionals and managers (often known as "technicians" in Cuba). The occupational backgrounds of émigrés from post-Soviet Cuba are thus extremely diverse.

Increased Undocumented Migration

At the beginning of the Special Period, most Cubans attempting to leave their country did not have immigrant visas from the United States. Between 1982 and 1988 the U.S. Coast Guard intercepted only 236 Cubans at sea. However, the number soared to 45,930 people between 1989 and 1994 (see the second column of table 7.2). The *balsero* crisis began when the U.S. Coast Guard detained 30,879 Cubans in the Straits of Florida between August 13 and September 13, 1994 (Rodríguez Chávez 1997: 112). This figure represented the largest number of Cuban immigrants in a single month since the Mariel boatlift. Signaling a major shift in U.S. policy toward Cuban immi-

TABLE 7.2 Cuban Migration to the United States, 1989–2009

Year	Legal[a]	Undocumented[b]
1989	10,046	257
1990	10,645	443
1991	10,349	1,722
1992	11,791	2,066
1993	13,666	2,882
1994	14,727	38,560
1995	17,937	525
1996	26,466	411
1997	33,587	421
1998	17,375	903
1999	14,132	1,619
2000	20,831	1,000
2001	27,703	777
2002	28,272	666
2003	9,262	1,555
2004	20,488	1,225
2005	36,261	2,712
2006	45,614	2,810
2007	29,104	2,868
2008	49,500	2,199
2009	38,954	799
Total	486,710	66,420

Sources: U.S. Citizenship and Immigration Services 2002–9; U.S. Coast Guard 2009; U.S. Department of Justice 1989–95, 1996–2001.

[a]Persons of Cuban birth admitted as immigrants in the United States.

[b]Cubans interdicted at sea by U.S. Coast Guard.

gration, the Coast Guard took the rafters to the U.S. naval base in Guantánamo, where they were detained until May 1995. All future *balseros* would be returned to Cuba and required to apply for a visa at the U.S. Interests Section in Havana.

In hindsight, the antecedents of the migratory crisis were clear. Between 1989 and 1993 the United States admitted only 56,497 Cubans, at an average of 11,299 per year (U.S. Department of Justice 1989–93). Consequently, unauthorized exits became the main way of leaving Cuba in the early 1990s. Cubans also took advantage of temporary visits to stay permanently in the United States. About 18 percent of them remained in the country, thus becoming undocumented (Rodríguez Chávez 1997: 135). On the one hand, the

U.S. Interests Section in Havana granted barely 7.1 percent of the maximum visa quotas between 1987 and 1994 (Henken 2005: 398). On the other hand, the long-standing policy of welcoming Cubans who arrived clandestinely in the United States promoted further migration. Thus, when the Cuban government decided not to interfere with unauthorized exits from the island on August 12, 1994, the stage was set for another Mariel.

Reducing Undocumented Migration

The *balsero* crisis concluded when the U.S. and Cuban governments renewed their migration accords in September 1994 and May 1995. One of the main agreements was the repatriation of Cubans intercepted at sea. As a result, the U.S. Coast Guard only interdicted 20,490 *balseros* between 1995 and 2009 (table 7.2). In addition, the U.S. Border Patrol located 7,887 undocumented Cubans who had gained access to U.S. territory between 1997 and 2002. According to Max Castro (2002: 8), the U.S. Coast Guard did not capture almost 60 percent of the *balseros* during this period. According to the Cuban sociologist Ernesto Rodríguez Chávez, nearly 80 percent of the rafters were intercepted and returned to Cuba between 1995 and 2004 (e-mail letter to the author, March 17, 2004). At any rate, the number of undocumented Cubans decreased abruptly after 1995.

The migration accords between Cuba and the United States exemplify what Cuban American political scientist Jorge Domínguez (1992) earlier dubbed "cooperating with the enemy." Despite their discrepancies, both governments defined the *balsero* crisis as a threat to their national security and took swift measures to eliminate it (albeit for different reasons). From the U.S. standpoint, the agreements guaranteed the legal and orderly departure of Cubans and the repatriation of 2,746 "excludable" delinquents, who remained in the United States since the Mariel exodus. From Cuba's perspective, the agreements undermined the privileged treatment of Cubans as refugees and redefined them as undocumented immigrants, similar to those from other Caribbean countries (Arboleya 1996). Both parties benefited from the provision of at least twenty thousand immigrant visas per year, including a lottery that would grant around five thousand visa applications. The success of the negotiations to terminate the crisis shows that the U.S. and Cuban governments can collaborate on issues of common interest, such as undocumented migration, drug trafficking, natural disaster management, and perhaps lifting the embargo.

Stabilizing Legal Migration

Between 1989 and 2009 the United States admitted 486,910 Cubans, at an annual average of 23,177 persons. These figures exceed those for any other period of Cuban emigration. Since the mid-1990s the volume of visas has approximated the annual quota of twenty thousand. The U.S.-Cuba agreements thus have channeled the bulk of the exodus through legal means.

Nevertheless, Cuba's migratory potential is much greater than the number of visas allotted by the U.S. government. In 1996 Cuban scholars estimated that between 490,000 and 733,000 persons would leave Cuba if they had the opportunity to do so (Aja Díaz, Milán Acosta, and Díaz Fernández 1996: 155). An index of the growing desire to emigrate is the number of participants in the visa lottery (*el bombo*, as it is popularly known in Cuba). Lottery applicants rose from 189,000 persons in 1994, to 436,277 in 1996, to 541,500 in 1998 (Aja Díaz 2002; Henken 2005; *Migration News* 1998a). At an annual rate of twenty thousand visas, it would take two more decades to satisfy the existing demand. As a result, Cubans have resorted to multiple forms of displacement — emigrating clandestinely, remaining in other countries after their travel documents expire, residing abroad temporarily, marrying foreigners, or using other countries as way stations to the United States.

Rising Temporary Migration

Since the mid-1990s, the Cuban government has selectively granted permits to reside abroad (*permisos de residencia en el exterior*, or PRE) to Cuban citizens in countries such as Mexico, Venezuela, and Spain. The PRE authorizes its bearer to enter and exit Cuba without losing his or her rights, benefits, and property on the island. People who obtain such permits may live outside Cuba for up to eleven months, as long as they pay the required fees. By and large, these permits are given to young women who marry foreign citizens, as well as to artists, physicians, scientists, and other professionals. Although the Cuban government has not released exact figures on the topic, Cuban scholars estimate that more than thirty thousand people received the PRE between 1995 and 2004 (Martín Fernández et al. 2007).

While numerically minuscule within the overall exodus, this new category of Cubans abroad merits further study. Until now, the possibility of returning to the island for long periods has eluded most émigrés. For the first time since 1959, some of those Cubans temporarily abroad could become

TABLE 7.3 Cuban Migration to the United States, Florida, and the
Miami Metropolitan Area, 1996–2009

Year	United States	Florida	Miami	Percentage of U.S. Total in Miami
1996	26,466	22,217	20,061	75.8
1997	33,587	28,433	24,682	73.4
1998	17,375	14,265	12,308	70.8
1999	14,132	10,293	8,861	62.7
2000	20,831	15,883	13,356	64.1
2001	27,703	21,729	18,425	66.5
2002	28,272	22,262	18,468	65.3
2003	9,262	6,303	5,283	57.0
2004	20,488	14,992	11,897	58.1
2005	36,261	30,624	26,087	71.9
2006	45,614	37,711	31,431	68.9
2007	29,104	23,605	19,167	65.9
2008	49,500	40,946	34,041	68.8
2009	38,954	31,928	26,666	68.4
Total	397,549	321,191	270,733	68.1

Sources: U.S. Citizenship and Immigration Services 2002–9; U.S. Department of Justice 1996–2001.

Note: Data are for persons of Cuban birth admitted as immigrants in the United States.

part of a circular flow. Some authors have even discussed the desirability of allowing émigrés to retire in Cuba (Monreal 1999). Cuban migration thus would increasingly resemble the circular patterns established in the remainder of the Caribbean.

The Persisting Concentration of Migrants in the United States

During the 1990s roughly three-fourths of all Cuban émigrés settled in the United States. Two-thirds of those who traveled with temporary visas went there (Aja Díaz 1999: 13, 14). Today the Cuban flow continues to be primarily oriented toward the United States, especially South Florida. Between 1996 and 2009 more than two-thirds of all Cubans admitted to the United States intended to live in Miami (table 7.3). The operation of social networks among the émigrés, as well as the asymmetry in employment opportunities and wages between Cuba and the United States, largely explains this

TABLE 7.4 Top Twenty Countries with Population of
Cuban Origin Outside Cuba, ca. 2000–2002

Country	Number	Percentage
United States	888,280	80.2
Spain	50,765	4.7
Puerto Rico	19,973	1.8
Germany	18,265	1.6
Pakistan	13,050	1.2
Venezuela	9,621	0.9
Italy	9,569	0.9
Mexico	6,558	0.6
Kuwait	6,259	0.6
Canada	5,412	0.5
Haiti	4,951	0.4
Russia	3,878	0.4
Congo	3,259	0.3
Dominican Republic	3,191	0.3
Chile	3,176	0.3
Uzbekistan	3,041	0.3
Jordan	2,803	0.3
Jamaica	2,453	0.2
Ukraine	2,207	0.2
Netherlands Antilles	2,048	0.2

Sources: University of Sussex, Development Research Centre
on Migration, Globalisation and Poverty 2007; U.S. Census
Bureau 2009a.

geographic concentration (Monreal 1999). The data confirm that *la Yuma*,
as the United States is colloquially known in Cuba, remains the preferred
destination for Cubans. Miami is still the principal external referent of the
island's collective imaginary.

Diverse Destinations

According to Cuban sources, in 2007 more than 258,000 Cubans lived
outside Cuba and the United States, especially in Spain, Venezuela, and
Mexico, as well as in Puerto Rico, which is usually excluded from U.S. statistics on immigration (Martín Fernández et al. 2007). Between 2000 and
2002 the censuses of various nations besides Cuba and the United States
counted 219,406 persons of Cuban origin (see table 7.4). Several former

republics of the Soviet Union have attracted Cubans, including Russia, Uzbekistan, and Ukraine. During the Special Period, Cuban migrants expanded their destinations to various Latin American and Caribbean countries, such as the Dominican Republic, Chile, and Jamaica, as well as European countries, such as Germany, Italy, and France. Canada has also become an important place for settlement or sojourning. The difficulty of traveling to the United States has partly redirected the Cuban migrant flow to other countries. Although these new destinations have not been studied in detail, some follow the trade and tourist routes developed during the Special Period.

Using Other Countries to Reach "The Promised Land"

The well-established tendency to move temporarily to another country and later relocate in the United States continues. Panama was one of the main bridges for Cubans into the United States until the U.S. invasion of that country in 1989. Venezuela also served as a relay station to the United States during the 1980s. More recently, the Dominican Republic has become a springboard to travel without documents to Puerto Rico and from there to the U.S. mainland. The presence of approximately ten thousand Cuban citizens in the Dominican Republic (Casaña Mata 2002b) suggests that this country serves largely as a temporary haven rather than as a permanent abode, given the economic difficulties experienced by Dominicans and the incentive to improve their living standards abroad. Other countries, such as Mexico and Canada, have also received Cubans hoping to cross over to the United States. Despite its growing significance, this angle of the contemporary Cuban exodus has attracted little academic attention.

Projecting the Cuban Exodus

A Continuing Flow

In the short and medium term, the accumulation of unsatisfied pressures to migrate will ensure a substantial movement of Cubans to the United States. As I have noted, the volume of immigrant visas granted by the U.S. Interests Section in Havana cannot meet the growing demand. At the same time, the prolonged Special Period has frustrated the hopes of improving living conditions for many Cubans, especially youth. Continuing economic scarcity will sustain a high outmigration rate in the coming decade. A substantial alteration of these conditions is unlikely in the near future.

Migration as a Survival Strategy

As I have mentioned, more than half a million Cubans registered for the last *bombo* in Havana, suggesting that many more desire to migrate. The relaxation of Cuba's travel restrictions, as well as the official insistence that the post-1989 exodus is driven economically more than ideologically, has helped legitimize migration. As the Cuban sociologist María Isabel Domínguez has observed, leaving the island during the Special Period became one of the main ways of "solving immediate, personal, and family needs" (Hernández et al. 2002: 77). "Under current conditions in Cuba," notes Cuban economist Pedro Monreal (1999: 56), "emigration can be a much more attractive way than employment in the national state and nonstate sectors as a mechanism to improve one's income." Insofar as other alternatives — such as working for mixed enterprises or the informal economy — are limited, emigration constitutes an increasingly popular survival strategy, as it has been in other Caribbean countries for decades. How such a strategy will be channeled — through authorized or unauthorized forms, temporarily or permanently, to the United States or other countries — is still unclear.

The Difficulty of Stemming the Exodus

During the 1990s changes in U.S. policy toward Cuba, particularly the migration accords between the two governments, slowed down unauthorized migration. Nonetheless, this policy has maintained an artificially low outmigration rate. As Max Castro (2002) underlines, the U.S. government no longer fosters mass migration to undermine the Cuban regime. Nonetheless, some juridical and ideological elements continue to stimulate the exodus. For instance, the 1966 Cuban Adjustment Act still applies, and Cuba is the only country with a minimum annual quota of twenty thousand visas from the United States. At the same time, the Cuban government has resorted to emigration as a safety valve for its economic woes. This combination of a restrictive immigration policy by the U.S. government and a more laissez-faire emigration policy by the Cuban government is potentially explosive.

After the Embargo, What?

Even under the current embargo, the United States became one of Cuba's leading suppliers of agricultural and food products during the first decade of the twenty-first century (Office of Global Analysis 2008). The gradual or complete elimination of U.S. trade sanctions against Cuba could have mixed effects. On the one hand, it could help improve the economic conditions of the Cuban population and thereby attenuate one of the main motivations to leave the island. But this dissuasive effect will probably take years to materialize, and it is difficult to predict how many disgruntled people will stay or leave the country. On the other hand, lifting the embargo will surely facilitate the movement of people, capital, goods, and ideas between Cuba and the United States, which might in turn reinforce the propensity to migrate. In other Caribbean countries, trade, investment, and tourism have tended to augment emigration, not to reduce it. It is still too early to determine which of these two effects will prevail in Cuba.

The Future of the Cuban Diaspora

Based on the trends and premises above, I foresee three plausible scenarios for the second decade of the twenty-first century: (1) the continuation of the current migration pattern; (2) a significant reduction of emigration; or (3) a substantial increase in emigration. In any event, I presuppose that the United States and Cuba will establish closer economic and perhaps diplomatic relations.

Current Migration Levels Continue

In this scenario, around twenty thousand Cubans would migrate legally every year to the United States by means of the established quotas. During the next decade, as many as thirty thousand would attempt to migrate clandestinely, half of whom would be intercepted by the U.S. Coast Guard and returned to Cuba. The Cuban government would extend the PRE to more than thirty thousand citizens living abroad. Under such conditions, at least a quarter of a million Cubans would migrate between 2010 and 2019. The prolongation of the status quo is highly unlikely if relations between Cuba and the United States are normalized. Terminating the embargo would probably destabilize the migration equation established at the end of the twentieth century.

Moreover, the opening up of the Cuban economy to U.S. trade, investment, and tourism would likely lead to revising the migration accords and perhaps the Cuban Adjustment Act. Once these conditions are modified, the current migration model would collapse.

Emigration Declines Significantly

Let us assume that ending the embargo would ease Cuba's reincorporation into the world economy and that this reincorporation would ameliorate the living standards of the Cuban population. The greater availability of food-stuffs — especially cereals such as wheat, corn, and rice, as well as meat, milk, and eggs — at lower prices would reduce the nutritional deficit on the island (Aguilar Trujillo 2001; Coleman 2001; Office of Global Analysis 2008). A more equitable income distribution, which has become increasingly lopsided during the Special Period, would decrease social tensions in Cuba. Expanding trade between Cuba and the United States could prepare the ground for diplomatic ties between the two countries. Unrestricted travel between Miami and Havana would promote transnational contacts among relatives, friends, tourists, and entrepreneurs. Eliminating the embargo could also encourage Cuban American remittances. Under such conditions, the exodus would diminish, perhaps reaching the level of the 1980s, when the United States admitted fewer than 164,000 Cubans. This scenario seems utopian in light of the demographic and economic trends prevalent in Cuba since 1989. Even if it did occur, its effects on the exodus would probably not be visible for several years.

Emigration Increases Substantially

In the third scenario, the process of family reunification would continue to draw Cubans to the United States. Deteriorated living conditions (including nutrition, health care, housing, and transportation) would push thousands to leave the country with or without government authorization. The expansion of self-employment (*trabajo por cuenta propia*) would hardly compensate for the massive loss of government jobs. The inability of the Cuban economy to absorb many professionals and technicians would accentuate the "brain drain" (see Brundenius 2000; and Casaña Mata 2002a). Popular dissatisfaction with a stagnant, state-run economy would persist and perhaps deepen. Consequently, one could anticipate a tidal wave of migrants from Cuba during the second decade of the twenty-first century, even larger than during the first decade. The figure of half a million migrants is thus not far-fetched. This seems to be the most plausible scenario for the Cuban diaspora in the short and medium term, even if the embargo ceases and U.S.-Cuba relations improve. Everything points to a new Cuban migration crisis in the near future.

Transnationalism during a Time of Crisis

Officially begun in 1990, the Special Period in Peacetime has sharpened economic shortages and social inequalities in Cuba, and these have become powerful incentives to emigrate. From the outset of the economic crisis in 1989 to the *balsero* crisis in 1994, unauthorized exits became the main form of leaving the island. After September 1994 the reassessment of U.S. policy toward Cuban refugees and, above all, negotiations between the U.S. and Cuban governments reduced undocumented migration. Since then the Cuban exodus has followed a relatively steady course, although it has enormous potential to overflow current visa quotas.

In the short run, the Cuban exodus will probably expand because of the accumulation of migratory pressures, the strength of transnational family ties, and the incapacity of U.S. and Cuban policies to curb the flow of people between the two countries. The material hardships of the seemingly endless Special Period are bound to persist during the second decade of the twenty-first century. Eliminating U.S. trade restrictions, whenever it occurs, should have a favorable impact on Cuba's economy. But lifting the embargo will not necessarily improve the living conditions of most Cubans in the short run. Reestablishing economic exchanges between Cuba and the United States may even enhance the propensity to migrate.

Although I am no futurologist, I expect the Cuban exodus to swell over the next decade. The most reasonable projections range between a quarter of a million and half a million people per decade. By itself, ending the U.S. embargo is insufficient to stem mass migration from Cuba. Other economic and political changes are necessary to satisfy the pressing needs and aspirations of Cuban citizens. Among other requirements, Cuba would have to sustain high rates of economic growth. Unfortunately, recent forecasts by experts on the Cuban economy — both on and off the island — are quite sobering (see Brundenius 2009; Comisión Económica 2009; Mesa-Lago 2007;

Pérez-López 2006; and Vidal Alejandro 2009). Should economic stagnation persist, the large-scale displacement of Cuba's population to the United States will proceed unabated. In any case, the transnational ties between Cubans on and off the island will probably strengthen, just as they have for Dominicans, as I show in the next two chapters.

Los Países

Transnational Migration from the Dominican Republic

In the 1990s the Dominican Republic became one of the top migrant-sending countries to the United States, after Mexico, the Philippines, Vietnam, and China.[1] Only Mexico, Puerto Rico, Cuba, and El Salvador were larger sources of the population of Hispanic ancestry in the United States. In 2009 the census estimated that 1,356,361 persons of Dominican origin lived in the United States (U.S. Census Bureau 2010). This figure represented 14.1 percent of the population of the Dominican Republic (9.7 million). The massive displacement of people to the United States and elsewhere is popularly known in the Dominican Republic as *irse a los países* (literally, "moving to the countries"). As I argue in this chapter, the plural and generic way that Dominicans refer to their migration patterns suggests the development of multiple transnational communities and diasporic identities.

Unlike Cuba, the Dominican Republic has been deemed a prototype of transnationalism. The approval of dual citizenship by the Dominican legislature in 1994 is a classic example of transnational politics. As I noted in chapter 3, remittances are the second-largest source of foreign currency in the Dominican Republic. In 2008 this small nation was the eighth most important destination for international telephone calls billed in the United States, as measured both by the number of messages and minutes (Federal Communications Commission 2010). Dominican transnationalism is embedded in long-distance kinship networks, households, and child-rearing practices. The circulation of cultural values, practices, and identities between the Dominican Republic and the United States has been well documented (Duany 2008b [1994]; Flores 2008; Guarnizo 1994; Itzigsohn et al. 1999; Levitt

2001, 2005). Nevertheless, not all Dominican migrants are equally transnational, as they are internally divided by age, birthplace, residence, class, and other factors.

This chapter traces the main contours of the contemporary Dominican diaspora. After reviewing recent academic controversies about Dominican transnationalism, I highlight the large volume and settlement patterns of Dominicans in the United States. The number of Dominicans has also increased in Western Europe, other countries of the Caribbean, and Latin America. In New York City, Dominicans have developed transnational spaces and cultural identities. Furthermore, expatriates have become key actors in the Dominican economy and politics, while also incorporating themselves into the economy and politics of the United States. Nowadays, the Dominican Republic is a full-fledged transnational nation-state, encompassing its diaspora to a much larger extent than either Cuba or Puerto Rico.

Are Dominicans Transnational or Diasporic?

According to many scholars, contemporary Dominican immigrants epitomize transnationalism. However, the Dominican American literary critic Silvio Torres-Saillant (2000) has rejected the transnational paradigm as it has been applied to Dominicans in New York City. Furthermore, Dominican American sociologist Milagros Ricourt (2002) doubts that all sectors of the Dominican American population can be dubbed transnational. More recently, Ana Aparicio (2006) has rebutted the transnational view of Dominican American politics. Still, the model of Dominicans as quintessential transnationals prevails in academic publications (Duany 2008b [1994]); Itzigsohn and Dore-Cabral 2000; Itzigsohn et al. 1999; Levitt 2001, 2005; Pantoja 2005; Sagás and Molina 2004; Sørensen 1996, 1997). Here I only have space to sketch the basic positions in dispute.

According to Torres-Saillant, transnationalism became "a fashionable mode of analysis that stresses the point that migration transforms social relations, producing new forms of identity that transcend traditional notions of physical and cultural space" (8). Torres-Saillant believes that "the apparent bidirectionality of life" (7) among Dominican Americans has dazzled non-Dominican scholars. He identifies Luis Guarnizo, Peggy Levitt, Pamela Graham, José Itzigsohn, and Ninna Nyberg Sørensen as the leading researchers of Dominican transnationalism. (Torres-Saillant generously exempts my own monograph from bitter criticism.) In Torres-Saillant's judgment, the transnational perspective "exaggerate[s] the existential options that the global society affords regular Dominicans" (21). In particular, he decries the depiction of ordinary migrants as borderless people without roots in the United States.

Instead of transnationalism, Torres-Saillant interprets the contemporary experiences of Dominicans in the United States as diasporic. He feels that this term — with its dual implication of uprooting and taking root in a new land — better describes transplanted Dominicans in New York City and elsewhere. In my mind, diasporic and transnational identities are not mutually exclusive. Throughout this book, I have used the two terms interchangeably to refer to scattered peoples who remain connected to their countries of origin, despite long distances and periods of residence abroad.

Ricourt (2002) contends that the Dominican community in New York City is fractured by gender, generation, and place of residence. Thus, the meaning of transnationalism differs between men and women, older and newer immigrants, and those who live in Washington Heights and other neighborhoods with smaller concentrations of Dominicans. She concludes that "transnationalism only tells a partial story" (14) that underestimates immigrants' engagement with community building and neighborhood politics. Dominican social service agencies, Ricourt argues, have helped form "a permanent community, with more roots in the host society, and more powerful politically" (6). Although her point is well taken, it does not invalidate a transnational approach to Dominican migration.

Aparicio (2006) argues that the rise of second-generation community leaders has shifted Dominican organizations in New York City from a transnational to a local focus. She rightly faults scholars for paying insufficient attention to political coalitions between Dominican Americans and other ethnic and racial minorities, especially Puerto Ricans and African Americans. However, following Graham (1998, 2001), I would argue that Dominican immigrants expanded their political participation in New York City as well as in the Dominican Republic during the 1990s. Aparicio reacts against the excessive "deterritorialization" of transnational politics, but she makes the equally exaggerated claim that Dominican Americans are no longer concerned with their homeland and have become fully absorbed as yet another racialized minority in the United States. In my view, the most intriguing dimension of Dominican American politics is precisely its bifocality — its dual focus on host and sending societies.

Despite the criticisms, transnationalism has proven a resilient paradigm to understand Dominican migration. In the introduction to their edited collection of essays, Ernesto Sagás and Sintia Molina (2004: 5) assert that "the Dominican Republic provides a textbook example of a transnational migration," echoing similar claims by Guarnizo (1994), Itzigsohn and colleagues (1999), and Levitt (2001). Sagás and Molina probably overstate their case when they add that "Dominicans have created a borderless nation outside the national territory with which they do not feel disconnected" (9). Transnational scholars have tended to overlook that national identities are always grounded in specific territories, even when the bearers of these identities are far removed from their places of origin. Also, in portraying Dominicans as transnationalists, scholars should not neglect their diversity, the result of different migrant waves, social classes, generational differences, and geographic locations.

Nonetheless, the contributors to Sagás and Molina's collection profitably extend a transnational perspective to a wide range of issues, from politics and economics to literature and music. Their work shows that transnational Dominican communities have mushroomed in New York, San Juan, Providence, Madrid, and Miami. Overseas Dominicans now vote in Dominican presidential elections, send millions of dollars back home, and nurture a vibrant and hybrid culture, especially through creative literature, popular music, and dance. Such practices do not contradict the rise of locally oriented organizations and allegiances in the communities of settlement. Instead, transnationalism may foster migrants' simultaneous participation in their home and host societies (Levitt and Glick Schiller 2004).

The Rise of Transnational Communities

The most outstanding feature of contemporary Dominican emigration is its sheer massiveness. Censuses conducted in 2000–2002 counted 965,228 persons of Dominican origin outside the Dominican Republic, mostly in the United States, Puerto Rico, and Spain (table 8.1). Substantial émigré communities also have emerged in Venezuela, Panama, Canada, and several other countries. (Chapter 9 focuses on Dominicans in Puerto Rico.) Sizable Dominican populations now exist in European nations such as Germany, Italy, the Netherlands, Switzerland, and even Russia and Uzbekistan. Within the Caribbean region, aside from Puerto Rico, most Dominicans have settled in the Netherlands Antilles, Guadeloupe, Aruba, and the U.S. Virgin Islands.

A second feature of the Dominican diaspora is its extraordinary growth

TABLE 8.1 Top Twenty Countries with Population of Dominican
Origin Outside the Dominican Republic, ca. 2000–2002

Country	Number	Percentage
United States	702,684	77.3
Puerto Rico	56,146	5.8
Spain	49,100	5.1
Germany	17,280	1.8
Venezuela	13,896	1.4
Italy	13,442	1.4
Pakistan	10,868	1.1
Haiti	7,143	0.7
Netherlands	6,107	0.6
Panama	5,775	0.6
Guadeloupe	5,674	0.6
Switzerland	5,668	0.6
Canada	5,302	0.5
Kuwait	5,211	0.5
Aruba	3,905	0.4
Philippines	3,866	0.4
Russia	3,229	0.3
U.S. Virgin Islands	3,165	0.3
Congo	2,713	0.3
Uzbekistan	2,532	0.3

Sources: University of Sussex, Development Research Centre on
Migration, Globalisation and Poverty 2007; U.S. Census Bureau 2009a.

over the last five decades. The number of Dominicans admitted in the
United States was so small until the mid-1960s that the Immigration and
Naturalization Service (INS, now called the U.S. Citizenship and Immigra-
tion Services) did not report separate data for them before 1925. In 1950 the
Census Bureau found only forty-two hundred people of Dominican birth in
the United States (figure 2.2). Large-scale population movements from the
Dominican Republic began shortly after the end of the Trujillo dictatorship
in 1961. Changes in the U.S. economy and immigration policy fostered the
Dominican exodus, such as an increasing demand for cheap labor in northeastern cities and the abolition of immigration quotas by national origin in
1965. Accordingly, Dominican migration to the United States soared from
9,915 people in the 1950s to 84,065 in the 1960s. The outflow continued to
rise in the 1970s, when the United States admitted 141,578 Dominicans. During the 1980s the INS counted 227,483 Dominican immigrants, a figure sur-

passed by the 365,545 people admitted during the 1990s (table 2.4). (These figures exclude undocumented immigrants, discussed in chapter 9.)

Compared to Cubans and Puerto Ricans, Dominican population movements are relatively recent. More than 98 percent of the 1,128,538 Dominicans admitted to the United States between 1925 and 2009 arrived after 1961. The statistics suggest a rising tide of immigrants from the Dominican Republic between the 1960s and 1990s. By the 1980s Dominicans had become one of the fastest growing segments of the foreign-born population in the United States. Today, the majority are still members of the first generation, which is one reason why they maintain such strong transnational attachments.

A third significant pattern is the geographic concentration of Dominicans within the United States. In 2009 nearly half of the immigrants and their descendants (678,881 people) lived in the state of New York. Secondary concentrations existed in New Jersey and Florida (table 3.1). Smaller communities have appeared in Massachusetts, Pennsylvania, and Rhode Island, as well as Puerto Rico. For many Dominicans, moving abroad (to *los países*) is practically synonymous with relocating in New York. Hence, a popular 1996 movie and its 1997 sequel about the Dominican diaspora, directed by Ángel Muñiz, were simply titled *Nueba Yol* (New York) and *Nueba Yol 3*.

In 2009 the leading metropolitan areas for Dominicans in the United States were New York, Miami, Boston, Providence, and Orlando (table 3.2). In particular, New York City has the second-largest number of Dominican residents in the world, after Santo Domingo. As one informant told the Danish anthropologist Ninna Nyberg Sørensen (1996), "New York is just another Dominican capital." Sørensen (176) interprets this statement to mean that, for many Dominicans, maintaining or improving their social status has become associated with living in New York City. Nowadays, the sobriquet *Dominican-York* alludes to Dominicans residing anywhere in the United States.

Carving Transnational Spaces

Dominican migrants occupy distinctive niches in their primary destinations, especially in New York. Among other practices, they have recreated their homeland in the diaspora by establishing businesses with names reminiscent of their country, establishing hometown associations, and celebrating festivals based on their folk traditions. In Santurce, Puerto Rico, Dominicans started chains of popular cafeterias with names like El Mangú (a typical Dominican staple made with boiled plantain and pork) and El Padrino (The Godfather). In Madrid, the Corona Boreal Square of Aravaca has a small stone plaque in homage to Lucrecia Pérez, the Dominican domestic worker who was murdered there in 1992. Every January 21, Dominicans in Queens commemorate the feast of the Virgin of Altagracia, the patron saint of the Dominican Republic (Ricourt and Danta 2003: 67). Transnational connections are especially evident in the Dominican neighborhoods of Washington Heights, the main focus of this section.

During the summer of 1993 I conducted fieldwork in Washington Heights (Duany 2008b [1994]). Four out of five residents of the block I studied were Dominicans. Itinerant traders sold oranges, corn, flowers, music cassettes, and ice cones (*frío-fríos*). Dozens of small carts offered *frío-fríos* in main traffic intersections. Children opened fire hydrants and played with water in the streets. Men usually spoke Spanish, listened to merengue, complimented young women walking by, played dominoes, drank Presidente beer, and read Dominican newspapers like *El Nacional*, *El Siglo*, and *Listín Diario*. Women pushed their baby strollers, shopped in neighborhood bodegas, and chatted with friends in front of their buildings. Teenagers walked to the nearby George Washington High School, swam in neighborhood pools, or listened to rap and house music on enormous cassette players.

In the mornings, many people took the subway to work in downtown Manhattan and returned home in the afternoons. Others traveled by bus to factories in New Jersey, across the Hudson River. Near the subway station, several businesses, such as Banco Dominicano, specialized in sending remittances to the Dominican Republic. Gypsy cabs from the Dominican-owned Riverside Company, usually large dark American cars, drove up and down the streets searching for customers. A newspaper stand in the corner of West 181st Street and Saint Nicholas Avenue offered ten newspapers, which arrived daily from the Dominican Republic.

Many cafeterias and restaurants sold typical Dominican food, featuring entrées such as *mangú*, *carne guisada*, *sancocho*, *mondongo*, *locrio cocido*, and *cabeza de cerdo*; side orders such as *moros*, *tostones*, and *empanada de yuca*; drinks such as *jugo de caña*, *morir soñando*, and *batida de fruta*; and desserts such as *pastelillos de guayaba*, *yaniqueque*, *habichuelas con dulce*, *dulce de coco*, and *pan dulce relleno*. Local grocery stores imported assorted tropical fruits and vegetables, ranging from plantains to *mamey*. A beauty parlor sold a wide variety of Dominican brand products, such as Lafier and Capilo. Small businesses specializing in telephone calls to the Dominican Republic prolif-erated. Many store owners displayed their national origin by playing loud music in front of their stores, usually merengue and salsa, and occasionally *bachata* and bolero. Some businesses were local subsidiaries of enterprises from the Dominican Republic, such as Nitín Bakery. Others sold Dominican drinks such as Cola Quisqueya, Refrescos Nacionales, and Presidente beer.

Commercial signs confirmed the strong presence of residents from the Cibao region, such as Acogedor Cibao Supermarket, Cibao Vision Center, Cibao Meat Products, and Hielo Cibao. A Dominican immigrant who longed to have his own "small Cibao" in New York planted corn and black beans at the corner of Broadway Avenue and West 153rd Street. During my fieldwork, a young man paraded down the sidewalk with two fighting roosters, a com-mon sight in the Dominican countryside. Dozens of hometown associations carried the names of Cibao places such as Moca and Tamboril. Some Do-minicans even referred to Washington Heights as "El Cibao."

Most immigrants maintained their cultural traditions at home. Some tenants placed Spanish signs on their apartment doors, as if to announce their national origin, especially religious messages such as "Jesus is our only hope," "Christ will change your life," and "Let's build peace with Christ." Within their households, many Dominicans hung pictures with religious motifs on the walls, such as the Sacred Heart of Jesus and the Last Supper.

Some families had Spanish-language calendars with an image of the Vir-gin Mary, acquired in a local bodega. Others hung the Dominican flag or coat of arms prominently in the living room. Many displayed the faceless ceramic dolls that have become emblems of the Dominican Republic, as well as colorful painted plates with their country's folk themes, usually a rural landscape, a peasant scene, the Santo Domingo Cathedral, or a tropical beach. Such objects recreated the iconography of the Dominican Republic in Washington Heights.

Many Dominican households and businesses had small niches with stat-ues of the Catholic saints and the Virgin Mary in a corner of the main room or private area. These humble shrines were usually surrounded with flow-ers, candles, food, and glasses of water, wine, and other drinks. Although the most popular figures were the Virgin of Altagracia and Saint Lazarus, the altars represented a wide variety of religious images: Saint Claire, Saint Anthony of Padua, Saint Barbara, the Holy Child of Atocha, the Sacred Heart, the Sacred Family, the Virgin of Fatima, and the Virgin of Mercedes, among others. Like other devout Catholics, many Dominicans believe that the saints protect them from evil and help them progress economically. A woman who carried a medallion of the Virgin of Altagracia told me, "When you're away from your country, you need protection. And your country, too." In sum, the popular Dominican devotion to the saints and the Virgin has been transplanted to a new transnational space.

Transnational Businesses and Economic Incorporation

According to Alejandro Portes and Luis Guarnizo (1991), Dominicans have created an emergent enclave economy in Washington Heights. This enclave consists of a thriving network of small businesses catering to the immigrants and to the sending country. In the early 1990s Dominicans owned nearly twenty thousand businesses in New York City. In 1988 Sarah Mahler (1989) counted an average of twelve Dominican-owned businesses per block in Washington Heights. The block I studied in 1993 had seven Dominican-owned businesses, including two bodegas, two beauty parlors, a restaurant, and a bakery.

Portes and Guarnizo classified Dominican businesses in New York City into four types, depending on their main product or service. First, bodegas, butcher shops, supermarkets, and packing businesses distributed Dominican foods. Second, beauty parlors, restaurants, and discotheques provided services related to the immigrants' social and cultural preferences. Third, local intermediary services included processing tax, accounting, immigration, and other forms required by local, state, and federal agencies. Finally, binational service businesses featured travel agencies, remittance agencies, moving and real estate companies.

Although Dominican immigrants show high levels of ethnic entrepreneurship, most are not business owners. In 2009 only 6.7 percent of Dominicans in New York City were self-employed (table 8.2). Moreover, they had the second-highest poverty rate among the major ethnic and racial groups in the city, after Puerto Ricans. Dominicans and Puerto Ricans both had a 13.4 percent unemployment rate, the highest of all groups. Dominicans had the lowest median household income and per capita income. Few had well-paid white-collar jobs such as professionals and managers. Only 14.1 percent of Dominicans twenty-five years and older had completed college, compared to 51.2 percent of white New Yorkers. Finally, Dominicans had the highest proportion of female-headed households.

TABLE 8.2 Selected Socioeconomic Indicators of the Main Ethnic and Racial Groups in New York City, 2009

Indicator	Dominicans	Puerto Ricans	All Hispanics	Non-Hispanic Whites	Non-Hispanic Blacks
Female-headed households (%)	39.1	31.6	28.7	7.2	32.5
Bachelor's degree or higher (%)	14.1	12.1	14.7	51.2	21.7
Unemployed (%)	13.4	13.4	13.1	7.6	12.8
Managers and professionals (%)	16.2	26.8	20.0	54.4	30.4
Self-employed (%)	6.7	2.9	6.4	7.6	4.9
Median household income (US$)	28,226	29,536	34,028	69,487	40,566
Per capita income (US$)	13,394	16,852	16,534	50,664	21,216
Poverty rate (%)	31.7	32.0	28.1	11.0	19.9

Source: U.S. Census Bureau 2010.

Expanding Transnational Economic Ties

Despite their relative disadvantage in the United States, expatriates have expanded their role in the Dominican economy, especially since the 1990s. As I discussed in chapter 3, the value of private monetary transfers to the Dominican Republic soared between 1970 and 2009. In the latter year, the Inter-American Development Bank (IADB 2010) estimated that Dominicans abroad sent home almost US$2.8 billion. In addition, every year, thousands of Dominicans travel to their home country and spend millions of dollars there. According to the Dominican Central Bank, Dominicans living abroad represented 15.8 percent of all international visitors to the Dominican Republic between 2000 and 2009 (see figure 8.1).

Increased Dominican emigration, especially since the 1980s, has had the primary effect of providing additional income for those remaining home. Like many other developing economies, the Dominican Republic depends on remittances to square off its balance of payments and generate new economic ventures. Similarly, the Dominican economy relies on massive expenditures by international visitors, including Dominicans living abroad. Remittances and ethnic tourism have strengthened economic ties between the United States and the Dominican Republic. Whether such links are beneficial or detrimental to self-sustained economic growth remains in dispute.

According to Itzigsohn and his colleagues (1999), remittances became central to the Dominican economy during the 1980s, just as political lead-

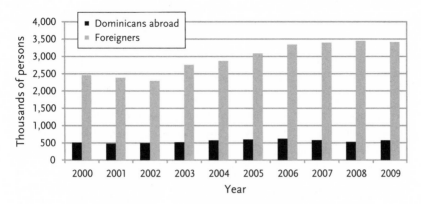

FIGURE 8.1 International Tourists in the Dominican Republic: Arrivals by Air, 2000–2009

Source: Banco Central de la República Dominicana 2010.

ers in the Dominican Republic acknowledged the diaspora's growing clout. The conjunction of these two factors prompted a profound reassessment of *dominicanos ausentes* (absent Dominicans), now usually called *dominicanos en el exterior* (Dominicans abroad). Like other countries with large overseas populations, the Dominican government amended its constitution and public policies toward citizenship in the 1990s. By this time the diaspora had gained substantial economic and political influence, and the official as well as popular discourse of Dominican identity became increasingly transnational. I elaborate this point later in this chapter.

Organizing a Transnational Community

During the 1960s Dominican business people and diplomats formed small social clubs in New York City. The earliest associations were the Centro Cívico Cultural Dominicano (Dominican Civic and Cultural Center), founded in 1962, and the Club Juan Pablo Duarte, founded in 1966 (Sainz 1990). These groups tended to be politically conservative and geared toward preserving Hispanic customs and values in the United States. At this time working-class Dominicans lacked social institutions such as ethnic churches to assist them in the resettlement process. Later on, community organizations reflected more closely the immigrants' predominantly proletarian and peasant backgrounds, as well as their largely black and mulatto membership. Such organizations included the Centro Cultural Ballet Quisqueya and the Club María Trinidad Sánchez.

As New York's Dominican population swelled in the late 1960s and early 1970s, new social and political groups emerged. Many radical and liberal leaders had gone into exile in the United States to avoid persecution in their home country. The number of Dominican associations in New York City multiplied; by the early 1980s, at least 125 of them were operating in the city, ninety of them in Washington Heights, where the bulk of the immigrants eventually settled (Georges 1984). Self-help associations with various recreational, cultural, civic, and political objectives proliferated. Formal organizations often revolved around places of origin, such as a city or town in the Dominican Republic. For example, in New York City the Club de Tamborileños and the Asociación de Banilejos represented two Dominican hometowns. Informal webs of relatives, friends, and neighbors helped organize the community. Political ideology, party affiliation, and class interests often fractured ethnic ties.

Two of the three major political parties of the Dominican Republic were established abroad. In 1939 Juan Bosch founded the Partido Revolucionario Dominicano (PRD), or Dominican Revolutionary Party, in Havana, Cuba, which led the opposition to Trujillo's dictatorship. In 1963, while exiled in New York City, Joaquín Balaguer formed the Partido Revolucionario Social Cristiano (PRSC), or Revolutionary Social Christian Party, later renamed the Reformist Social Christian Party. In 1973 Bosch resigned from the PRD and created the Partido de la Liberación Dominicana (PLD), or Dominican Liberation Party. During the 1970s the two main opposition parties, the PRD and the PLD, developed large followings in New York City, San Juan, and other centers of the diaspora. While right-wing groups persisted abroad, left-wing exiles organized the community at the grassroots. Most of these efforts were initially oriented toward domestic issues in the Dominican Republic, particularly government repression of political dissidents. Over time, they tended to shift their main concerns to the United States, although many of them remained bifocal.

Hometown Associations as Transnational Liaisons

Scholars have increasingly studied migrant organizations that maintain a link with their places of origin and a sense of community based on that origin (Orozco 2002a). These hometown associations are primarily interested in supporting the local development of their sending communities through collective funds. The best known case is that of Mexican associations in the

United States, which number in the thousands. Luin Goldring (2003) and Robert Smith (2006) have shown that such groups have built roads, bridges, and dams; purchased computers for schools and ambulances for hospitals; reconstructed soccer fields and churches; and paved streets and plazas in their hometowns. Most analysts concur that such public works are beneficial to the receiving communities, helping the Mexican state provide for the basic needs of its citizens. A well-regarded model for infrastructural development is the program Tres por Uno (Three for One), where municipal, state, and federal governments match collective remittances. Less studied is the role of Dominican associations in the United States in funneling resources to their places of origin (but see Levitt 2001; Orozco 2002a; and Portes, Escobar, and Radford 2005).

Deepak Lamba-Nieves (2009) has recently examined two Dominican hometown associations in Boston: the Sociedad Progresista de Villa Sombrero (SOPROVIS), or Progressive Society of Villa Sombrero, and the Movimiento para el Desarrollo de Boca Canasta (MODEBO), or Movement for the Development of Boca Canasta. Both were founded in the southwest of the Dominican Republic during the 1970s to address local community needs, especially in education and health care. Both started chapters in the United States, as many of their members relocated in Boston and New York in the late 1970s and early 1980s. SOPROVIS and MODEBO have raised substantial funds for infrastructural projects in their hometowns, such as building a central plaza, a baseball park, a community center, and a funeral home. Their solid financial base has strengthened their role in local community and state structures. Lamba-Nieves concludes that the two organizations have become successful transnational actors in the Dominican Republic. However, the Dominican state has yet to promote community development through partnerships with hometown associations, as has Mexico's Tres por Uno.

Mobilizing and Empowering Migrants

In the 1980s Dominican Americans created umbrella organizations to address their most pressing needs in New York City, such as education, housing, and health (see Aparicio 2006). The largest of these groups is Alianza Dominicana (Dominican Alliance), a comprehensive service and community development agency founded in 1987 that helps children, youth, and families. Alianza began as a support group for various community organizations focusing on local educational issues (Sainz 1990). Nowadays, it operates in fifteen different sites in northern Manhattan and the West Bronx with a budget of more than US$12 million and a staff of more than 350 people.

During the 1980s activists also mobilized the Dominican community to participate in local politics. This mobilization led to the election of several of their compatriots to Manhattan school boards. Former elementary schoolteacher Guillermo Linares was first elected in 1983 to the community board of District 6 in northern Manhattan. In 1991 Washington Heights chose Linares as its first Dominican representative to the New York City Council. In 1996 Adriano Espaillat won the New York State Assembly seat from the 72nd district, which includes Washington Heights. Today, Dominicans are one of the best organized and well-represented Latino communities in New York.

Two important voluntary associations were created in the 1990s: the Dominican American National Roundtable (DANR) and Dominicanos 2000. Founded in Washington, D.C., in 1997, DANR promotes the educational, economic, cultural, and political interests of Dominican Americans through community empowerment, economic development, and planning. It includes representatives from most states with large Dominican populations, such as New York, New Jersey, Rhode Island, Massachusetts, Pennsylvania, and Florida, as well as Puerto Rico and the Dominican Republic. Founded in 1997 in New York City, Dominicanos 2000 is a community-based organization with a strong following among college and high school students, especially those enrolled at the City University of New York. Like DANR, Dominicanos 2000 focuses on the educational advancement and political empowerment of the Dominican American community.

Dominicans have expanded their political representation in the United States, although not yet proportionate to their numbers. While the U.S. House of Representatives does not yet have a Dominican member, several have been elected to state assemblies, in addition to Espaillat. In 2002 José Peralta won a seat in the New York State Assembly, followed by Nelson Castro in 2008. William Lantigua became the first Hispanic state senator in Massachusetts in 2002 and the first Hispanic mayor of Lawrence in 2008. In 2002 Juan Pichardo was elected state senator in Rhode Island, while Grace Díaz was elected state representative in 2004. In 2006 Joselin Peña Melnyk became a Maryland state delegate. As of 2009 at least twenty-one Dominicans were elected officials in city governments throughout the United States. As these figures indicate, Dominican Americans have increased their visibility in U.S. politics, particularly in the northeastern states where they cluster.

Still, Dominican Americans have a long road ahead to empower themselves. In 2009 only 48.2 percent of all foreign-born Dominicans in the United States were naturalized U.S. citizens. Dominicans have one of the lowest naturalization rates among recent migrants, lower than such groups as Cubans (57.9 percent) and Chinese (60.9 percent) (U.S. Census Bureau 2010). In addition, many Dominicans (as many as ninety-one thousand, according to 2000 estimates by the former INS) are undocumented in the United States. Nonetheless, Dominican Americans increased their electoral participation in the United States after the 1994 approval of dual citizenship by the Dominican legislature, which allowed expatriates to become U.S. citizens without relinquishing their Dominican nationality. Dual citizenship offers practical advantages to those who move back and forth between the United States and the Dominican Republic, whether as tourists, returnees, or circular migrants (Weyland 1998).

Like other transnational migrants, Dominicans maintain strong political ties to their home country and cultivate links to the host society. Transnational connections helped elect Dominican leaders in New York, such as Linares and Espaillat (Graham 1998, 2001). Conversely, fundraising trips to New York and San Juan have become standard for presidential candidates in the Dominican Republic. Moreover, ordinary immigrants have developed numerous transnational political practices. Table 8.3 summarizes the findings of a recent survey of Dominicans and other Latinos in the United States. The results show that Dominicans were much more likely than Puerto Ricans, Mexicans, and Salvadorans to engage politically with their home country, except belonging to transnational organizations and seeking assistance from their embassies or consulates.

The Emergence of a Transnational Nation-State

Since the 1960s Dominican politicians have favored migration as a safety valve for demographic and economic pressures, such as overpopulation and unemployment. Between 1966 and 1978 the Balaguer administration exported both surplus workers and political dissidents (Torres-Saillant and Hernández 1998: 42–44). In contrast, Dominican officials have usually perceived Haitian immigration as a threat to national security and identity.

TABLE 8.3 Transnational Political Practices of Latinos in the United States, 2002 (in Percentages)

Practice	Dominicans	Puerto Ricans	Mexicans	Salvadorans
Followed politics of nation of origin in Spanish-language media	67.1	66.5	63.6	48.0
Voted in nation of origin's elections	15.0	14.6	9.5	8.5
Contributed money to candidate running for office or political party in nation of origin	6.3	5.3	2.0	2.8
Attended rally in United States in which home-nation candidate or representative of home-country political party spoke	17.3	11.6	2.7	2.3
Was contacted by home-nation representative to become involved in home-nation political or cultural affairs	11.5	8.1	3.0	1.8
Attended meeting to discuss home-country politics	21.8	14.6	6.2	5.8
Attended cultural or educational event related to home country	43.9	42.7	26.6	23.1
Been member of organization promoting cultural ties between United States and home country	12.8	15.2	6.7	5.6
Been member of organization of people from respondent's hometown	22.6	12.1	8.5	7.8
Sought assistance from embassy or consulate (for non–Puerto Rican respondents) or Puerto Rican government (for Puerto Rican respondents)	3.0	4.5	6.0	5.0

Source: DeSipio et al. 2003.

Since the 1980s government authorities have expressed concern for migrants returning from the United States, blaming them for the Dominican Republic's crime rate and drug addiction. Immigration thus has officially been labeled as a social problem, while emigration has usually appeared as a short-term economic solution. Return migration has also been deemed problematic culturally and linguistically.

The Dominican state has created numerous institutional mechanisms to incorporate its diaspora. In 1991 the Dominican Congress exempted overseas Dominicans from import duties for gifts brought to the country during the Christmas season. In 1994 it extended to migrants all the political rights of their compatriots, except running for president and vice president (Itzigsohn and Villacrés 2008; Ríos 1995). The constitutional amendment also granted Dominican citizenship to those born abroad to Dominican parents. In 1994 José Fernández was elected to the Dominican Congress while living in New York.

In 1996 Leonel Fernández — who spent much of his childhood and adolescence in Washington Heights — was elected president of the Dominican Republic and subsequently reelected in 2004 and 2008. Under his presidency, the Dominican government has encouraged investment in the Dominican Republic by overseas Dominicans, as well as their repatriation. In October 2000 the Dominican House of Representatives held a seminar in Puerto Rico to identify the needs of the émigré community, including the protection of its civil rights and political participation back home (Cámara de Diputados 2002). The right to vote from abroad in the country's presidential elections, approved in 1997, was first implemented in 2004. That year, some 52,500 Dominicans living in the United States, Puerto Rico, Spain, Venezuela, Canada, Italy, the Netherlands, Switzerland, and other countries registered to vote in Dominican presidential elections.

In 2006 Leonel Fernández created the Presidential Program to Support Dominican Communities Abroad. This initiative was part of the president's commitment to integrate the Dominican exodus into the country's development. In 2008 the Dominican Congress passed a law establishing the National Council for Dominican Communities Abroad. Moreover, the Fernández administration has increased the number of consular appointments among émigré leaders in New York City, San Juan, and other cities. In short, the Dominican Republic has become a transnational nation-state that extends "beyond the state's territorial boundaries and incorporates dispersed populations" (Fouron and Glick Schiller 2001: 20).

Dominicans from "Here" and "There"

Whether deemed "transnational" or "diasporic," Dominicans retain multiple connections at home and abroad (*los países*), especially in the United States. During the first half of the twentieth century, the United States established a commanding presence in the Dominican Republic. During the second half of the century, the Dominican population dispersed widely. The two phenomena — neocolonial domination and mass migration — are closely intertwined. Today, the Dominican Republic has extensive political, economic, and cultural ties with the United States, as well as with Puerto Rico, Spain, and other countries where migrants have resettled in large numbers.

The Dominican Republic has become one of the chief examples of a transnational nation-state that defines its members not according to birthplace, residence, or even citizenship, but according to blood ties and shared descent (Glick Schiller 1999). Regardless of where they were born or what passport they hold, Dominican migrants and their descendants are officially deemed part of the Dominican nation. Like other transnational nation-states, the Dominican Republic has reclaimed its emigrants even if they become citizens of other countries. As members of a transnational community, many Dominicans shuttle between "here" and "there" in their daily lives. In the next chapter, I explore the transnational practices of Dominicans in Puerto Rico.

The Dominican Diaspora to Puerto Rico

A Transnational Perspective

Since the 1960s the secondary concentration of overseas Dominicans has been in Puerto Rico, a U.S. territory with higher living standards than the Dominican Republic but with a similar geography, history, culture, and language.[1] Although Puerto Rico has often served as a springboard to the U.S. mainland, a bustling Dominican community has emerged in San Juan, displacing Cubans as the leading sector of the foreign-born population. By 1980 San Juan had the second-largest number of Dominicans outside the Dominican Republic, after New York City. Their demographic and cultural significance for contemporary Dominican transnationalism cannot be overlooked.

Elsewhere I have argued that Dominican migration is "characterized by a constant flow of people in both directions, a dual sense of identity, ambivalent attachments to two nations, and a far-flung network of kinship and friendship ties across state frontiers" (Duany 2008b [1994]: 24). In chapter 8 I elaborated a transnational framework to understand the massive flow of people between the Dominican Republic and the United States. Here I show that Dominicans in Puerto Rico retain strong social, economic, and political links with their homeland. This case exemplifies how contemporary migrants reconstruct their national, ethnic, and racial identities across borders and boundaries.

This chapter provides a panoramic view of transnational migration from the Dominican Republic to Puerto Rico, emphasizing several themes. First, the two neighboring countries have had extensive ties at least since the days of Spanish colonialism. Second, although political disturbances initiated the

Dominican diaspora in the 1960s, it is now driven primarily by economic forces. Third, the migrants' regional and socioeconomic origins as well as their incorporation into the host economy have shifted over time. Finally, Dominicans have developed many transnational practices in Puerto Rico, particularly through political parties, hometown clubs, and other voluntary associations.

Historical Background

Transnational Connections

Close links between what are now the Dominican Republic and Puerto Rico date back to pre-Columbian times, when Arawak peoples from the Amazon basin of South America settled both territories. Spain conquered the two countries in the late fifteenth and early sixteenth centuries and remained in control until the nineteenth century. Throughout the Spanish colonial period, a small number of state bureaucrats, soldiers, clerics, professionals, students, artisans, and slaves shuttled between the two territories. In addition to official trade, contraband flourished across the Mona Channel dividing Hispaniola from Puerto Rico (Pérez Memén 1989; Rosario Natal 1990). During the nineteenth century, hundreds of residents of Hispaniola sought refuge in Puerto Rico, primarily as a result of political upheavals, such as Spain's cession of Hispaniola to France (1795), the triumph of the Haitian Revolution (1804), and the Haitian occupation of Santo Domingo (1822–44). The émigrés included white property owners, black slaves, and free colored workers who tended to settle in Puerto Rico's western cities, particularly Mayagüez, San Germán, and Cabo Rojo (Camuñas Madera 1999; Chinea 2005; Marazzi 1974; Rosario Natal 1995).

The primary direction of the migrant flow reversed itself at the end of the nineteenth century and the beginning of the twentieth. As I noted in chapter 4, increasing numbers of Puerto Ricans sought employment in the Dominican Republic. The development of the Dominican sugar industry, centered in the provinces of San Pedro de Macorís, La Romana, and Puerto Plata, attracted thousands of workers from other Caribbean islands, including Puerto Rico. Historians have documented the growing Puerto Rican presence in the Dominican Republic during the first three decades of the twentieth century (del Castillo 1990 [1981]; Pérez Memén 1989; Rosario Natal 1983; Soto Toledo 1998). In 1920 the Dominican census counted 6,069

Puerto Ricans, representing 12.2 percent of all foreign-born residents (Secretaría de Estado 1923: 129).

Because of their linguistic, cultural, and religious affinities, Puerto Ricans and Dominicans quickly intermarried. The children of such unions usually identified themselves as Dominican. The two most famous cases are former presidents Joaquín Balaguer and Juan Bosch, both of whom had Dominican and Puerto Rican parents. Pedro Mir, one of the most distinguished poets of the Dominican Republic, had a Puerto Rican mother. The prominent Puerto Rican writer José Luis González was born in Santo Domingo but moved to Puerto Rico at a young age; his father was Puerto Rican and his mother Dominican.

Between 1930 and 1960 few Puerto Ricans migrated to the Dominican Republic and few Dominicans migrated to Puerto Rico. In 1935 the Dominican census counted 3,221 Puerto Ricans (Senior 1947: 69). During the 1940s Puerto Rican migration to the Dominican Republic practically ceased. After World War II the vast majority of Puerto Rican migrants relocated to the U.S. mainland, especially New York City (ch. 4). By 1950 the Dominican census found only 2,216 Puerto Ricans (Oficina Nacional del Censo 1958: 135). Because of strict controls by the Trujillo regime, most Dominicans were unable to travel abroad; those who did were mostly entrepreneurs, professionals, or exiles, including several hundred who settled in Puerto Rico (Herrera Mora 2008). In 1960 the Puerto Rican census counted 1,812 Dominican-born residents (U.S. Census Bureau 1961). Some of these were descendants of earlier Puerto Rican migrants.

Large-scale migration from the Dominican Republic to Puerto Rico took off after 1965. That year the INS reported only 4,709 alien residents of Puerto Rico, born in the Dominican Republic (Duany 1990: 30). Between 1966 and 2009 134,834 Dominican immigrants were admitted in San Juan (see figure 9.1). This figure represents 12.5 percent of the Dominican exodus to the United States during this period (U.S. Citizenship and Immigration Services 2009). In addition, thousands have entered the island without government authorization or overstayed their tourist visas. Census data confirm the spectacular growth of Puerto Rico's Dominican population, multiplying nearly forty times between 1960 and 2009 (figure 9.2). At the same time, Dominicans increased their share of the foreign-born more than threefold. No other sector of Puerto Rico's population has grown as quickly as the Dominican-born over the last three decades. Dominicans are now the largest and most visible minority group in Puerto Rico.

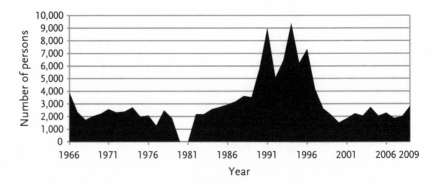

FIGURE 9.1 Dominican Immigrants Admitted to Puerto Rico, 1966–2009

Sources: U.S. Citizenship and Immigration Services 2002–9; U.S. Department of Justice 1967–77, 1978–95, 1996–2001.

Note: The INS did not report separate data for Dominican immigrants in Puerto Rico before 1966. No data were reported for 1980 and 1981. For 2007 the available data refer to U.S. dependencies.

A Politically Motivated Exodus

Political instability largely drove the first stage of Dominican emigration during the 1960s (Georges 1984; Grasmuck and Pessar 1991; Torres-Saillant and Hernández 1998). The earliest groups to leave the Dominican Republic after 1961 were primarily those linked with the Trujillo dictatorship. Among those who briefly sought refuge in Puerto Rico in 1962 was former President Balaguer. A year later, a civic-military coalition overthrew President Bosch, who went into exile in San Juan, where he had previously lived. The 1965 civil war and U.S. invasion of Santo Domingo led to further migration to Puerto Rico.

Political factors have continued to play a role in the Dominican exodus, even during periods of relative democratization. Figure 9.1 shows that migration to Puerto Rico has tended to peak in years of presidential elections in the Dominican Republic. For instance, Balaguer's election in 1966 and reelection in 1970, 1974, 1986, and 1990 spurred migration to Puerto Rico. When Balaguer died in 2002, many expatriates in San Juan felt relieved because of his prominent role during the Trujillo era and subsequent repressive tactics. Today, the immigrant community is split among the three major parties in the Dominican Republic — the PRD, the PLD, and the PRSC. Because of their ideological diversity, Dominicans in Puerto Rico do not form a single voting bloc or lobbying group; nor do they have a unified voice in the Dominican Republic. I will return to this point shortly.

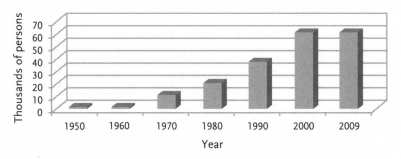

FIGURE 9.2 Dominican-Born Population of Puerto Rico, 1950–2009

Sources: U.S. Census Bureau 1953, 1961, 1973, 1984, 1993, 2010.

Searching for a Better Life

As I discussed in chapter 8, material hardship has increasingly motivated the Dominican exodus. When asked why they moved to Puerto Rico, many Dominicans simply reply, "searching for a better life [*buscando mejor vida*]." Three-fifths of those surveyed in Santurce, an area of San Juan with a large Dominican population, said they were looking for a job or higher salaries (Thompson 1990: 107). Most had been employed in the Dominican Republic, many as skilled workers such as mechanics, masons, seamstresses, and nurses. Other studies have confirmed that Dominican migration to Puerto Rico draws primarily on the employed labor force (Pascual Morán and Figueroa 2000; Peralta 1995). The basic economic rationale for the large-scale displacement of Dominicans to Puerto Rico is the wide discrepancy between the wage levels of the two countries — especially since the U.S. dollar, the currency used in Puerto Rico, is much stronger than the Dominican peso. Hence, emigration has become a common survival strategy for lower- and middle-class Dominicans. Economic and political crises under President Hipólito Mejía (2000–2004) prompted further emigration, which continued unabated during President Leonel Fernández's second and third terms (2004–12).

Differences between Puerto Rico–Bound and U.S.-Bound Migration

Dominican migration to Puerto Rico differs from migration to the United States on several counts. First, the volume of Dominican migrants to the island is much smaller than the one to the mainland (about one-eighth of all those admitted between 1966 and 2009). Second, Dominicans in Puerto Rico tend to be less educated than those in the United States.[2] In 2009 only 49.7 percent of Dominicans in Puerto Rico had completed high school, compared to 64.1 percent in the United States. Third, Dominicans in Puerto Rico are more likely to be service, construction, maintenance, and repair workers (59.5 percent) than in the United States (40.3 percent). Fourth, most Dominicans in Puerto Rico are employed in construction, domestic service, and retail trade, whereas Dominicans in the United States concentrate in education, health care, food services, and retail trade (U.S. Census Bureau 2010). Finally, as I elaborate below, a much larger proportion of Dominicans is undocumented in Puerto Rico than in the United States.

The main contrasts between Puerto Rico–bound and U.S.-bound migration can be attributed to geographic, economic, and cultural factors. A flight from Santo Domingo to San Juan lasts only about forty-five minutes, and even an unauthorized trip in a makeshift boat (*yola*) across the sixty-mile Mona Channel usually takes between twenty-six and twenty-eight hours, depending on weather conditions and travel routes. Furthermore, a ferry service provides cheap transportation for passengers, vehicles, and other heavy items between Santo Domingo and San Juan, as well as Mayagüez. One reason Dominicans often mention for settling in Puerto Rico is that it is much closer than the United States, and many plan to go back home (Romero Anico 1984). Moreover, the Puerto Rican economy continues to demand cheap labor, particularly in the service, construction, and agricultural industries. Compared to the U.S. mainland, the island provides proportionally more opportunities for low-wage and unskilled employment. Culturally, Puerto Rico and the Dominican Republic have much in common, from similar Caribbean dialects of Spanish, to a shared Catholic heritage, to popular tastes in food, music, and sports. A transnational lifestyle is easier to sustain for Dominicans in Puerto Rico than in the United States.

The Rise of Undocumented Migration

Because Puerto Rico is so near to the Dominican Republic, undocumented migration from the Dominican Republic is much more common in Puerto Rico than on the U.S. mainland (see Enchautegui 2000). Many Dominicans have used Puerto Rico as a stepping stone to the continental United States. As a result, U.S. immigration authorities have increased their presence at

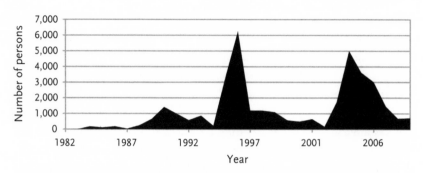

FIGURE 9.3 Undocumented Dominicans Interdicted at Sea by the U.S. Coast Guard, 1982–2009

Source: U.S. Coast Guard 2009.

San Juan's international airport and have even stationed Puerto Rican officers at airports in New York City and Philadelphia, to detain Dominicans trying to pass as Puerto Ricans.

It is extremely difficult to assess the size of the undocumented population in Puerto Rico and in the United States. In 1996 U.S. immigration officials estimated that thirty-four thousand undocumented immigrants — mostly from the Dominican Republic — lived in Puerto Rico, compared to seventy-five thousand undocumented Dominicans in the United States (*Migration News* 1997; U.S. Department of Justice 1998). According to these figures, the ratio of undocumented to documented Dominicans is almost six times higher in Puerto Rico than on the mainland.

The first unauthorized trip from the Dominican Republic to Puerto Rico was reported in 1972, when a small group tried to sail across the Mona Passage in a *yola*. Between 1982 and 2009, the U.S. Coast Guard intercepted nearly thirty-seven thousand undocumented Dominicans at sea (see figure 9.3). Moreover, the INS office in San Juan removed an annual average of about thirty-five hundred undocumented immigrants during the 1990s (U.S. Department of Justice 1990–95; U.S. Department of Justice 1996–2000). More than 90 percent of the deportees were from the Dominican Republic, although other Latin American and Caribbean countries were represented in the figures, including Colombia, Ecuador, Haiti, and Cuba (Duany, Hernández Angueira, and Rey 1995). The Mona Passage has become a major entry route into U.S. territory for alien smugglers, after the land frontier with Mexico. This point becomes even more dramatic when one remembers the calamities suffered by those who travel clandestinely. Although no one knows exactly how many *yolas* capsize every year, hundreds of Dominicans have drowned in the perilous sea journey. In 1980 the suffocation of twenty-two Dominican stowaways aboard the cargo ship *Regina Express*, bound for Miami, drew international attention to the human costs of smuggling undocumented immigrants.

Several scholars have traced a profile of undocumented migrants from the Dominican Republic to Puerto Rico (del Castillo 1989; Duany, Hernández Angueira, and Rey 1995; Graziano 2006; Hernández and López 1997; Pascual Morán and Figueroa 2000; Ricourt 2007; Selman Fernández, Tavarez María, and Puello Nina 1990). The *yolas* usually depart from the eastern ports of Higüey, Samaná, Boca de Yuma, and La Romana in the Dominican Republic and arrive on the western coast of Puerto Rico, especially in Rincón, Añasco, Aguadilla, Aguada, Mayagüez, and Cabo Rojo. In 2010, the cost of a trip ranged between US$400 and US$2,000 per person. Most of the passengers are young men with an elementary education and an unskilled job in the Dominican Republic. Some are poor women who were employed as domestic and factory workers or informal traders. Once in Puerto Rico, they tend to move to the San Juan metropolitan area, where relatives and friends help them find work and housing. Many end up in the urban informal sector, particularly in itinerant trade, construction, or domestic service. Others continue their journey to New York City and elsewhere on the U.S. mainland.

The proportion of undocumented immigrants in Puerto Rico varies widely by time and place of settlement. Only 7 percent of those interviewed in the early 1980s said they had entered U.S. territory without authorization, while 35 percent overstayed their tourist visas (Romero Anico 1984). In Barrio Gandul in Santurce, about a third of the Dominican residents were undocumented in 1990 (Duany, Hernández Angueira, and Rey 1995). In Barrio Capetillo in Río Piedras, nearly 59 percent of the Dominican interviewees admitted they had arrived in Puerto Rico without legal documents; most had regularized their status by marrying U.S. citizens or permanent residents (Peralta 1995). A similar proportion of undocumented Dominicans was found in the highland *municipios* (counties) of Lares, Maricao, Las Marías, San Sebastián, and Yauco (Pascual Morán and Figueroa 2000). It is difficult to calculate the exact number of unauthorized immigrants for Puerto Rico as a whole, because field studies have focused on small and statistically unrepresentative samples. One estimate based on census and immigration data suggests that roughly 28 percent of all Dominicans in Puerto Rico in 1996 were undocumented (Enchautegui 2000).

In his memoirs, Raúl Martínez Rosado (2006) has chronicled the complications of traveling from the Dominican Republic to Puerto Rico by *yola*. He begins his account in 1986 in La Romana, where the boat's captain organized the trip and met his nearly seventy passengers. Then they moved on to Higüey, where they embarked early the next morning, but Martínez Rosado was forced to go back home because the overcrowded boat capsized near the Dominican coast.

After staying a few days in his poor neighborhood in Santo Domingo, Martínez Rosado attempted to travel again from La Romana. Three weeks later, he boarded another *yola* in Punta Cana, along with sixty-six passengers. After more than twenty-four hours at sea, the group landed in Desecheo, an uninhabited island off the west coast of Puerto Rico. Five hours later, the boat docked in Cabo Rojo. Martínez Rosado and most of his shipmates eventually found their way to Santurce, especially Barrio Obrero, and Río Piedras. In Santurce, Martínez Rosado stayed with an uncle for several months, but he decided to relocate to Chicago, where a Dominican friend would help him find a job. He bypassed the immigration officer at San Juan's airport by speaking English when asked about his citizenship.

Transnational Origins and Destinations

Regional Origins

Table 9.1 compares the migrants' place of birth and last residence in the Dominican Republic, according to two surveys of Dominicans in Santurce and Río Piedras. In 1987 slightly less than half was born in the four largest cities, with about a third in Santo Domingo. Another third was born in the Cibao region. The proportion of migrants who lived in Santo Domingo, however, was 12 percent larger than those who were born there. The proportion of those who were born and resided in Santiago de los Caballeros, San Pedro de Macorís, and the southeast was about the same. By 2006 the share of immigrants born in major urban areas had risen to more than 56 percent, while those from the Cibao had decreased to less than 13 percent. Most Dominicans thus had urban experience before moving to Puerto Rico.

Even undocumented Dominicans in Puerto Rico's coffee industry have a predominantly urban background (Pascual Morán and Figueroa 2000: 17). However, most Dominicans in Barrio Capetillo were born in the eastern provinces of the Dominican Republic, especially the coastal towns of Nagua,

TABLE 9.1 Regional Origins of the Dominican Population of San Juan, 1987 and 2006 (in Percentages)

Place	1987 Birthplace	1987 Last Residence in D.R.	2006 Birthplace
MAIN CITIES			
Santo Domingo	33.5	45.5	40.4
Santiago de los Caballeros	4.2	1.8	2.6
La Romana	4.2	5.5	8.4
San Pedro de Macorís	3.2	0.0	1.3
San Francisco de Macorís	—	—	3.9
Subtotal	45.1	52.8	56.6
OTHER AREAS			
Cibao	31.9	31.8	12.9
Southeast	14.5	10.0	7.9
Southwest	1.3	1.8	—
Unclassified	7.1	3.6	22.6
Subtotal	54.8	47.2	43.4

Sources: Duany 1990, 2007.
Note: First column does not add up to 100 percent because of rounding.

Miches, and Higüey (Duany 2007; Peralta 1995). These towns send many undocumented Dominicans to Puerto Rico. Such differences suggest that the migrants' regional origins vary according to their community of settlement, as well as the sampling frames used by researchers.

Socioeconomic Backgrounds

Most studies agree that the contemporary Dominican diaspora originates primarily among the lower middle sectors of Dominican society (Báez Evertsz and d'Oleo Ramírez 1985; Castro and Boswell 2002; Ramona Hernández 2002; Levitt 2001; Pessar 1995; Ugalde, Bean, and Cárdenas 1979). Most of the immigrants surveyed in Santurce had been skilled or semiskilled workers in their home country. Almost 43 percent had white-collar jobs, such as sales and administrative occupations, prior to moving abroad. In addition, 58 percent worked in trade and services, especially personal, business, and repair services. Only about 11 percent was employed in agriculture (Duany 1990). These data confirm that Dominican migrants to Puerto Rico tend to

TABLE 9.2 Occupational Distribution of Dominican and Puerto Rican Workers in Puerto Rico, 1970–2009 (in Percentages)

	1970		1980		1990		2009	
Occupation	Domini-can	Puerto Rican	Domini-can	Puerto Rican	Domini-can	Puerto Rican	Domini-can	Puerto Rican
Managerial, profes-sional, and related	24.3	10.8	12.3	19.5	15.7	23.1	12.9	29.1
Technical, sales, and administrative support	19.2	24.5	22.0	26.1	21.1	26.0	17.4	28.2
Precision production, craft, and repair	20.5	15.2	16.7	12.8	13.7	12.2	10.2	12.2
Operators, fabricators, and laborers	16.2	20.7	14.9	23.0	16.2	21.0	16.6	9.8
Service	19.2	13.2	33.7	14.9	31.9	14.9	42.9	20.1
Farming, forestry, and fishing	0.6	8.4	0.4	3.7	1.4	2.8	0.1	0.7

Sources: For 1970, Vázquez Calzada and Morales del Valle 1979; for 1980, U.S. Census Bureau 1984; for 1990, Rivera Román 2004; for 2009, U.S. Census Bureau 2010.

Note: Seventh and eighth columns do not add up to 100 percent because of rounding.

be more skilled than the population of the Dominican Republic and to come from the tertiary sector of the economy. An exception to this trend is the high proportion (nearly 61 percent) who were agricultural workers in the Dominican Republic and now work as coffee pickers in Puerto Rico (Pascual Morán and Figueroa 2000: 22).

Economic Incorporation

Census data collected since 1970 confirm the presence of two main waves of Dominican immigrants in Puerto Rico. As the Dominican sociologist José del Castillo (1989: 56) has pointed out, a largely middle-class and documented cohort arrived during the 1960s, whereas the working-class and undocu-mented flow rose since the 1980s. In 1970 Dominican immigrants included a larger share of upper-status workers, such as managers and professionals, than among natives of Puerto Rico (see table 9.2). An early demographic study described Dominicans in Puerto Rico as an occupationally "select

TABLE 9.3 Industrial Distribution of Dominican and Puerto Rican Workers in Puerto Rico, 1970–2009 (in Percentages)

	1970		1980		1990		2009	
Industry	Domini- can	Puerto Rican	Domini- can	Puerto Rican	Domini- can	Puerto Rican	Domini- can	Puerto Rican
Agriculture, forestry, fishing, and mining	1.2	9.4	0.8	4.8	1.5	4.0	0.4	1.3
Manufacturing	9.9	20.0	20.5	21.4	11.3	17.0	3.9	10.1
Construction	16.8	12.2	6.7	8.6	10.9	8.6	14.0	6.7
Transportation and communications	5.6	8.4	4.3	6.8	6.0	8.8	3.2	5.2
Trade	30.4	15.9	29.7	16.5	27.9	16.4	12.8	15.8
Finance, insurance, and real estate	0.6	2.3	3.2	3.1	2.3	3.6	2.7	5.5
Public administration	2.5	7.9	4.4	12.8	5.3	15.1	1.6	10.4
Services	33.0	23.9	30.3	26.1	34.8	26.5	61.4	44.8

Sources: For 1970, Vázquez Calzada and Morales del Valle 1979; for 1980, U.S. Census Bureau 1984; for 1990, Ruggles et al. 2009; for 2009, U.S. Census Bureau 2010.

Note: Eighth column does not add up to 100 percent because of rounding.

group," a "privileged" minority, and "an elite from an educational viewpoint" (Vázquez Calzada and Morales del Valle 1979: 18, 31, 33). This characterization coincides with other studies of the Dominican diaspora during the 1960s and 1970s (Funkhouser and Ramos 1993; Grasmuck and Pessar 1991; Pessar 1995).

After 1970 the proportion of Dominican service workers in Puerto Rico grew substantially, while the proportion of managers and professionals declined abruptly. By 1980 Dominicans concentrated in the lower rungs of Puerto Rico's labor force. In 2009 more than two-fifths were service workers such as housekeepers, maids, cashiers, and security guards; one-fourth were operators, laborers, craft, and repair workers, including those in construction. Among white-collar workers, only sales and office employees represented a sizable proportion. Compared to natives of Puerto Rico, Dominican immigrants were more likely to have lower-status jobs. In sum, most Dominicans have incorporated into Puerto Rico's secondary labor market, characterized by low wages, poor working conditions, limited opportunities for upward mobility, and job instability.

Table 9.3 shows that the industrial distribution of Dominican workers in Puerto Rico has increasingly concentrated in services and construction. Between 1970 and 1990 three-fifths of the immigrants clustered in services (particularly domestic and other personal services) and in trade (especially retail trade). The proportion of Dominican workers in manufacturing increased between 1970 and 1980 but decreased between 1980 and 2009; conversely, those employed in the construction industry first decreased and then increased during the same period. By 2009 three out of five Dominican workers in Puerto Rico were in service industries. In Santurce and Río Piedras, women are predominantly employed in domestic service, while men concentrate in retail trade, repair services, and construction (Duany 1990; Duany, Hernández Angueira, and Rey 1995; Peralta 1995). In the inner highlands of Puerto Rico, Dominican men are primarily seasonal agricultural workers (Pascual Morán and Figueroa 2000). These patterns of economic incorporation reflect a split labor market between Dominicans and Puerto Ricans. They also suggest that most Dominican workers have not displaced Puerto Rican workers but have filled a void in the island's low-wage labor force.

Transnational Practices

Political Parties

The primary form of organization among Dominicans in Puerto Rico is the political party. As I have mentioned, the leading Dominican parties have been active in San Juan for decades. All have been important fundraising venues for presidential candidates in the Dominican Republic. In turn, the Dominican consulates in San Juan, Mayagüez, and Ponce have become symbolic prizes for immigrant leaders affiliated with the ruling party in the home country. A study of these leaders has documented their extensive activities, community bases, and strong links to the Dominican power structure (Iturrondo 2000). Dominican parties operating in Puerto Rico as well as in the United States provide the best example of political transnationalism (Graham 2001; Itzigsohn et al. 1999; Levitt 2001). So far, they have promoted the immigrants' participation in Dominican politics more than in Puerto Rican politics.

Hometown Associations

A second type of transnational organization is the hometown club — a social or cultural association based on its members' regional origins. For instance, former residents of Cotuí, Jarabacoa, La Romana, La Vega, and Puerto Plata have formed their own groups in Puerto Rico (table 9.4). These clubs usually organize trips back home, donate medical supplies to their compatriots, and celebrate special occasions such as Carnival. Most are highly informal organizations centered on strong leaders and their personal cliques. The Puerto Rican sociologist Milagros Iturrondo (2000: 85) provides a gloomy assessment of these voluntary associations: "Some organizations are created with the goal of institutionalizing themselves as entities at the service of their community. The goal is often lost, however, when the leadership faces a power struggle. We also observe a pattern in which organizations usually end up disintegrating. . . when the leadership does not consult its base in decision-making processes. The panorama is one of multiple atomized organizations that appear and disappear, even after being legally registered."

Religious Groups

Researchers have identified only one voluntary association with an explicit religious focus among Dominicans in Puerto Rico. The Asociación 21 de Enero, founded in Río Piedras in 1980, is a Catholic organization devoted to the Virgin of Altagracia. With only eighteen members in the early 1990s, this group sponsored religious and charitable activities, such as rosaries, pilgrimages, masses, and donations. However, according to the Dominican planner Reyna Peralta (1995), it constituted a very small, closed, and informal group with few connections to the Dominican community of Barrio Capetillo.

Iturrondo (2000) mentions a few other Dominican associations loosely centered on the cult of the Virgin in Santurce and Río Piedras. Dominicans also are active in Protestant denominations, such as Seventh-Day Adventists, Baptists, Episcopalians, Lutherans, and Pentecostals. A homegrown church, the Iglesia de Mita, has expanded into the Dominican Republic and other Latin American countries. Dominicans have also contributed to the growth of Gagá (an African-derived religion from Haiti and the Dominican Republic), Afro-Cuban Santería, and *espiritismo* (spiritism) in Puerto Rico. Unfortunately, the linkages of these religious organizations with the Dominican Republic have not been studied to date.

Social Clubs

According to anthropologist Eugenia Georges (1984: 22–23), Dominican social clubs in New York "have as their overtly stated objective to bring members together for informal socializing, as well as more formally organized activities such as competitive sports, raffles, dances, lectures, and so on." Dominicans have established several recreational associations in Puerto Rico, such as La Casa Dominicana del Oeste in Mayagüez and smaller social clubs in Santurce (see table 9.4). La Casa Dominicana was founded in 1977 under the motto "Unity, peace, and harmony" to foster "the healthy recreation and improvement of our cultural heritage within the framework of fraternal links with the Puerto Rican people" (*Hablando de Quisqueya en Borinquen* 1992: 14). With more than five hundred members, the club celebrated a family day in honor of all mothers in the western region of Puerto Rico. Other activities included sponsoring a softball team, a domino tournament, and public lectures. Unfortunately, La Casa Dominicana lacked its own locale and physical structure. A similar initiative in San Juan has faced the same problem.

Other Voluntary Associations

The largest number of Dominican organizations in Puerto Rico includes a wide variety of professional and occupational groups (table 9.4). Some voluntary associations represent the entrepreneurial, commercial, and academic sectors of the immigrant community, while others are composed of engineers, journalists, radio announcers, tailors, and workers. Until now, umbrella organizations, such as the Concilio de Organizaciones Dominicanas and the Unión Internacional de Dominicanos Inmigrantes, have been short-lived. Dominican associations in San Juan are fewer, weaker, and less integrated than in New York, which boasted around 125 such groups in the 1980s (Georges 1984). Although more than forty Dominican organizations have been reported in Puerto Rico (José Germán Gómez, personal communication, March 16, 1995), most are small, fragmented, and unable to articulate a unified voice.

A formerly active member of the Dominican community in Puerto Rico who relocated to New York has identified four of its main organizational challenges (Gómez 1993). First, the reproduction of Dominican institutions — especially political parties, labor unions, and newspapers — continues to

TABLE 9.4 Main Dominican Organizations in Puerto Rico, ca. 2000

Organization	Year Founded	Main Location	Representative
POLITICAL PARTIES			
Partido Reformista Social Cristiano (PRSC)	1963	Santurce	Martín Taveras Guzmán
Partido de la Liberación Dominicana (PLD)	1973	Río Piedras	Ismael Luna
Partido Revolucionario Dominicano (PRD)	1966	Santurce	Rolando Acosta
HOMETOWN ASSOCIATIONS			
Amigos de Cotuí	—	Santurce	Cristina Salas de Saviñón
Amigos de Jarabacoa	—	—	Generoso Hernández
Asociación de Veganos	1996	Santurce	Frank Capellán
Asociación Hijos y Amigos de Puerto Plata	1994	—	Rosa Torréns
Asociación Hijos y Amigos de La Romana	—	—	Luis Antonio Island Eusebio
RELIGIOUS ASSOCIATION			
Asociación 21 de Enero	1980	Río Piedras	Reynaldo Cruz
SOCIAL AND CULTURAL CLUBS			
Asociación Cultural Antillana	—	—	—
Centro Cultural Dominicano	—	Santurce	—
Casa Dominicana del Oeste	1977	Mayagüez	Paulina Concepción
Club Cultural Dominicanos Unidos	1973	Santurce	Fernando Rodríguez
Comunidad de Confraternidad Dominicana	1992	Trujillo Alto	Francisco Cabrera
Fraternidad de Dominicanos Radicados en Puerto Rico[a]	—	Cayey	—

TABLE 9.4 (*continued*)

Organization	Year Founded	Main Location	Representative
CIVIC AND PROFESSIONAL GROUPS			
Asociación de Ingenieros, Arquitectos y Agrimensores Dominicanos Residentes en Puerto Rico	1980	—	José Acevedo Alfam
Asociación de Investigadores y Profesores Universitarios Dominicanos en Puerto Rico	1986	Río Piedras	César Lozano
Asociación de Periodistas Dominicanos en Puerto Rico	1985	—	Héctor Julio Hernández
Asociación de Sastres y Modistas en Puerto Rico	1980	—	Miguel de la Cruz
Centro de la Mujer Dominicana	2003	Río Piedras	Romelinda Grullón
Círculo Dominicano de Locutores	—	—	—
Comité Pro Mejor Imagen Dominicanos	—	—	José Germán Gómez
Concilio de Organizaciones Dominicanas en Puerto Rico	1992	—	—
Dominicanos 2000	1994	—	Elvin Santana
Federación de Comerciantes y Empresarios Dominicanos	—	Santurce	Pablo Puello
Federación de Mujeres Socialdemócratas	1996	Santurce	Celeste Reyna
Fundación Domínico Puertorriqueña	1993	—	Héctor Julio Hernández
Movimiento de Orientación al Emigrante	—	Santurce	Rodolfo de la Cruz
Movimiento de Unidad Obrera Dominicana	—	—	Saúl Pérez
Unión Internacional de Dominicanos Inmigrantes	—	—	Felipe Brazobán Fortunato

Sources: Adapted from Iturrondo 2000 and Peralta 1995.

divide the immigrants. Second, Dominicans' apparent lack of interest in integrating into Puerto Rican society increases their social and political marginality. Third, the constant movement of people among the Dominican Republic, Puerto Rico, and the United States contributes to the turnover of community leaders and followers. Finally, discrimination against Dominicans in Puerto Rico militates against the creation of ethnic organizations.

Gender Matters

Several essays, theses, and films have focused on Dominican women in Puerto Rico (María Casal 1992; de la Rosa Abreu 2002; Fritz 1990; Hernández and López 1997; Hernández Angueira 1990, 1997; Herrera Mora 2008). The 1987 survey that I directed found that three out of five Dominicans in Santurce were women (Duany 1990). In 2009 the Puerto Rico Community Survey estimated that 55.3 percent of the Dominican population was female (U.S. Census Bureau 2010). The predominantly female character of the Dominican exodus is primarily a function of the demand for cheap labor in Puerto Rico, particularly in domestic service, home care, restaurants, and cafeterias. In 2009 more than half (56.9 percent) of all Dominican women in Puerto Rico were service workers (ibid.).

Most Dominican women in San Juan are relatively young, between twenty and forty years of age, single or divorced, with an average of eight years of schooling and prior experience in domestic service before migrating. Many leave their immediate family in the Dominican Republic because of the high risk of traveling (often illegally) and the cost of living in Puerto Rico. Women are often the first household members to move abroad, initiating a chain migration as other relatives later join them in San Juan. Once settled there, many women legalize their status through marriage with U.S. citizens and eventually "ask for" their sons and daughters who remain back home under the care of grandparents, uncles and aunts, and other kin.

For many Dominican women, the migration experience represents a rupture in their family structure. In our 1987 and 2006 samples, Dominican women headed 56 percent of all households, with or without husbands present. Barely half of all Dominican households were nuclear families; the rest were extended families or single-person households (Duany 1990, 2007). In many cases, wives and mothers were temporarily separated from their husbands and children. Thus, migration is often associated with marital disruption and divorce. Such shifts in gender and family roles are primarily due to women's incorporation into the paid labor force, as well as changing fertility patterns, and frequently lead to more egalitarian relations between men and women. Consequently, men are more likely than women to plan to return to the Dominican Republic, where they can reestablish conventional patterns of male authority. Dominican women in Puerto Rico as well as in the United States tend to postpone going back home, for fear of losing their increased autonomy as wives, mothers, and workers (see Grasmuck and Pessar 1991; Guarnizo 1995; Hernández Angueira 1990; and Pessar 1995). While many Dominican men believe they have the right to control women, the latter often resist gender subordination (Hernández and López 1997; Ricourt 2002).

The Problem of Racial Identity

Several studies have documented the difficulties faced by Dominican immigrants because of their dark complexion (see, e.g., Bailey 2002; Candelario 2007; Duany 1998b; and Itzigsohn and Dore-Cabral 2000). Although the vast majority of Dominicans consider themselves *indios* (literally "Indians," figuratively brown-skinned), they are usually regarded as black or mulatto in Puerto Rico and in the United States. According to the 2009 Puerto Rico Community Survey, 28.8 percent of Dominicans described themselves as white, 36.4 percent said they were black, and 30.1 percent responded that they were members of "some other race" or "two or more races." In contrast, 73.1 percent of Puerto Ricans classified themselves as white, 6.6 percent said they were black, and 20 percent chose "some other race" or "two or more races" (Ruggles et al. 2010).

Puerto Ricans tend to represent Dominicans as darker-skinned than themselves, underlining their Negroid facial features and hair texture and treating them as black (Cruz Caraballo 1998; López Carrasquillo 1999; Martínez–San Miguel 2003). Dominicans in Puerto Rico thus often experience intense stigmatization, stereotyping, prejudice, and discrimination. The racialization of Dominicans as black justifies their social exclusion — from jobs, housing, schooling, and marriage, even in the second generation. In all these areas, the coupling of *dominicano* with *negro* hampers the immigrants' incorporation.

Ethnic humor is a case in point. Like other disadvantaged minorities around the world, Dominicans in Puerto Rico are targets of an extensive repertoire of ethnic jokes, racial slurs, anecdotes, and quips. (In the early

1990s, Iturrondo [2000: 17] collected a sample of more than one thousand Dominican jokes in Puerto Rico.) Numerous studies have documented the increasing hostility toward Dominican immigrants on the island since the 1980s (Benítez Nazario 2001; de Maeseneer 2002; Martínez–San Miguel 2003; Mejía Pardo 1993; Ríos 1992; Romero Anico 1984). Popular radio and television programs in Puerto Rico have tended to ridicule Dominicans as comic, ignorant, vulgar, and unruly characters, such as the domestic worker Altagracia in the television comedy *Entrando por la cocina* (de la Rosa Abreu 2002). Puerto Rican folk humor often portrays Dominicans as strange, incomprehensible, dangerous, inept, dirty, undesirable, illegitimate, and dishonest subjects. Dominican immigrants are usually scorned because of their foreign accent, physical features, cultural idiosyncrasy, and undocumented status. Graffiti calling for "Death to Dominicans" has occasionally appeared on public murals in San Juan, and anonymous leaflets denouncing "the Dominican plague" have been distributed in academic conferences. Ironically, the prevalent discourse on Dominicans in Puerto Rico resembles those on Haitians in the Dominican Republic and Puerto Ricans and Dominicans in the United States (see Duany 2006b).

Dominican Transnationalism in Puerto Rico

The Dominican experience in Puerto Rico can be analyzed productively from a transnational perspective. For centuries, geography, history, culture, language, and religion have bound together the Dominican Republic and Puerto Rico. Before 1930 several thousand Puerto Ricans worked in the Dominican Republic, primarily in the sugar mills of San Pedro de Macorís, Puerto Plata, and La Romana. Since 1961 tens of thousands of Dominicans have sought a better life in Puerto Rico, usually taking low-wage service jobs in the San Juan metropolitan area. Over the past few decades, large-scale migration, tourism, trade, and investment have tightened the social, economic, and political links between the two countries. The continuing tide of undocumented migrants is a dramatic expression of those ties, despite efforts by U.S. and Dominican authorities to curb the illegal traffic of people.

Dominicans have established vibrant communities in San Juan, especially in the urban centers of Santurce and Río Piedras. These communities function very much like "transnational villages" in Peggy Levitt's (2001) sense of places tied together through continuous flows of people, money, ideas, practices, organizations, and resources. Migrants from the Cibao, Miches, or

Santo Domingo often resettle in working-class neighborhoods of San Juan, such as Barrio Obrero and Barrio Capetillo. The vast majority are unskilled service and blue-collar workers such as domestic workers, cleaners, waitresses, security guards, and construction workers. By and large, Dominicans have incorporated into the secondary segment of Puerto Rico's labor market.

Transnationalism pervades the daily life of Dominicans in Puerto Rico. Two of the major political parties (the PLD and the PRD) from the Dominican Republic have large followings among expatriates, dividing their ideological loyalties and sense of community. Class, regional, gender, racial, and legal differences fragment Dominican associations, both formal and informal. Nonetheless, many Dominicans have managed to reconstruct their cultural identities in a transnational context. The growing Dominican presence in Santurce and Río Piedras has transformed the physical and cultural landscape of several neighborhoods, which now vie for the title of Little Santo Domingo or Little Quisqueya. The Dominican influence is most evident in popular music, language, religion, and food preferences. The immigrants have also made inroads into the local mass media — in radio, television, and the press — that help them preserve ties to the Dominican Republic.

Dominicans in Puerto Rico form part of dense transnational fields with the Dominican Republic, the United States, Spain, and other countries. As I document in chapter 10, they represent a significant portion of the multimillion-dollar remittance market, and they make significant investments in small businesses in the Dominican Republic. They raise large amounts of funds for Dominican presidential candidates. They travel frequently between San Juan and Santo Domingo, especially during Christmas vacations, carrying gifts, letters, cassettes, and bags full of merchandise to be resold back home. They constantly circulate capital, goods, and information, as well as values, images, and identities, between their home and host countries. In sum, Dominicans in Puerto Rico have contributed to redrawing the symbolic contours of their nation of origin through numerous transnational practices. The next chapter compares the remittance practices of Dominicans and Puerto Ricans.

Transnational Crossroads

The Circulation of People and Money in
Puerto Rico and the Dominican Republic

During the 1990s remittances became the second-largest source of foreign exchange for many Latin American and Caribbean countries, including Mexico, Guatemala, the Dominican Republic, and Cuba.[1] In 2009 the Inter-American Development Bank (IADB 2010) estimated that Latin American and Caribbean immigrants worldwide dispatched US$58.8 billion to their nations of origin. Most adult Hispanics regularly send *migradólares* (as they are often dubbed in Mexico) to family members back home (Bendixen and Associates 2001; DeSipio 2002; Orozco et al. 2005). Although the U.S. recession and the global economic crisis have slowed the growth of remittances, they continue to play a key role in Latin America and the Caribbean. In smaller economies such as Haiti, Jamaica, Guyana, Honduras, El Salvador, and Nicaragua, remittances rival revenues from agriculture, manufacturing, and tourism (World Bank 2008). In most cases, private transfers of money exceed direct foreign investment and development aid from wealthier to poorer countries. Everywhere, remittances help sustain local economies, particularly households with few assets.

Remittances are one of the strongest transnational economic links between sending and receiving communities (Basch, Glick Schiller, and Szanton Blanc 1994; Goldring 2003; Guarnizo 2003; Levitt and Glick Schiller 2004; Levitt and Nyberg-Sørensen 2004; Robert Smith 2006; Vertovec 2009). These massive transfers of resources are embedded in far-flung webs of solidarity and reciprocity between relatives across nations. Contrary to other monetary transfers, remittances reach the poorer sectors of the population, especially helping women, children, and the elderly meet subsistence needs, such as food, shelter, clothing, and health care. Aside from being spent on necessities, remittances are used to settle debts, finance education, save, purchase property, obtain consumer goods, cover the costs of emergencies, and pay for professional services, thus generating additional employment and income (Durand, Parrado, and Massey 1996). Hence, remittances are a classic form of transnationalism from below, insofar as they represent grassroots initiatives by the poor (see chapter 1). As Alejandro Portes (1996: 1) has quipped, transnational migrant communities are "labor's analog to the multinational corporation."

One of the central questions in the study of contemporary migrants is how frequently they participate in transnational activities such as sending money home, especially beyond the first generation (see Levitt and Waters 2002; and Waldinger 2007). As a rule, foreign-born persons remit more than those born in the United States (de la Garza and Lowell 2002; Itzigsohn 2006). Nonetheless, second- and third-generation immigrants also retain economic, social, and political attachments to their ancestral homelands (see Fouron and Glick Schiller 2001; Robert Smith 2006; and Toro-Morn and Alicea 2003). For instance, many Latinos in the United States visit their places of origin, plan to return to live there, and attend cultural events related to their home countries (DeSipio and Pantoja 2004; Portes, Escobar, and Arana 2009). The issue of dual allegiance within transnational communities is not merely academic but has broader practical implications. How immigrants shed or cling to their national and ethnic identities while becoming full-fledged citizens in the receiving society has long concerned scholars and policymakers, as illustrated by Randolph Bourne's call in 1916 for a cosmopolitan "trans-national America."

These issues are particularly relevant for Puerto Rico, a primary source of emigrants to the United States since World War II, a major destination for return migrants and their descendants, and more recently a recipient of immigrants from other countries. In 2009 the U.S. Census Bureau estimated that 53.4 percent of all persons of Puerto Rican birth or origin lived in the United States. The 4.4 million people of Puerto Rican descent residing stateside represent the second-largest number of U.S. Latinos, after Mexicans, and the largest proportion relative to the sending population. At the same time, 8.1 percent of the island's population was born abroad, especially in the United States, the Dominican Republic, and Cuba (U.S. Census Bureau 2010). As the Cuban American anthropologist Samuel Martínez (2003: 147) has argued, Puerto Rico has become a transnational migrant crossroads, "the scene of multiple, cross-cutting, back-and-forth geographic displacements of people of different national origins." Similarly, the Dominican Republic has sent hundreds of thousands of migrants to the United States and Puerto Rico, while receiving hundreds of thousands of Haitians. One result of this fluid demographic situation is the massive circulation of people and money to and from Puerto Rico and the Dominican Republic. Yet the cumulative effect of migradollars on the Puerto Rican economy over the last half century, and the island's current role as the third-largest source of remittances to the Dominican Republic after the United States and Spain, have been neglected.

In 2004 the IADB estimated that Dominicans in Puerto Rico transmitted approximately US$240 million or 9 percent of all remittances to the Dominican Republic (Bendixen and Associates 2004; Suki 2004). This figure represented almost half the private transfers of money received in Puerto Rico (Junta de Planificación 2004).[2] In 2006 Dominican households in San Juan sent an average of US$189 per month, a considerable amount given the immigrants' low wages and the high cost of living in Puerto Rico (Duany 2007). This practice has created a growing demand for businesses specializing in the sending of valuables (*envío de valores*), including money, packages, and gifts, to the Dominican Republic. Such businesses are typically found in neighborhoods with large concentrations of Dominican residents, such as Barrio Obrero in Santurce and Barrio Capetillo in Río Piedras.

One enterprising Dominican photographer, Vinicio Peña, established forty remittance agencies throughout Puerto Rico during the 1990s (Iturrondo 2000: 392). Dozens of companies have since specialized in transferring money to the Dominican Republic, including Consorcio Oriental, El Rapidito Express, Envíos Mi Tierra, Fernández Ventura y Asociado, Remesas Quisqueyanas, and Rafael Express. More recently, several Dominican-owned firms have expanded their share of the remittance market: La Nacional, Quisqueyana, BHD, Ría Envía, and Uno. Most of these companies offer multiple services, such as prepaid phone cards, telephone booths, money orders, photocopying, fax transmittal, and airplane and ferry tickets. Financial conglomerates such as MoneyGram, Western Union, Visa, and Banco Popular de Puerto Rico have also tapped into the business of sending money to the Dominican Republic. In 2004 MoneyGram announced that it would provide money transfer services at 350 locations in Puerto Rico, including twelve WalMart stores (MoneyGram International 2004). In 2006 Western

Union began to offer door-to-door delivery service in the Dominican Republic, at a cost of US$4.99 per transaction, plus a transfer fee (Avilés Inostroza 2006).

Puerto Rico thus has become a major exporter of migradollars to the Dominican Republic as well as an importer from the United States. To my knowledge, the simultaneous inflow and outflow of remittances has not been scrutinized in a single country. Yet many Latin American and Caribbean nations — including the Dominican Republic, Costa Rica, Ecuador, Brazil, and Argentina — have experienced substantial inflows and outflows of both migrants and remittances. The large-scale transnational exchange of funds has important repercussions for an open and stagnant economy such as Puerto Rico's. Among other reasons, it might help explain increasing spending on consumer goods even as the island's economy contracts as a result of recession, public debt, and unemployment.

The Dominican economy increasingly relies on the transfer of funds by expatriates in the United States, Spain, Puerto Rico, and other countries. In 2007 a nationwide survey of the Dominican Republic found that 20 percent of all households received remittances (Oficina Nacional de Estadística 2009b). Other studies have estimated even higher proportions of remittance receivers, reaching 38 percent of Dominican households, the highest for all the Latin American countries polled (Bendixen and Associates 2006). In 2009 remittances represented 6.2 percent of the gross domestic product (GDP) of the Dominican Republic. In addition, Haitians in the Dominican Republic dispatched around US$33 million to Haiti in 2006 (IADB 2007). In the rest of this chapter, I focus on the Dominican Republic as a remittance receiver.

Measuring the Significance of Remittances

As others have observed, remittances are the largest source of external finance for many developing economies (Kapur 2003; Orozco 2004). In 2009 the Dominican Republic was the sixth-largest remittance destination in the Americas, after Mexico, Brazil, Colombia, Guatemala, and El Salvador. The balance of payments accounts compiled by the Junta de Planificación (2010) would place Puerto Rico at number twenty in the Americas, after Costa Rica. Even though these are conservative estimates, they show a steady increase over the past three decades, especially since the 1990s (figure 3.1). Still, according to these figures, Dominicans currently transfer over seven times more money than Puerto Ricans to their country of origin.

A second way to assess the significance of remittances is to calculate the ratio of funds received relative to a country's population. In 2009 the Dominican Republic was the seventh-highest per capita remittance receiver (with US$289) in Latin America and the Caribbean, while Puerto Rico ranked nineteenth (US$92). The top six per capita receivers of migradollars in the region were Jamaica, El Salvador, Guyana, Belize, Honduras, and Guatemala (IADB 2010).

A third strategy considers remittances as a percentage of the GDP. Again, the smaller Central American and Caribbean economies lead the Western Hemisphere, especially Guyana, Haiti, Honduras, and El Salvador, where remittances represent more than 15 percent of the GDP (IADB 2010). According to this criterion, Puerto Rican remittances are among the lowest in the region, with less than 1 percent of the GDP (Junta de Planificación 2010).

A fourth approach used to compare remittances focuses on average amounts sent home by various immigrant groups. Mariano Sana (2003) has found that migrants from Puerto Rico transmitted a monthly average of only US$118, compared to US$148 for the Dominican Republic and US$268 for western Mexico. Similarly, Elizabeth Fussell (2005) estimated that annual remittances from Puerto Ricans in the United States were the lowest (US$1,140 per household) of the five groups she studied (the others were Costa Ricans, Dominicans, Mexicans, and Nicaraguans). The paradox of relatively low levels of remittances to Puerto Rico despite a high outmigration rate warrants further investigation.

It is difficult to study remittances to Puerto Rico because of the lack of adequate data. Even gross estimates of the monetary transfers vary widely from one source to another. Based on an unpublished survey of island-born residents of the United States, the Puerto Rican political scientist Angelo Falcón (2004) has speculated that stateside Puerto Ricans might remit as much as US$1 billion a year to the island. The lower estimates of the local planning board — US$364.5 million in 2009 — pale before the US$12.9 billion in transfers from the U.S. government (Junta de Planificación 2010) (see figure 10.1).

Federal disbursements, especially for nutritional assistance, housing subsidies, and educational grants, may well be the safety net in Puerto Rico that remittances are in other countries. In addition, most Puerto Ricans have

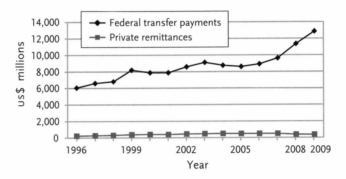

FIGURE 10.1 Federal Transfer Payments and Private Remittances to Puerto Rico, 1996–2009

Source: Junta de Planificación 2000–2010.

unemployment and disability insurance; and many have earned benefits such as Social Security, Medicare, and veterans' pensions. The latter benefits have displaced the former as the primary form of government subsidy to the island's low-income population (Duany and Pantojas-García 2005; Pantojas-García 2007) (see figure 10.2). Unlike federal transfer payments, remittances are one of the most overlooked variables in academic and public discussions about the Puerto Rican economy (see, e.g., Collins, Bosworth, and Soto-Class 2006; and Irizarry Mora 2001).

Studying Puerto Rican and Dominican Remittances

I have identified serious gaps in the existing knowledge about remittances in Puerto Rico, compared with other Latin American and Caribbean countries. The most intriguing issue is that the island has one of the largest migrant populations but one of the lowest levels of remittances in the Western Hemisphere. So why do Puerto Ricans in the United States send less money to their country of origin than most other Latinos? What effect do transfer payments from the U.S. government have on Puerto Rican remittances? How does Puerto Rico's relatively high living standard affect private transfers from the U.S. mainland? Finally, how do the transnational practices of Puerto Rican migrants differ from those of other groups that remit more funds to their home countries?

The data for this chapter come from the Puerto Rican and Dominican

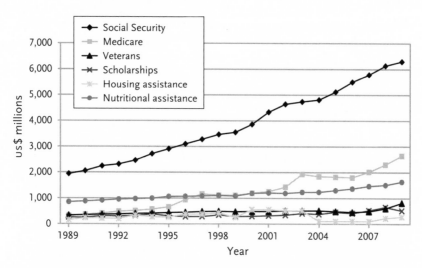

FIGURE 10.2 Composition of Major Federal Transfers to Individuals in Puerto Rico, 1989–2009

Source: Junta de Planificación 2000–2010.

samples of the Latin American Migration Project (LAMP). The communities chosen for this study represent a broad range of population sizes, regions, ethnic compositions, and economic bases in Puerto Rico and the Dominican Republic. The sample size varied between one hundred and two hundred households for each community. Each community was enumerated on a house-by-house basis, and households were selected using simple random sampling.

Table 10.1 summarizes the main characteristics of the samples. Overall, the Puerto Rican sample is more female, older, less likely to be single, more educated, less likely to be engaged in agricultural labor, and more likely to be born in the fifty United States than the Dominican sample. Furthermore, Puerto Ricans tended to move abroad earlier, remain on the U.S. mainland, have more migratory experience, and spend more time abroad than Dominicans.

The LAMP instruments were adaptations of the ethnosurvey designed for the Mexican Migration Project (MMP). Developed by Douglas Massey, Jorge Durand, and their colleagues, the ethnosurvey was originally employed to collect information on migration between Mexico and the United States; it was later applied in Puerto Rico, the Dominican Republic, and other Latin American and Caribbean countries. The questionnaire followed a semistruc-

TABLE 10.1 Basic Characteristics of the Ethnosurvey Samples

Characteristic	Puerto Rico (N=2,878)	Dominican Republic (N=5,913)
Sex (%)		
Male	46.9	48.2
Female	53.1	51.8
Median age (years)	37.0	28.0
Marital status (%)		
Never married	31.3	45.8
Married	41.9	28.7
Consensual union	7.4	15.6
Widowed	6.7	2.6
Divorced	8.4	2.5
Separated	4.3	4.8
Median school years completed	12	8
Occupation (%)		
Professionals and technicians	17.2	15.8
Managers and administrators	3.5	3.0
Sales and administrative support	24.2	20.2
Skilled and repair workers	16.3	15.3
Unskilled operators and laborers	15.8	13.4
Service workers	22.7	22.9
Agricultural workers	0.3	9.4
Born in the United States (%)	10.4	2.4
Median year of first U.S. migration	1972	1988
Currently on last U.S. migration (%)	12.5	10.2
One or more U.S. migrations (%)	26.4	12.9
Mean number of months of U.S. experience	48.7	17.8

Source: LAMP database (2009), PERS file.

tured format to generate a flexible, unobtrusive, and nonthreatening interview schedule. Although interviewers obtained identical information from each respondent, they decided how to word and order questions. (For more details on the ethnosurvey, see LAMP 2009.) Local research assistants, supervised by a field coordinator, conducted interviews in Spanish, with the household head serving as the principal respondent for all people in the sample.

The questionnaires were applied in three phases. First, interviewers gathered basic data on all household members, including sex, age, birthplace, marital status, education, and occupation. The interview began by identifying the household head (as defined by respondents) and enumerating the spouse and children, whether or not they lived at home. If a son or daughter was a member of another household, this fact was recorded as well. A child was considered to be living in a separate household if he or she was married, maintained a separate house or kitchen, and organized expenses separately. After listing the head, spouse, and children, interviewers identified other household members and clarified their relationship to the head. Second, interviewers compiled a year-by-year life history for all household heads and their spouses. This phase of the fieldwork focused on business formation, labor, migration, property, and housing. Finally, interviewers detailed the household head's last trip to the United States, including the amount and purposes of remittances, and the number of relatives and friends currently living abroad. If necessary, households were revisited to complete or clarify information.

Remitting in Comparative Perspective

In prior fieldwork, I found that only 5 percent of Puerto Ricans on the island regularly received money from relatives or friends from abroad (Duany 2007). This proportion is even lower than that found for Costa Rica, which received the lowest share of remittances (5.4 percent) in a comparison of four countries using LAMP data. The corresponding percentage for Mexico was 13.3; for Nicaragua, 15; and for the Dominican Republic, 29.2 (Sana and Massey 2005: 518). According to the present study, slightly more than one-third of Puerto Ricans sent money to their home country while living in the United States, compared to more than two-thirds of Dominicans. On average, Puerto Ricans transferred just under US$85 per month, while Dominicans transmitted US$192 (see table 10.2).

In most cases, remittances were used to meet household maintenance expenses such as food and medicine. However, Puerto Ricans were more likely than Dominicans to purchase consumer goods, to save, and to spend these funds on recreation and entertainment. Conversely, Dominicans devoted a

TABLE 10.2 Remittances Sent to Puerto Rico and the Dominican Republic by Household Heads in the United States

Remittances	Puerto Rico (N=272)	Dominican Republic (N=168)
Sent remittances (%)	34.8	66.5
Mean monthly amount (US$)	84.8	192
Median monthly amount (US$)	50	150
Primary purpose of remittances (%)		
Food and maintenance	52.4	66.5
Construction and house repair	—	—
Purchase house or lot	—	1.0
Purchase vehicle	—	—
Purchase livestock	—	—
Purchase agricultural inputs	—	—
Purchase consumer goods	20.2	—
Start or expand business	—	—
Education	—	4.9
Health	7.1	1.0
Debt	1.2	—
Special event	2.4	—
Recreation or entertainment	7.1	—
Savings	9.5	—
Other	—	25.5

Source: LAMP database (2009), MIG file.

larger share of money to other, unspecified activities (probably paying rent, which was not coded separately). Thus, Puerto Rican remittances served as complementary sources of income more often than Dominican remittances.

Table 10.3 compares the main characteristics of remittance senders and nonsenders in the two samples. According to these results, the typical profile of a remittance sender is a middle-aged, married Dominican man with twelve years of formal education. Most often, remitters are blue-collar or service workers, especially in repair services, who moved to the United States in the early 1980s. On average, remittance senders have lived in the United States for eleven years. Conversely, nonsenders are more likely to be female, older, Puerto Rican, unmarried, and less educated than remittance senders. They also tend to be earlier migrants to the United States and to

TABLE 10.3 Selected Characteristics of Puerto Rican and Dominican
Remittance Senders and Nonsenders

Characteristic	Senders (N=216)	Nonsenders (N=224)
Sex (%)		
Male	69.4	53.1
Female	30.6	46.9
Median age (years)	49.5	52.0
Country of origin (%)		
Puerto Rico	46.3	76.8
Dominican Republic	53.7	23.2
Marital status (%)		
Never married	7.4	5.4
Married	48.6	37.5
Consensual union	14.4	8.9
Widowed	6.9	16.1
Divorced	12.0	18.8
Separated	10.6	13.4
Median school years completed	12.0	10.0
Occupation (%)		
Professionals and technicians	10.6	10.4
Managers and administrators	9.2	5.7
Sales and administrative support	24.8	26.6
Skilled and repair workers	23.4	26.7
Unskilled operatives and laborers	16.3	13.2
Service workers	14.9	16.0
Agricultural workers	0.7	4.7
Median year of first U.S. migration	1981	1971
Median number of months of U.S. experience	132	224

Source: LAMP database (2009), MIG file.

have lived there longer. Once again, Dominicans were three times as likely
as Puerto Ricans to remit.

I propose six interrelated reasons why Puerto Ricans in the United States
transmit less money home than Dominicans do. First, as a rule, Puerto Ricans have fewer close relatives (especially parents, siblings, and cousins)

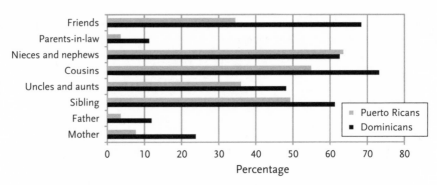

FIGURE 10.3 Relatives and Friends of Puerto Rican and Dominican Household Heads Currently Residing in the United States

Source: LAMP 2009.

and friends abroad than Dominicans (figure 10.3). This finding suggests that Puerto Ricans have weaker moral incentives to remit than Dominicans because Puerto Ricans have fewer family ties overseas.

Second, the median year of departure for Puerto Rican migrants to the United States was sixteen years earlier (1972) than for Dominican migrants (1988) (table 10.1). Also, the Puerto Rican sample had four times more people born in one of the fifty United States (10.4 percent) than the Dominican sample (2.4 percent). Similarly, a larger percentage of Puerto Ricans (65.9) than Dominicans (42.7) in the 2009 American Community Survey were second-generation immigrants (table 10.4). Consequently, Puerto Ricans have usually had more time to reunite with their families abroad and often have lost touch with relatives left behind. These findings confirm that the likelihood of remitting declines as kinship ties and norms of reciprocity between migrants and nonmigrants weaken over time.

Third, the demographic profile of Dominican migrants is more closely associated with remitting than the profile of Puerto Rican migrants (table 10.4; see also table 3.5). According to the 2009 American Community Survey, Dominicans in the United States were slightly more likely to be married and less educated than Puerto Ricans. A larger proportion of Dominicans than Puerto Ricans was born in the country of origin. Furthermore, Dominicans tend to have less skilled occupations and earn less income than Puerto Ricans in the United States. Despite their low socioeconomic status, working-class immigrants dispatch the bulk of migradollars. Among Mexicans, the most typical remitter is a man with little formal education employed as a temporary laborer in the United States (Sana 2003).

TABLE 10.4 Selected Demographic Characteristics of Puerto Ricans and
Dominicans in the United States, 2009

Characteristic	Puerto Ricans	Dominicans
Male (%)	49.5	47.5
Female (%)	50.5	52.5
Median age (years)	28.5	29.3
Married (%)	36.3	37.1
Born abroad (%)	34.1	57.3

Source: U.S. Census Bureau 2010.

TABLE 10.5 Selected Economic Characteristics of Puerto Rico and the
Dominican Republic, 2008–2009

Characteristic	Puerto Rico	Dominican Republic
Gross domestic product (GDP), 2009 (US$ millions)	95,708.2	46,711.6
GDP per capita, 2009 (US$)	24,165	4,815.6
Unemployment rate, 2009 (%)	13.5	14.9
Poverty rate, 2008 (%)	44.8	44.3
Average hourly wage in manufacturing, 2008 (US$)	12.1	1.23[a]

Sources: Banco Central 2010; Comisión Económica 2010; International Labour Organization
2009; Junta de Planificación 2010.

[a] Available data refer to 2004.

Fourth, living conditions are more precarious in the Dominican Republic than in Puerto Rico. Table 10.5 shows that Puerto Rico's GDP per capita is more than five times higher than that of the Dominican Republic and that average wages in manufacturing are almost ten times higher in Puerto Rico than in the Dominican Republic. According to the World Bank (2009), Puerto Rico is a high-income economy, whereas the Dominican Republic is a lower middle-income economy. Although official poverty rates are higher in Puerto Rico, its poor population is economically better off than the poor population in the Dominican Republic, especially given massive federal transfer payments to Puerto Rico.

Fifth, Puerto Ricans have access to more varied sources of income than Dominicans do in their country of origin, including retirement and disability pensions, as well as public assistance. As U.S. citizens, Puerto Ricans qualify for many federally funded social programs, such as the Nutritional

Assistance Program, Temporary Assistance for Needy Families, Section 8, and Medicaid (Burtless and Sotomayor 2006; Hernández Angueira 2001). According to the 2009 Puerto Rico Community Survey, 42.4 percent of all households on the island received Social Security income, while 35.1 percent received food stamps (U.S. Census Bureau 2010). Dominican migrants who are not U.S. citizens or permanent residents do not qualify for such benefits. In the Dominican Republic, much of the population does not have medical insurance or social security. Consequently, migradollars represent a key survival strategy for low-income households in the Dominican Republic but not for those in Puerto Rico (Itzigsohn 1995; Sana and Massey 2005).

Finally, remittances have greater economic value in the Dominican Republic than in Puerto Rico because of favorable exchange rates for the U.S. dollar in the first country. Stateside Puerto Ricans do not have that incentive to remit, because the island uses the U.S. dollar as its only currency.

Remittances and Transnational Engagement

Remittances are one of the most tangible expressions of transnationalism. The LAMP surveys have documented the extensive transnational engagement of Dominicans and Puerto Ricans in the United States with their countries of origin. The results reported here support previous work on the persistent ties between Puerto Ricans on and off the island (Alicea 1997; Aranda 2007; DeSipio and Pantoja 2004; Flores 2008; Gina Pérez 2004; Toro-Morn and Alicea 2003). Elsewhere I have argued that the Puerto Rican diaspora remains connected with the island through a steady circulation of people, money, and cultural practices (Duany 2002). This is especially true of recent migrants to the mainland and return migrants to Puerto Rico, who tend to have more social ties on the U.S. mainland than those who have never lived abroad. Puerto Ricans can move between the island and the mainland without any of the legal impediments faced by undocumented Dominicans. According to the LAMP, twice as many Puerto Ricans (26.4 percent) as Dominicans (12.9 percent) had traveled to the United States.

The data also suggest that, as a group, Dominicans are more involved transnationally than Puerto Ricans. In particular, Dominicans had more personal contacts living abroad — including parents, siblings, cousins, in-laws, and friends — than did Puerto Ricans (figure 10.3). My previous fieldwork showed that proportionally more Dominican than Puerto Rican migrants sent clothes, food, medicine, and electrical appliances to their relatives back home. Dominicans in Puerto Rico were also more likely to hold assets such as bank accounts, businesses, and other properties in their home country than were Puerto Ricans living in the fifty United States (Duany 2007). The socioeconomic field of transnationalism was thus more extensive for Dominicans than for Puerto Ricans.

As other research has shown, Dominicans abroad remain more strongly attached to their country of origin than do most other Latinos (DeSipio and Pantoja 2004; Levitt and Waters 2002; Pantoja 2005; Waldinger 2007). According to a recent study, Dominicans in the United States traveled to their country of origin and made long-distance calls to their relatives there more frequently than did immigrants from ten other Latin American and Caribbean countries (Orozco et al. 2005). For many Dominican households, transnational connections have become customary and even necessary for survival.

For their part, many Puerto Ricans participate in "broad" or "expanded" transnational practices, such as celebrating ritual occasions — especially baptisms, weddings, anniversaries, and funerals — in both Puerto Rico and the United States (see chapter 1). But these practices seldom involve a monthly flow of money from Puerto Ricans on the mainland to the island. Moreover, many Puerto Rican women travel back and forth to take care of elderly parents, pregnant daughters, and small children (Alicea 1997; Aranda 2007). However, fewer than 4 percent of the Puerto Ricans in my earlier study had moved two or more times between the island and the mainland. Only one out of four Puerto Rican households on the island telephoned their relatives abroad at least once a week, compared to four out of five Dominican households in Puerto Rico (Duany 2007).

In contrast to Puerto Rican migrants, Dominican migrants exemplify a more institutionalized and habitual engagement with their country of origin, a "narrow" or "core" transnationalism. Dominicans often belong to hometown clubs, vote in Dominican elections, and preserve religious ties to Catholic parishes in the Dominican Republic (DeSipio and Pantoja 2004; Levitt 2001; Portes, Escobar, and Arana 2009; Waldinger 2007). The distinction between broad and narrow transnationalism helps explain why Dominicans send migradollars more regularly than Puerto Ricans do. Future studies should probe the differences and similarities between Puerto Rican and Dominican transnationalism. Among other issues, researchers should assess more carefully the impact of free movement between Puerto Rico and the United States as a result of common citizenship. Comparisons with other "colonial immigrants" from the Caribbean would be revealing.

Migration, Remittances, and the Transnational Colonial State

In this chapter, I have sought to explain the paradox of a high migration rate combined with a low level of remittances to Puerto Rico, compared with the Dominican Republic. Like many Latin American and Caribbean countries, Puerto Rico has experienced an exodus to the United States. Unlike most migrant-sending countries, the island has also received a growing influx of immigrants, primarily from the Dominican Republic. In addition, many Puerto Ricans have returned from the United States or moved back and forth between the island and the mainland. Thus, the circulation of people and money in Puerto Rico follows more complex routes than elsewhere.

This study confirmed that Puerto Ricans in the United States send fewer migradollars than do Dominicans. Furthermore, the share of households receiving remittances in the Dominican Republic greatly exceeds the share in Puerto Rico. Although Puerto Rico has a higher percentage of migrants relative to the sending population, the Dominican Republic receives more money from its expatriates.

One of the main reasons for this contrast is the availability of substantial government subsidies for low-income families in Puerto Rico. Federal transfer payments to the island ensure a minimum level of public welfare, which migradollars sustain in poorer countries such as the Dominican Republic. In Puerto Rico, several federally funded programs mitigate the basic needs of the poor — especially nutrition, housing, health care, and education. Remittances are thus a supplementary source of support for lower-class Puerto Rican households. In this regard, Puerto Rico differs from most migrant-sending countries of Central America and the Caribbean, such as El Salvador, Guatemala, Jamaica, Haiti, and Cuba. The island experience is closer to that of Costa Rica, with a very low percentage of remittance receipts, a relatively high living standard, and substantial immigration from neighboring Nicaragua. Unlike Costa Rica, however, Puerto Rico has exported more than half of its population to the U.S. mainland.

The data presented in this chapter confirm that most remittances help meet subsistence needs in the recipient communities, such as food, medicine, and clothes. A very small fraction of migradollars was used to save, start a business, buy a house, or acquire land. Likewise, relatively few households invested their remittances in human capital formation, as measured by expenses in formal education. Remittances therefore should not be deemed a primary engine for economic development but, rather, a basic mechanism for the social reproduction of poor households, especially in the Dominican Republic. Typically, remittances substitute for a well-developed welfare state such as exists in Puerto Rico, as a result of its transnational colonial ties.

On average, Puerto Ricans remit less than Dominicans, a finding explained by the demographic, socioeconomic, and historical characteristics of the two population flows, notably the timing of the migration and the persistence of kinship ties across borders. The data I have presented also suggest that Puerto Ricans in the United States currently engage in transnational practices less commonly than Dominicans. One of the basic causes of this difference is that many Puerto Ricans moved to the U.S. mainland well before Dominicans began to move abroad en masse. As migrant flows mature, social ties between those who left and those who remain behind tend to wane. As a rule, Dominicans abroad now maintain tighter networks with their country of origin than Puerto Ricans do. This seems to be the primary reason why Dominicans in the United States send much larger sums of migradollars.

Conclusion

How Do Borders Blur?

The concern with shifting borders and boundaries, rather than with the contents of such spaces, is a recurring theme in contemporary social thought. As Hastings Donnan and Thomas Wilson (1999) write, this intellectual trend largely reflects political changes in the world since 1989, such as the fall of the Berlin Wall, the end of the Cold War, the disintegration of the Soviet Union, and the rise of the European Union. Numerous boundary disputes have accompanied such transformations, not just in Eastern Europe and the former Soviet Union but also in the Middle East, Africa, and Asia. Furthermore, globalization has accelerated the movement of capital, goods, information, and people across international boundaries. In particular, the growth of migrant, refugee, and displaced populations has attracted increasing attention. Consequently, social scientists and humanists have reexamined their sedentary notions of nation-states as the sole containers of cultural identities.

Among other scholars, the Mexican American anthropologist Renato Rosaldo (1989) has contributed to refiguring the contours of culture, ideology, class, and power.[1] His analysis of "culture in the borderlands," based on the U.S.-Mexican experience, underlines migrants' constant transgression of national, ethnic, racial, class, and gender divisions in their daily lives. Rosaldo proposes that "ethnographers look less for homogeneous communities than for the border zones within and between them" (217) as a point of departure for analyzing cultural identities, especially in the context of transnational migration.

Recent scholarship has reconceptualized migrants as part of extended webs of economic, political, and cultural exchange. Transnational practices cut across state boundaries in ways that are difficult to grasp from a nation-centered perspective. Current approaches to transnationalism discard the conventional image of immigration as a form of cultural stripping away and complete absorption into the host society, as Rosaldo observed. Rather, such approaches show that immigrants belong to multiple communities with fluid and hybrid identities, grounded in subjective affiliations more than geopolitical criteria. For example, Mexicans and Puerto Ricans in the United States often straddle U.S. and Latin American cultures. As Juan Flores (1993: 215) has underlined, the "Latino experience in the U.S. has been a continual crossover, not only across geopolitical borders but across all kinds of cultural and political boundaries."

Border crossing becomes an apt image not just for the act of moving to another country but also for the crossover between cultures, languages, and nations in which migrants participate. An intense process of cultural hybridization usually takes place as people relocate. Transnationalism therefore involves imagining communities beyond the nation-state, defying stationary models of physical and cultural space. The massive dispersal and resettlement of people away from their homelands unsettles customary linkages among territories, states, and citizenships. Among other changes, diasporas often call into question ethnic, racial, and national identities as defined in both their home and host countries.

Throughout this book, I have argued that Hispanic Caribbean migrants blur the borders of their countries with the United States. In so doing, they create hybrid zones of contact between their places of origin and destination. Thus, they constantly shuttle along the social, cultural, political, and economic edges between two or more nations. In the Puerto Rican case, the border with the United States is more permeable than elsewhere because of the island's nebulous definition as an unincorporated territory. However, migrants cannot obliterate altogether the entrenched legal and administrative divisions between their home countries and the United States. As many scholars have underscored, borders and boundaries still matter, and not just in a metaphorical sense (see, e.g., Donnan and Wilson 1999; Saldívar 1997).

Despite the pressures of globalization, nation-states continue to frame the daily lives of most people, including those who live outside their country of birth. For instance, patrolling the boundaries of the United States has become a national security issue, especially after the terrorist attacks of

September 11, 2001. Responding to "transnational threats" such as smuggling migrants, controlled substances, and weapons, the U.S. government has militarized its southern boundaries, not just with Mexico, but also with the Dominican Republic and Cuba. In the Cuban case, the boundary is even more ominous given the lack of official relations with the United States. Comparing the three cases presented in this book has broader implications for understanding the continuing significance of state boundaries in the contemporary world, despite their growing irrelevance for cultural practices and identities.

Table c.1 recapitulates the main differences and similarities in the transnational experiences of Cubans, Dominicans, and Puerto Ricans. Following Peggy Levitt and Nina Glick Schiller (2004), I have characterized Cuba as a disinterested and denouncing state that traditionally excluded its diaspora for political reasons. The Cuban government has not recognized dual citizenship or extended other legal rights (such as voting from abroad) to those who leave the country permanently. A Spanish colony before 1898, Cuba remained a neocolonial dependency of the United States until 1958. The postrevolutionary government's antagonism toward the United States may be considered postcolonial. The leaders of the Cuban Revolution insist on defending the island's sovereignty at all costs and perceive outside pressures for political reform as signs of imperialistic interference.

During the Cold War the U.S. government embraced Cubans as refugees fleeing communism. Since the 1994 *balsero* crisis the U.S. Coast Guard has detained undocumented Cubans at sea, while admitting those who reach U.S. soil (the "wet foot/dry foot" policy). A highly favorable context of reception (at least until the 1980 Mariel exodus) facilitated the rise of Miami's Cuban enclave. Moreover, the presence of upper- and middle-class refugees, especially during the first two stages of the postrevolutionary exodus, smoothed Cubans' economic progress in the United States and Puerto Rico. However, the enmity between Washington and Havana, embodied in the decades-old U.S. embargo of Cuba, has restrained émigrés' contacts with their relatives and return trips home, except for short visits (and then only allowed after the 1978 *Diálogo*). Hence, Cuban transnationalism has emerged despite persistent confrontations between the Cuban and U.S. governments. The Cuban case shows the need to include nonstate or informal practices in the comparative analysis of transnationalism.

So far, the Cuban diaspora has been primarily a unilateral flow to the United States and transnationalism has taken place largely outside official

TABLE C.1 Basic Types of Transnational Migration from the Hispanic Caribbean

Type	Cuba	Dominican Republic	Puerto Rico
Sending country policy toward emigration	Disinterested and denouncing state	Transnational nation-state	Transnational colonial state
Recognition of dual citizenship	No	Yes	No
Voting from abroad	No	Yes	No
Relationship with United States	Postcolonial	Neocolonial	Colonial
Immigrants' legal status upon arrival in United States	Refugees (between 1959 and 1994); wet foot/dry foot policy	Immigrants (legal or undocumented)	U.S. citizens (since 1917)
U.S. policy toward migration	Open arms during Cold War	Restrictive (after 1966)	Laissez-faire (since 1904)
Context of reception	Highly favorable (until 1980)	Unfavorable	Unfavorable
Class composition	Initially middle- and upper-class; later, broader representation	Largely lower middle-class	Predominantly lower-class
Racial composition according to U.S. census	Mostly white	Mostly some other race and black	Largely white and some other race
Basic mode of labor incorporation	Enclave economy	Secondary labor market	Secondary labor market
Type of migration	One-way	Two-way	Two-way
Transnational ties with country of origin	Limited and unofficial	Narrow or core	Broad or expanded
Level of remittances	Moderate	High	Low

channels. The economic, political, and emotional costs of maintaining family ties with Cuba are still relatively high (Eckstein 2009). On average, Cubans call, travel, and send money home less frequently than other Latinos in the United States (Orozco et al. 2005; Waldinger 2007). They rarely retain property on the island and bring few ethnic products back when they return to the United States. But Cuba's prolonged economic crisis, beginning in 1989, revitalized kinship networks between Cubans on and off the island. Consequently, remittances have reached a moderate level compared to other Caribbean and Central American countries.

In contrast, the Dominican Republic is a well-developed transnational nation-state. The Dominican government encourages the diaspora's participation in the country's political and economic affairs. During the 1990s the Dominican Congress recognized dual citizenship and external voting. Nowadays, overseas Dominicans, including those holding another passport, can run for office in the Dominican Republic. At the same time, the Dominican Republic maintains a neocolonial relationship with the United States, rooted in a long history of customs receivership and military interventions. The country's foreign trade, investment, and tourism remain oriented toward the United States. Yet the U.S. government did not make special concessions to Dominican immigrants after the mid-1960s. On the contrary, U.S. policy toward the Dominican exodus has been increasingly restrictive. Together with the migrants' predominantly lower middle-class origins and nonwhite racial classification, a hostile context of reception confined most Dominicans to the secondary labor market of the United States and Puerto Rico.

Over the past few decades, the Dominican diaspora has become a large-scale two-way flow, including a substantial return migration. This back-and-forth movement among the Dominican Republic, the United States, and other countries has strengthened ties between Dominicans at home and abroad. Today, Dominicans in the United States engage more frequently than most other Latinos in transnational practices such as attending cultural events, belonging to hometown associations, and voting in their country of origin. Overseas Dominicans also call home, travel, and send money more regularly than many immigrant communities (DeSipio et al. 2003; Levitt and Waters 2002; Orozco et al. 2005; Waldinger 2007). Compared to other Latin American and Caribbean nations, the level of remittances received by the Dominican Republic is extremely high.

Finally, Puerto Rico may be deemed a transnational colonial state that remains politically and economically subordinated to the United States. Even though Puerto Ricans are U.S. citizens, they have no electoral representation in the federal government unless they reside in one of the fifty United States; conversely, they cannot vote in Puerto Rico unless they reside on the island. This distinction is at the heart of Puerto Rico's predicament as an unincorporated territory that "belongs to but is not part of" the United States. Because the U.S. government does not regard Puerto Ricans as "aliens" for immigration purposes, it has no official policy toward the Puerto Rican diaspora. Still, U.S. public opinion toward Puerto Rican immigrants has been largely disapproving since the mid-twentieth century. Because of the lack of legal restrictions to migration, the Puerto Rican diaspora overrepresents the lower classes and racially mixed sectors of the island's population. Like Dominicans, most Puerto Ricans have incorporated into the secondary labor market of the United States.

The contemporary Puerto Rican diaspora is a massive bilateral movement between the island and the U.S. mainland, which scholars have dubbed a revolving-door, commuter, circular, or swallow migration (Duany 2002; Clara Rodríguez 1989). After more than six decades of constant migration, kinship ties between the island and the diaspora have matured and expanded. Today, most Puerto Ricans in the United States remain bound to their country of origin through occasional transnational practices, such as attending family gatherings, following the island's status debate, or consuming ethnic goods. Paradoxically, Puerto Rican remittances are among the lowest in the Americas, even though the island is one of the main sources of Hispanic migration to the United States. This paradox is largely a consequence of the growing influx of federal funds, which provide a safety net for the island's poor population.

In sum, migrant transnationalism depends very much on preexistent political and economic ties between sending and receiving countries. Direct external control, such as the one the United States exercises over Puerto Rico, tends to produce a larger and longer lasting population movement than indirect hegemony, such as the current U.S. presence in the Dominican Republic. In the long run, the first type generates broad or expanded transnational practices, whereas the second type results in narrow or core practices. Lastly, the absence of diplomatic ties and long-standing animosity between sending and receiving countries, such as between Cuba and the United States, produce an irregular, episodic, and often chaotic migrant stream, as well as restricted and unofficial transnational networks.

Each of the cases discussed in this book illustrates different ways in which transnationalism blurs borders but does not erase them altogether. Increasing numbers of Puerto Ricans, Dominicans, and Cubans in the United States and Puerto Rico maintain social, political, economic, cultural, and emotional contacts with their places of origin. Many transnational immigrants (and their descendants) lead bifocal lives, bridging two (or more) states, markets, cultures, and languages. In this way, they challenge dominant discourses of the nation based on the equation between places of birth and residence, between cultural and legal definitions of identity and citizenship, between borders and boundaries. The incessant crossing of borders makes them more porous, even as states attempt to draw their boundaries more clearly to protect themselves from external threats. In short, transnationalism has redrawn the lines between the Spanish-speaking Caribbean and the United States.

Notes

1 As one of the anonymous reviewers of this manuscript noted, transnationalism often flourishes in areas where the state is absent, such as smuggling activities between the Caribbean and the English colonies of North America during the eighteenth century. Analyzing such illicit practices lies beyond the scope of this book.

2 The following section draws on my essay "Becoming Cuba-Rican," in *The Portable Island: Cubans at Home in the World*, edited by Ruth Behar and Lucía M. Suárez (New York: Palgrave Macmillan, 2008), 197–208, reprinted with the permission of Palgrave Macmillan.

3 To my knowledge, the Cuban American sociologist Alejandro Portes (1969) was the first to use the expression *Golden Exile* in an academic article. The term has become synonymous with the first migrant wave (1959–62) after the Cuban Revolution, which drew mostly on the middle and upper classes. See also Duany 1993.

4 Rumbaut coined the term "1.5 generation" to refer to the children of Indochinese refugees who arrived in California after reaching school age but before puberty. The literary critic Gustavo Pérez Firmat (1994) later developed the concept in a Cuban American setting, arguing that persons born in Cuba but raised in the United States are neither fully Cuban nor fully American. They straddle the linguistic and cultural boundaries between the first and second generations of Cuban immigrants. More recently, Rumbaut (2004) has written of a "1.75 generation": people who were born abroad but moved to the United States before the age of five, and whose experiences are closer to the second than to the first generation.

5 Although I did not belong to the Brigada Antonio Maceo and the Círculo de Cultura Cubana, I traveled to Cuba as part of two trips sponsored by these organizations in the early 1980s. For an account of the first group of young radicalized Cubans who returned to the island, see Grupo Areíto 1978. For other personal narratives of traveling back to Cuba, see Behar 1996; Behar and Suárez 2008; de la Campa 2000; and Herrera 2007.

6 Here I use "Cuba-Rican" to designate someone born in Cuba and raised in Puerto Rico. Other scholars have employed the term to refer to the extensive cultural exchanges between Cuba and Puerto Rico since the nineteenth century, especially

in popular music, creative literature, and the mass media (Rivero 2004; Salgado 2009). Yolanda Martínez–San Miguel (2007) has aptly analyzed "the constitution of a diasporic Cuban-Rican imaginary" in the scant literature produced by Cubans in Puerto Rico. For more information on Cubans in Puerto Rico, see Cobas and Duany 1997.

7 Padilla included the poem "Siempre he vivido en Cuba" ("I Have Always Lived in Cuba") in his controversial collection *Fuera del juego* (1968). The Cuban émigré Lourdes Casal later wrote a poem with a similar line, included in her posthumous anthology *Palabras juntan revolución* (1981). I thank Eliana Rivero for reminding me of Casal's poem. See also Román de la Campa's memoirs, *Cuba on My Mind: Journeys to a Severed Nation* (2000).

CHAPTER ONE

1 This chapter incorporates portions of my essay "*Los Países*: Transnational Migration from the Dominican Republic to the United States," in *Dominican Migration: Transnational Perspectives*, edited by Ernesto Sagás and Sintia E. Molina (Gainesville: University Press of Florida, 2004), 29–52, reprinted with the permission of the University Press of Florida; and the "Preface to the Second Edition" of my monograph *Quisqueya on the Hudson: The Transnational Identity of Dominicans in Washington Heights* (New York: CUNY Dominican Studies Institute, 2008), 1–22.

2 From a different perspective, Ramón Crespo-Soto (2009: xii) considers Puerto Rico a "borderland state — a state embodying a sustained deinstitutionalization of the nation-state form . . . whose influence extends beyond geographic borders" to the United States. Although I disagree with Crespo-Soto's apology for the commonwealth's ideology and his dismissal of the island's colonial status, his discussion of "an anomalous state formation spreading its influence across its borders" (xxi) dovetails with my thinking about the transnational colonial state.

CHAPTER TWO

1 This chapter is based on my essay "Migration from the Spanish-Speaking Caribbean," written for the website project *In Motion: The African-American Migration Experience*, produced by the Schomburg Center for Research in Black Culture of the New York Public Library, 2005, http://www.inmotionaame.org/texts.

2 The Spanish folk term *guagua* (as a synonym for bus) is used throughout the Hispanic Caribbean and the Canary Islands. Although the origins of the word are uncertain, its diffusion throughout Cuba, the Dominican Republic, and Puerto Rico is an example of linguistic border blurring in the region.

CHAPTER THREE

1 Parts of this chapter are based on my essay "Migration from the Spanish-Speaking Caribbean," written for the website project *In Motion: The African-American Migration Experience*, produced by the Schomburg Center for Research in Black Culture of the New York Public Library, 2005, http://www.inmotionaame.org/texts.

CHAPTER FOUR

1 This chapter was originally published as "A Transnational Colonial Migration: Puerto Rico's Farm Labor Program," *New West Indian Guide* 84 (3–4) (2010): 225–51. Some portions will also appear in "The Puerto Rican Diaspora: A Postcolonial Migration?," in *Postcolonial Immigration and Identity Formation in Europe since 1945: Towards a Comparative Perspective*, edited by Ulbe Bosma, Jan Lucassen, and Gert Oostindie (forthcoming).

2 Although the island's name was the object of public controversy after the Spanish-Cuban-American War of 1898, most U.S. government and journalistic reports on the island retained the American spelling "Porto Rico" until 1932, when the U.S. Congress passed a resolution accepting the official name of Puerto Rico. As one of the reviewers of this manuscript noted, the common use of the terms "Porto Rico" and "Porto Ricans" reflects the colonial habit of removing foreign-sounding diphthongs from place names in order to Americanize them.

3 The best historical comparison with the Migration Division can be drawn with the Bureau for the Development of Migrations Concerning the Overseas Departments, or BUMIDOM (Bureau pour le Développement des Migrations Intéressant les Départements d'Outre-Mer), operated by the French metropolitan government between 1963 and 1982. According to the Martinican historian Monique Milia-Marie-Lucie (2002, 2007), Puerto Rico's Migration Division served as a model for BUMIDOM, especially its efforts to encourage mass migration, recruit workers, and facilitate their adjustment to the metropolitan country. Similar labor recruitment schemes were established in the British colonies of the Caribbean, particularly Barbados, Jamaica, and Trinidad, and in the Netherlands Antilles and Suriname, after World War II (Cervantes-Rodríguez et al. 2009: 5).

4 For an earlier study of the farmworkers' correspondence at the General Archive of Puerto Rico, see Stinson Fernández 1996.

CHAPTER FIVE

1 An earlier version of this chapter was published as "The Orlando Ricans: Overlapping Identity Discourses among Middle-Class Puerto Rican Immigrants," *CENTRO: Journal of the Center for Puerto Rican Studies* 22 (1) (2010): 84–115.

2 According to the U.S. Census Bureau (2009b), "the terms 'Hispanic' or 'Latino' refer to persons who trace their origin or descent to Mexico, Puerto Rico, Cuba, Spanish-speaking Central and South America[n] countries, and other Spanish cultures."

3 Research on middle-class Puerto Rican migrants is scanty. Historian Virginia Sánchez Korrol (1994: chap. 3) has documented their presence in New York City during the 1920s. They included health and legal professionals and owners of small businesses such as barbershops, boardinghouses, restaurants, bodegas, and *botánicas*. Sociologist Maura Toro-Morn (1995) interviewed middle-class Puerto Rican women in Chicago in 1989–90. For more recent studies, see Aranda 2007, 2009; and Ramos-Zayas 2003, esp. chap. 5.

4 In 2008 Patricia Silver and Natalie Underberg initiated the oral history project "Puerto Ricans in Central Florida, 1940s to 1980s: A History" at the University of Central Florida. See the project's website: http://www.prcf.info.

5 In 1947 the Puerto Rican government launched Operation Bootstrap, an industrialization program based on luring U.S. investment through tax exemption for manufacturing enterprises. The same year the Puerto Rican government created the Employment and Migration Bureau (later renamed the Migration Division) of the Labor Department "to follow its migrant citizens to facilitate their adjustment" to the U.S. mainland. For more details on the Migration Division as a "transnational" agency, see Duany 2002, esp. chap. 7.

6 For a useful analysis of the Mexican American borderlands, see Saldívar 1997. For other case studies ranging from Northern Ireland to Israel and Palestine to Spain and Morocco, see Donnan and Wilson 1999.

7 Although I did not inquire about my informants' residential locations, other researchers have found that middle-class Puerto Ricans tend to live in relatively affluent and dispersed suburban neighborhoods, away from the main Puerto Rican settlements in the city of Orlando, Kissimmee, and Poinciana (Concepción Torres 2008; Luis Sánchez 2009).

CHAPTER SIX

1 This chapter includes and updates fragments from "Revisiting the Cuban Exception: A Comparative Perspective on Transnational Migration from the Hispanic Caribbean to the United States," in *Cuba Transnational*, edited by Damián J. Fernández (Gainesville: University Press of Florida, 2005), 1–23, reprinted with the permission of the University Press of Florida; "Networks, Remittances, and Family Restaurants: The Cuban Diaspora from a Transnational Perspective," in *Cuba: Idea of a Nation Displaced*, edited by Andrea O'Reilly Herrera (Albany: State University of New York Press, 2007), 161–75; and "La diáspora cubana desde una perspectiva transnacional," in *Cuba 2009: Reflexiones en torno a los 50 años de la revolución de Castro*, edited by Andrzej Dembicz (Warsaw: Centro de Estudios Latinoamericanos, University of Warsaw, 2009), 189–207.

2 The social science bibliography on the Cuban exodus to the United States is voluminous. Useful books on the topic include Eckstein 2009; García 1996; González-Pando 1998; Grenier and Pérez 2003; Martínez et al. 1996; Masud-Piloto 1996; Pedraza 2007; Pérez Firmat 1994; Portes and Stepick 1993; Prieto 2009; Rodríguez Chávez 1997; and María de los Angeles Torres 1999. One of the key features of the bibliography is its narrow single-case approach, with little attention paid to the comparative dimensions of the Cuban diaspora (for important exceptions to this trend, see Pedraza-Bailey 1985; and Portes and Bach 1985).

3 For an overview of Cuban exceptionalism, see Whitehead and Hoffman 2007. For a critical position, see Buscaglia-Salgado 2002, which faults historian Louis Pérez (1999) for promoting "the myth of Cuban primacy and uniqueness" in his account of U.S.-Cuba relations since the nineteenth century. In a different context, Mark Sawyer (2006) has also questioned whether Cuban race relations are exceptional.

4 Susan Eckstein and Lorena Barbería (Barbería 2004; Eckstein 2003, 2004a, 2004b, 2009; Eckstein and Barbería 2001, 2002) have elaborated a transnational perspective on the Cuban diaspora. Margarita Cervantes-Rodríguez (2010) has recently applied a transnational framework to immigration and emigration in Cuba's history.

5 The other basic options have been self-employment and participation in the informal economy, including a huge black market that often provides goods and services stolen from state enterprises. Cubans commonly refer to such practices on the margins of the law as *resolver, inventar,* or *bisnear* (resolving, inventing, or "doing business") (Holgado Fernández 2000; Taylor 2009).

6 Writing from a prorevolutionary standpoint, Jesús Arboleya (1996, 1997) has emphasized the tight ideological association between emigration and counterrevolution.

7 For moving testimonies of the enduring transnational ties between Cubans on the island and in the diaspora, see Behar and Suárez 2008; and Herrera 2007.

8 According to the Cuban American economist María Dolores Espino (2010), the number of Cuban nationals residing abroad who traveled to Cuba rose from 224,700 in 2008 to 299,600 in 2009. These figures probably include Cubans with PREs in countries other than the United States. Another poll conducted in the United States estimated that 240,000 Cuban American adults planned to travel to Cuba during 2009–10 (Bendixen and Associates 2009).

CHAPTER SEVEN

1 This chapter is a revised, updated, and translated version of "La migración cubana: Tendencias actuales y proyecciones," *Encuentro de la Cultura Cubana* 36 (2005): 164–79; and "Más allá de las balsas: Tendencias recientes y proyecciones de la migración cubana," in *Cuba, el Caribe y el post embargo,* edited by Alejandra Liriano de la Cruz (Santo Domingo: Facultad Latinoamericana de Ciencias Sociales, 2005), 405–32. I presented summaries of this chapter at the conference "The Balsero Crisis, Ten Years Later: No Longer Adrift?," organized by Holly Ackerman and Damián J. Fernández at the Cuban Research Institute, Florida International University, and the Center for Latin American Studies, University of Miami, on July 16–17, 2004; and at the international seminar "Cuba and the Caribbean: Constructing Post-Embargo Scenarios" at the Facultad Latinoamericana de Ciencias Sociales, Santo Domingo, on March 26–27, 2004.

2 In this chapter, I use *embargo* and *blockade* as virtual synonyms, although I recognize the political overtones of each term. *Embargo,* preferred in the United States, has a more technical, juridical, and neutral connotation than *blockade,* preferred in Cuba, which suggests the political, military, and even moral obstruction of commerce and communication between the two countries.

CHAPTER EIGHT

1 Parts of this chapter were originally published in my essay "*Los Países:* Transnational Migration from the Dominican Republic to the United States," in *Dominican Migration: Transnational Perspectives,* edited by Ernesto Sagás and Sintia E.

Molina (Gainesville: University Press of Florida, 2004), 29–52, reprinted with the permission of the University Press of Florida. An online version appeared in *Migration Dialogue*, http://migration.ucdavis.edu/ceme/more.php?id=19_0_6_0. Some portions of the text are based on the "Preface to the Second Edition" of my monograph *Quisqueya on the Hudson: The Transnational Identity of Dominicans in Washington Heights* (New York: CUNY Dominican Studies Institute, 2008), 1–22.

CHAPTER NINE

1 The original version of this chapter was published as "Dominican Migration to Puerto Rico: A Transnational Perspective," *CENTRO: Journal of the Center for Puerto Rican Studies* 17 (1) (2005): 242–69. Spanish translations appeared as "La diáspora dominicana en Puerto Rico: Sus persistentes exclusiones por etnia, raza y género," in *La diversidad cultural: Reflexión crítica desde un acercamiento interdisciplinario*, edited by Rosalie Rosa Soberal (San Juan: Publicaciones Puertorriqueñas, 2007), 363–91; and as "La migración dominicana hacia Puerto Rico: Una perspectiva transnacional," in *Globalización y localidad: Espacios, actores, movilidades e identidades*, edited by Margarita Estrada Iguíniz and Pascal Labazée (Mexico City: Centro de Investigaciones y Estudios Superiores en Antropología Social, 2007), 397–430.

2 Based on a sample of the 1980 census, Edward Funkhouser and Fernando Ramos (1993) found that Dominicans in Puerto Rico were more educated, skilled, and professional than those in the United States. However, the 1990 census showed that the Dominican population in Puerto Rico included a larger proportion of service, precision production, craft, and repair workers than in New York City (Ramona Hernández 2002; Rivera Román 2004). Moreover, the census is known to underestimate undocumented immigrants, who tend to be less skilled and educated than legal residents.

CHAPTER TEN

1 This chapter draws on a report for the Center for the New Economy in San Juan (Duany 2007). It also incorporates ideas contained in two other publications: "To Send or Not to Send: Migrant Remittances in Puerto Rico, the Dominican Republic, and Mexico," in *Continental Divides: International Migration in the Americas*, edited by Katharine M. Donato, Jonathan Hiskey, Jorge Durand, and Douglas S. Massey, special issue of *Annals of the American Academy of Political and Social Science* 630 (1) (2010): 205–23; and "Enviar o no enviar migradólares: Migración y remesas en Puerto Rico, República Dominicana y México," *Camino Real* 1 (1) (2009): 27–52.

2 According to data compiled by the Office of the Commissioner of Financial Institutions in 2007, residents of Puerto Rico sent approximately US$524 million to other countries, especially the Dominican Republic (US$148.7 million), China, Colombia, the Philippines, and Mexico (Leal Calderón 2010).

CONCLUSION

1 The following three paragraphs are based on Duany 1998a: 20–21, 26–27.

Works Cited

Ackerman, Holly. 1997. "An Analysis and Demographic Profile of Cuban
Balseros, 1991–1994." *Cuban Studies* 26: 169–99.

Ackerman, Holly, and Juan M. Clark. 1995. *The Cuban "Balseros": Voyage of
Uncertainty.* Miami: Cuban American National Council.

Acosta-Belén, Edna, and Carlos E. Santiago. 2006. *Puerto Ricans in the United
States: A Contemporary Portrait.* Boulder, Colo.: Lynne Rienner.

Aders, Robert O. 1976. Letter to William D. Ford, Chairman, Subcommittee
on Agricultural Labor, January 26. Microfilm reel 145; series: Apple Harvest,
1959–81; box 2487; folders 1–19. Records of the Offices of the Government
of Puerto Rico in the United States. Centro de Estudios Puertorriqueños,
Hunter College, City University of New York.

Administration, Migration Division, Department of Labor, Government of Puerto
Rico. 1953–92. "Annual Reports." Microfilm reels 53–54; boxes 2733–39. Records
of the Offices of the Government of Puerto Rico in the United States. Centro de
Estudios Puertorriqueños, Hunter College, City University of New York.

Aguilar Trujillo, Alejandro. 2001. "Un escenario hipotético en la normalización
de las relaciones económicas Cuba–Estados Unidos." *Cuba Siglo XXI* 3. http://
www.nodo50.org/cubasigloXXI/economia/trujillo1_280201.htm. Accessed
September 14, 2009.

Aja Díaz, Antonio. 1999. "La emigración cubana en los años noventa." *Cuban
Studies* 30: 1–25.

———. 2002. *Tendencias y retos de Cuba ante el tema de la emigración.* Havana:
Centro de Estudios de Migraciones Internacionales, Universidad de La Habana.
http://bibliotecavirtual.clacso.org.ar/ar/libros/cuba/cemi/tenden.pdf. Accessed
September 11, 2009.

———. 2009. *Al cruzar las fronteras.* Havana: Centro de Estudios Demográficos/
Fondo de Población de las Naciones Unidas.

Aja Díaz, Antonio, Guillermo Milán Acosta, and Marta Díaz Fernández. 1996.
"La emigración cubana de cara al futuro: Estimación de su potencial migratorio
y algunas reflexiones en torno a la representación de los jóvenes en su compo-
sición." In *Anuario CEAP 1995: Emigración Cubana,* ed. Centro de Estudios de
Alternativas Políticas, Universidad de La Habana, 142–63. Havana: Universidad
de La Habana.

Alicea, Marixsa. 1990. "Dual Home Bases: A Reconceptualization of Puerto Rican Migration." *Latino Studies Journal* 1 (3): 78–98.

———. 1997. "'A Chambered Nautilus': The Contradictory Nature of Puerto Rican Women's Role in the Social Construction of a Transnational Community." *Gender and Society* 11: 597–626.

Allen, Charles H. 1902. *First Annual Report of Charles H. Allen, Governor of Porto Rico, Covering the Period from May 1, 1900, to May 1, 1901*. Washington, D.C.: U.S. Government Printing Office.

Anderson, Benedict R. O. 2001. "Western Nationalism and Eastern Nationalism: Is There a Difference That Matters?" *New Left Review* 2 (9): 31–42. http://newleftreview.org/A2320. Accessed September 8, 2008.

Aparicio, Ana. 2006. *Dominican Americans and the Politics of Empowerment*. Gainesville: University Press of Florida.

Aponte-Parés, Luis. 2000. "Appropriating Place in Puerto Rican Barrios: Preserving Contemporary Urban Landscapes." In *Preserving Cultural Landscapes in America*, ed. Arnold Robert Alanen, 94–111. Baltimore: Johns Hopkins University Press.

Appadurai, Arjun. 1996. *Modernity at Large: Cultural Dimensions of Globalization*. Minneapolis: University of Minnesota Press.

Apple Harvest File, Farm Labor Program, Migration Division, Department of Labor, Government of Puerto Rico. 1959–81. Microfilm reels 145–46; boxes 2487–88. Records of the Offices of the Government of Puerto Rico in the United States. Centro de Estudios Puertorriqueños, Hunter College, City University of New York.

Aranda, Elizabeth M. 2007. *Emotional Bridges to Puerto Rico: Migration, Return Migration, and the Struggles of Incorporation*. Lanham, Md.: Rowman and Littlefield.

———. 2009. "Puerto Rican Migration and Settlement in South Florida: Ethnic Identities and Transnational Spaces." In *Caribbean Migration to Western Europe and the United States: Essays on Incorporation, Identity, and Citizenship*, ed. Margarita Cervantes-Rodríguez, Ramón Grosfoguel, and Eric Mielants, 111–30. Philadelphia: Temple University Press.

Aranda, Elizabeth M., Rosa E. Chang, and Elena Sabogal. 2009. "Racializing Miami: Immigrant Latinos and Colorblind Racism in the Global City." In *How the United States Racializes Latinos: White Hegemony and Its Consequences*, ed. José A. Cobas, Jorge Duany, and Joe R. Feagin, 149–65. Boulder, Colo.: Paradigm.

Arboleya, Jesús. 1996. *Havana Miami: The U.S.-Cuba Migration Conflict*. Melbourne, Australia: Ocean.

———. 1997. *La contrarrevolución cubana*. Havana: Ciencias Sociales.

Asamblea Legislativa de Puerto Rico. 1947a. *Leyes de la Cuarta y Quinta Legislaturas Extraordinarias*. San Juan: Administración General de Suministros.

———. 1947b. *Leyes de la Tercera Legislatura Ordinaria de Puerto Rico*. San Juan: Administración General de Suministros.

Avilés Inostroza, María. 2006. "Al enviar dinero al exterior." *Primera Hora*, April 3. http://www.primerahora.com/noticia.asp?guid=6604F78BFAF4483BA6FDC38C 15A678E9. Accessed September 20, 2006.

Báez Evertsz, Franc, and Frank d'Oleo Ramírez. 1985. *La emigración de dominicanos a Estados Unidos: Determinantes socio-económicos y consecuencias*. Santo Domingo: Fundación Friedrich Ebert.

Bailey, Benjamin. 2002. *Language, Race, and Negotiation of Identity: A Study of Dominican Americans*. New York: LFB.

Banco Central de la República Dominicana. 2010. *Estadísticas económicas*. http://www.bancentral.gov.do. Accessed April 16, 2010.

Banco Gubernamental de Fomento para Puerto Rico. 2010. *Indicadores económicos mensuales de Puerto Rico — Series de tiempo. Transportación y carga*. http://www.gdb-pur.com/spa/economy/pr-monthly-economic-indicators-time-series.html. Accessed January 26, 2010.

Barberia, Lorena. 2004. "Remittances to Cuba: An Evaluation of Cuban and U.S. Government Policy Measures." In *The Cuban Economy at the Start of the Twenty-First Century*, ed. Jorge Domínguez, Omar Everleny Pérez Villanueva, and Lorena Barberia, 353–412. Cambridge: Harvard University Press.

Basch, Linda, Nina Glick Schiller, and Cristina Szanton Blanc. 1994. *Nations Unbound: Transnational Projects, Postcolonial Predicaments, and Deterritorialized Nation-States*. Basel, Switzerland: Gordon and Breach.

Behar, Ruth, ed. 1996. *Bridges to Cuba/Puentes a Cuba*. Ann Arbor: University of Michigan Press.

Behar, Ruth, and Lucía M. Suárez, eds. 2008. *The Portable Island: Cubans at Home in the World*. New York: Palgrave Macmillan.

Bendixen and Associates. 2001. *Survey of Remittance Senders: U.S. to Latin America*. http://www.bendixenandassociates.com/Presentations%20and%20Reports%20-%20website/IDB%20Remesas%202001.pdf. Accessed April 12, 2006.

———. 2004. *Remittances and the Dominican Republic: Survey of Recipients in the Dominican Republic. Survey of Senders in the United States*. http://www.bendixenandassociates.com/Presentations%20and%20Reports%20-%20website/IDB%20Dominican%20Republic%20Presentation%20FINAL%20 2004.pdf. Accessed April 11, 2006.

———. 2005. *Remittances to Cuba from the United States*. http://www.bendixen andassociates.com/studies/IAD%20Orozco%20Cuban%20Remittances%20 Presentation%202005.pdf. Accessed December 27, 2009.

———. 2006. *The Remittance Process in Brazil and Latin America*. http://www.bendixenandassociates.com/studies/IDB%20-%20Belo%20Horizonte.pdf. Accessed September 29, 2006.

———. 2009. *National Survey of Cuban Americans*. http://www.bendixenand associates.com/studies/National_Survey_of_Cuban_Americans_on_Policy_ towards_Cuba_FINAL.pdf. Accessed March 26, 2010.

Benítez Nazario, Jorge. 2001. *Reflexiones en torno a la cultura política de los puertorriqueños (Entre consideraciones teóricas y la evidencia empírica)*. San Juan: Instituto de Cultura Puertorrriqueña.

Black, Jan Knippers. 1986. *The Dominican Republic: Politics and Development in an Unsovereign State*. Boston: Allen and Unwin.

Blue, Sarah A. 2005. "From Exiles to Transnationals: Changing State Policy and the Emergence of Cuban Transnationalism." In *Cuba Transnational*, ed. Damián J. Fernández, 24–41. Gainesville: University Press of Florida.

Bonilla, Frank. 1994. "Manos que Sobran: Work, Migration, and the Puerto Rican in the 1990s." In *The Commuter Nation: Perspectives on Puerto Rican Migration*, ed. Carlos Alberto Torre, Hugo Rodríguez Vecchini, and William Burgos, 115–49. Río Piedras: Editorial de la Universidad de Puerto Rico.

Bonilla-Santiago, Gloria. 1988. *Organizing Puerto Rican Migrant Farmworkers: The Experience of Puerto Ricans in New Jersey.* New York: Peter Lang.

Boswell, Thomas D., and James R. Curtis. 1984. *The Cuban-American Experience: Culture, Images, and Perspectives.* Totowa, N.J.: Rowman and Allanheld.

Bourne, Randolph S. 1916. "Trans-national America." *Atlantic Monthly* 118 (July): 86–97.

Brubaker, Rogers. 2005. "The 'Diaspora' Diaspora." *Ethnic and Racial Studies* 28 (1): 1–19.

Brundenius, Claes. 2000. *The Role of Human Capital in Cuban Economic Development, 1959–1999.* CDR Working Paper 00.8, Centre for Development Research, Copenhagen. http://www.diis.dk/graphics/CDR_Publications/cdr_publications/working_papers/wp-00-8.pdf. Accessed September 14, 2009.

———. 2009. "Revolutionary Cuba at 50: Growth with Equity Revisited." *Latin American Perspectives* 36 (2): 31–48.

Burke, Nancy. 2002. *Pre-paid Phone Cards, "Cosas," and Photos of the Saints: Transnational Santería Practices in a Southwest City.* Research Paper no. 38, Latin American Institute. Albuquerque: University of New Mexico.

Burnett, Cristina Duffy, and Burke Marshall, eds. 2001. *Foreign in a Domestic Sense: Puerto Rico, American Expansion, and the Constitution.* Durham, N.C.: Duke University Press.

Burtless, Gary, and Orlando Sotomayor. 2006. "Labor Supply and Public Transfers." In *Restoring Growth in Puerto Rico: Overview and Policy Options*, ed. Susan M. Collins, Barry P. Bosworth, and Miguel A. Soto-Class, 19–30. Washington, D.C.: Brookings Institution/San Juan: Center for the New Economy.

Buscaglia-Salgado, José F. 2002. "Leaving Us for Nowhere: The Cuban Pursuit of the 'American Dream.'" *New Centennial Review* 2 (2): 285–98.

Cámara de Diputados, Comisión de Dominicanos Residentes en el Exterior. 2002. *Seminario "El futuro de la comunidad dominicana residente en Puerto Rico."* Santo Domingo: Cámara de Diputados de la República Dominicana.

Camuñas Madera, Ricardo. 1999. "Relaciones entre Santo Domingo y Puerto Rico: Una perspectiva histórica." In *La República Dominicana en el umbral del siglo XXI: Cultura, política y cambio social*, ed. Ramonina Brea, Rosario Espinal, and Fernando Valerio-Holguín, 525–43. Santo Domingo: Centro Universitario de Estudios Políticos y Sociales, Pontificia Universidad Católica Madre y Maestra.

Candelario, Ginetta E. B. 2007. *Black behind the Ears: Dominican Racial Identity from Museums to Beauty Shops.* Durham, N.C.: Duke University Press.

Casal, Lourdes. 1981. *Palabras juntan revolución.* Havana: Casa de las Américas.

Casal, María del C. 1992. "El impacto de la migración sobre la dinámica ocupacional, familiar y social de un grupo de mujeres dominicanas en Puerto Rico." Master's thesis, Division of Behavioral Sciences, Inter-American University of Puerto Rico, Río Piedras.

Casaña Mata, Ángela. 2002a. *Una contribución al estudio de la emigración calificada desde la perspectiva del país de origen.* Centro de Estudios de Migraciones Internacionales, Universidad de La Habana. http://www.uh.cu/centros/cemi/texto%20 completo/angela/Contribuci%F3n%20al%20estudio%20de%20la%20 emigraci%F3n%20calificada.htm. Accessed September 12, 2009.

———. 2002b. "Cubanos en República Dominicana: ¿Nueva tendencia de emigración?" In *Anuario CEMI, 1999–2001: Emigración Cubana,* ed. Centro de Estudios de Migraciones Internacionales, Universidad de La Habana. http:// bibliotecavirtual.clacso.org.ar/ar/libros/cuba/cemi/cubanos.pdf. Accessed March 29, 2010.

Castro, Max J. 2002. *The New Cuban Immigration in Context.* The North-South Agenda, Paper no. 58. Miami: North-South Center, University of Miami.

Castro, Max J., and Thomas D. Boswell. 2002. *The Dominican Diaspora Revisited: Dominicans and Dominican-Americans in a New Century.* North-South Agenda, Paper no. 53. Miami: North-South Center, University of Miami.

Central Intelligence Agency. 2009. *The World Factbook.* https://www.cia.gov/ library/publications/the-world-factbook. Accessed September 8, 2009.

Cervantes-Rodríguez, Margarita. 2010. *International Migration in Cuba: Accumulation, Imperial Designs, and Transnational Social Fields.* University Park: Pennsylvania State University Press.

Cervantes-Rodríguez, Margarita, Ramón Grosfoguel, and Eric Mielants, eds. 2009. *Caribbean Migration to Western Europe and the United States: Essays on Incorporation, Identity, and Citizenship.* Philadelphia: Temple University Press.

Chenault, Lawrence R. 1938. *The Puerto Rican Migrant in New York City.* New York: Columbia University Press.

Chinea, Jorge Luis. 2005. *Race and Labor in the Hispanic Caribbean: The West Indian Immigrant Worker Experience in Puerto Rico, 1800–1850.* Gainesville: University Press of Florida.

Christenson, Matthew. 2001. *Evaluating Components of International Migration: Migration between Puerto Rico and the United States.* Working Paper Series no. 64, Population Division, U.S. Bureau of the Census. http://www.census.gov/ population/www/documentation/twps0064.html#res. Accessed September 14, 2009.

Clark, Juan M. 1975. "The Exodus from Revolutionary Cuba (1959–1974): A Sociological Analysis." PhD diss., University of Florida.

Clark, Juan M., José I. Lazaga, and Rose S. Roque. 1981. *The 1980 Mariel Exodus: An Assessment and Prospect.* Washington, D.C.: Council for Inter-American Security.

Clegg, Peter, and Emilio Pantojas-García, eds. 2009. *Governance in the Non-independent Caribbean: Challenges and Opportunities in the Twenty-First Century.* Kingston: Ian Randle.

Clifford, James. 1994. "Diasporas." *Cultural Anthropology* 9 (3): 302–38.

Cobas, José A., and Jorge Duany. 1997. *Cubans in Puerto Rico: Ethnic Economy and Cultural Identity*. Gainesville: University Press of Florida.

Cobas, José A., Jorge Duany, and Joe R. Feagin, eds. 2009. *How the United States Racializes Latinos: White Hegemony and Its Consequences*. Boulder, Colo.: Paradigm.

Cohen, Robin. 1997. *Global Diasporas: An Introduction*. Seattle: University of Washington Press.

Coleman, Jonathan. 2001. "The Economic Impact of U.S. Sanctions with Respect to Cuba." In *Cuba in Transition*, vol. 11, ed. Association for the Study of Cuban Economy, 86–96. http://lanic.utexas.edu/project/asce/pdfs/volume11/coleman.pdf. Accessed September 14, 2009.

Collins, Susan M., Barry P. Bosworth, and Miguel A. Soto-Class, eds. 2006. *The Puerto Rican Economy: Restoring Growth*. Washington, D.C.: Brookings Institution/San Juan: Center for the New Economy.

Comisión Económica para América Latina y el Caribe. 2009. "Cuba." In *Balance preliminar de las economías de América Latina y el Caribe, 2009*. http://www.one.cu/publicaciones/cepal/bpalc2009/Cuba.pdf. Accessed January 8, 2010.

———. 2010. *Anuario estadístico de América Latina y el Caribe 2009*. http://websie.eclac.cl/anuario_estadistico/anuario_2009. Accessed April 16, 2010.

Committee on Insular Affairs, U.S. House of Representatives. 1945. *Report of the Committee on Insular Affairs, House of Representatives, 79th Congress, First Session*. Washington, D.C.: U.S. Government Printing Office.

Concepción Torres, Ramón Luis. 2008. "Puerto Rican Migration, Settlement Patterns, and Assimilation in the Orlando MSA." Master's thesis, Binghamton University, State University of New York.

Continuations Committee. 1959. *First Report of Continuations Committee*. Third Migration Conference, San Juan, January 19–26, 1958, New York, June 12, 1959.

Cordero-Guzmán, Héctor R., Robert C. Smith, and Ramón Grosfoguel, eds. 2001. *Migration, Transnationalization, and Race in a Changing New York*. Philadelphia: Temple University Press.

Crespo-Soto, Ramón. 2009. *Mainland Passage: The Cultural Anomaly of Puerto Rico*. Minneapolis: University of Minnesota Press.

Cruz, José E. 1998. *Identity and Power: Puerto Rican Politics and the Challenge of Ethnicity*. Philadelphia: Temple University Press.

———. 2010. "Barriers to Political Participation of Puerto Ricans and Hispanics in Osceola County, Florida: 1991–2007." *CENTRO: Journal of the Center for Puerto Rican Studies* 22 (1): 242–85.

Cruz Caraballo, Darwin. 1998. "'Tú eres dominicano': Las interacciones entre adolescentes dominicanos y puertorriqueños." Unpublished manuscript, McNair Program, University of Puerto Rico, Río Piedras, May.

Daniel, Justin. 2000. "Migration and the Reconstruction of Identity: The Puerto Rican Example." In *Politics and Identity: Migrants and Minorities in Multicultural States*, ed. Robert Hudson and Fred Réno, 3–23. London: Macmillan/St. Martin's.

Dávila, Arlene. 2001. *Latinos Inc.: The Marketing and Making of a People*. Berkeley: University of California Press.

―――. 2004. *Barrio Dreams: Puerto Ricans, Latinos, and the Neoliberal City*. Berkeley: University of California Press.

―――. 2008. *Latino Spin: Public Image and the Whitewashing of Race*. New York: New York University Press.

de Frank Canelo, Juan. 1982. *Dónde, por qué, de qué, cómo viven los dominicanos en el extranjero (Un informe sociológico sobre el proceso migratorio nuestro, 1961–1982)*. Santo Domingo: Alfa y Omega.

de Genova, Nicholas, ed. 2006. *Racial Transformations: Latinos and Asians Remaking the United States*. Durham, N.C.: Duke University Press.

de Genova, Nicholas, and Ana Y. Ramos-Zayas. 2003. *Latino Crossings: Mexicans, Puerto Ricans, and the Politics of Race and Citizenship*. New York: Routledge.

de Jesús, Anthony, and Daniel W. Vasquez. 2007. "Exploring the Education Profile and Pipeline for Puerto Ricans and Hispanics in Central Florida." Paper presented at the Second Hispanic Summit, Orlando Regional Chamber of Commerce, June 28–29. http://www.orlando.org/clientuploads/hsummit/ 07media/DeJesus.ppt. Accessed September 8, 2009.

de Jong, Lammert. 2005. "The Kingdom of the Netherlands: A Not So Perfect Union with the Netherlands Antilles and Aruba." In *Extended Statehood in the Caribbean: Paradoxes of Quasi Colonialism, Local Autonomy and Extended Statehood in the USA, French, Dutch and British Caribbean*, ed. Lammert de Jong and Dirk Krujit, 85–123. Amsterdam: Rozenberg.

de Jong, Lammert, and Dirk Krujit, eds. 2005. *Extended Statehood in the Caribbean: Paradoxes of Quasi Colonialism, Local Autonomy and Extended Statehood in the USA, French, Dutch and British Caribbean*. Amsterdam: Rozenberg.

de la Campa, Román. 2000. *Cuba on My Mind: Journeys to a Severed Nation*. London: Verso.

de la Garza, Rodolfo O., Louis DeSipio, F. Chris García, John García, and Angelo Falcón. 1992. *Latino Voices: Mexican, Puerto Rican, and Cuban Perspectives on American Politics*. Boulder, Colo.: Westview.

de la Garza, Rodolfo O., and Briant Lindsay Lowell, eds. 2002. *Sending Money Home: Hispanic Remittances and Community Development*. Lanham, Md.: Rowman and Littlefield.

de la Rosa Abreu, Aida Liz. 2002. "La identidad cultural de la mujer dominicana de clase trabajadora en Puerto Rico: Su articulación en la comedia televisiva." Master's thesis, School of Public Communication, University of Puerto Rico, Río Piedras.

del Castillo, José. 1989. "La inmigración dominicana en los Estados Unidos y Puerto Rico." In *Los inmigrantes indocumentados dominicanos en Puerto Rico: Realidad y mitos*, ed. Juan Hernández Cruz, 35–62. San Germán, P.R.: Centro de Publicaciones, Universidad Interamericana de Puerto Rico.

―――. 1990 [1981]. "Las inmigraciones y su aporte a la cultura dominicana (finales del siglo XIX y principios del XX)." In *Ensayos sobre cultura dominicana*, by Bernardo Vega, Carlos Dobal, Carlos Esteban Deive, Rubén Silié, José del Castillo, and Frank Moya Pons, 169–210. 2nd ed. Santo Domingo: Fundación Cultural Dominicana/Museo del Hombre Dominicano.

Delgado, José. 2001. "Clave la fuerza boricua en Florida." *El Nuevo Día*, December 31, 36.

————. 2008. "Voto puertorriqueño podría ser decisivo." *El Nuevo Día*, October 13, 46–47.

de Maeseneer, Rita. 2002. "Sobre dominicanos y puertorriqueños: ¿Movimiento perpetuo?" *CENTRO: Journal of the Center for Puerto Rican Studies* 14 (1): 52–73.

DeSipio, Louis. 2002. "Sending Money Home . . . for Now: Remittances and Immigrant Adaptation in the United States." In *Sending Money Home: Hispanic Remittances and Community Development*, ed. Rodolfo O. de la Garza and Briant Lindsay Lowell, 157–87. Lanham, Md.: Rowman and Littlefield.

DeSipio, Louis, Harry Pachón, Rodolfo O. de la Garza, and Jongho Lee. 2003. *Immigrant Politics at Home and Abroad: How Latino Immigrants Engage the Politics of Their Home Communities and the United States*. Claremont, Calif.: Tomás Rivera Policy Institute. http://www.trpi.org/PDFs/Immigrant_politics.pdf. Accessed November 19, 2009.

DeSipio, Louis, and Adrián Pantoja. 2004. *Puerto Rican Exceptionalism? A Comparative Analysis of Puerto Rican, Mexican, Salvadoran, and Dominican Transnational Civic and Political Ties*. http://perg.tamu.edu/lpc/DeSipio&Pantoja.pdf. Accessed September 6, 2009.

Diaz McConnell, Eileen, and Edward A. Delgado-Moreno. 2004. "Latino Panethnicity: Reality or Methodological Construction?" *Social Focus* 37 (4): 297–312.

Domínguez, Jorge. 1992. "Cooperating with the Enemy? U.S. Immigration Policies toward Cuba." In *Western Hemisphere Immigration and U.S. Immigration Policy*, ed. Christopher Mitchell, 31–88. University Park: Pennsylvania State University Press.

Domínguez, Jorge, Omar Everleny Pérez Villanueva, and Lorena Barberia, eds. 2004. *The Cuban Economy at the Start of the Twenty-First Century*. Cambridge: David Rockefeller Center for Latin American Studies, Harvard University.

Domínguez, Virginia. 1973. "Spanish-Speaking Caribbeans in New York: 'The Middle Race.'" *Revista/Review Interamericana* 3 (2): 135–42.

————. 1978. "Show Your Colors: Ethnic Divisiveness among Hispanic Caribbean Migrants." *Migration Today* 6 (1): 5–9.

Donnan, Hastings, and Thomas M. Wilson. 1999. *Borders: Frontiers of Identity, Nation and State*. New York: Berg.

Duany, Jorge. 1993. "Neither Golden Exile nor Dirty Worm: Ethnic Identity in Recent Cuban-American Novels." *Cuban Studies* 23: 167–83.

————. 1998a. "Of Borders and Boundaries: Contemporary Thinking on Cultural Identity." *Gestos: Teoría y Práctica del Teatro Hispánico* 13 (25): 15–33.

————. 1998b. "Reconstructing Racial Identity: Ethnicity, Color, and Class among Dominicans in the United States and Puerto Rico." *Latin American Perspectives* 25 (3): 147–72.

————. 2001. "Redes, remesas y paladares: La diáspora cubana desde una perspectiva transnacional." *Nueva Sociedad* 174: 40–51.

————. 2002. *The Puerto Rican Nation on the Move: Identities on the Island and in the United States.* Chapel Hill: University of North Carolina Press.

————. 2006a. "Más allá de El Barrio: La diáspora puertorriqueña hacia la Florida." *Nueva Sociedad* 201: 73–89.

————. 2006b. "Racializing Ethnicity in the Spanish-Speaking Caribbean: A Comparison of Haitians in the Dominican Republic and Dominicans in Puerto Rico." *Latin American and Caribbean Ethnic Studies* 1 (2): 231–48.

————. 2007. *A Transnational Migrant Crossroads: The Circulation of People and Money in Puerto Rico.* San Juan: Center for the New Economy. http://www.grupocne.org/publications/Transnational_Migrant_Crossroads.pdf. Accessed May 13, 2008.

————. 2008a. "Becoming Cuba-Rican." In *The Portable Island: Cubans at Home in the World*, ed. Ruth Behar and Lucía M. Suárez, 197–208. New York: Palgrave Macmillan.

————. 2008b [1994]. *Quisqueya on the Hudson: The Transnational Identity of Dominicans in Washington Heights.* 2nd ed. New York: Dominican Studies Institute, City University of New York.

————, ed. 1990. *Los dominicanos en Puerto Rico: Migración en la semi-periferia.* Río Piedras, P.R.: Huracán.

Duany, Jorge, Luisa Hernández Angueira, and César A. Rey. 1995. *El Barrio Gandul: Economía subterránea y migración indocumentada en Puerto Rico.* Caracas: Nueva Sociedad.

Duany, Jorge, and Félix V. Matos-Rodríguez. 2006. *Puerto Ricans in Orlando and Central Florida.* Policy Report 1, no. 1. New York: Centro de Estudios Puertorriqueños, Hunter College, City University of New York. http://www.centropr.org/documents/working_papers/FloridaBrief(F).pdf. Accessed September 6, 2009.

Duany, Jorge, and Emilio Pantojas-García. 2005. "Fifty Years of Commonwealth: The Contradictions of Free Associated Statehood in Puerto Rico." In *Extended Statehood in the Caribbean: Paradoxes of Quasi Colonialism, Local Autonomy and Extended Statehood in the USA, French, Dutch and British Caribbean*, ed. Lammert de Jong and Dirk Krujit, 21–58. Amsterdam: Rozenberg.

Duany, Jorge, and Patricia Silver, eds. 2010. *Puerto Rican Florida.* Special issue of *CENTRO: Journal of the Center for Puerto Rican Studies* 22 (1).

Durand, Jorge, Emilio A. Parrado, and Douglas S. Massey. 1996. "Migradollars and Development: A Reconsideration of the Mexican Case." *International Migration Review* 30 (2): 423–44.

Eckstein, Susan. 2003. *Diasporas and Dollars: Transnational Ties and the Transformation of Cuba.* http://web.mit.edu/cis/www/migration/pubs/rrwp/16_diasporas.pdf. Accessed September 7, 2009.

————. 2004a. "Dollarization and Its Discontents: Remittances and the Remaking of Cuba in the Post-Soviet Era." *Comparative Politics* 36 (3): 313–38.

———. 2004b. "Transnational Networks and Norms, Remittances, and the Transformation of Cuba." In *The Cuban Economy at the Start of the Twenty-First Century*, ed. Jorge Domínguez, Omar Everleny Pérez Villanueva, and Lorena Barberia, 319–52. Cambridge: David Rockefeller Center for Latin American Studies, Harvard University.

———. 2009. *The Immigrant Divide: How Cuban Americans Changed the U.S. and Their Homeland*. New York: Routledge.

Eckstein, Susan, and Lorena Barberia. 2001. *Cuban-American Cuba Visits: Public Policy, Private Practices*. http://web.mit.edu/cis/www/migration/pubs/mellon/5_cuba.pdf. Accessed September 7, 2009.

———. 2002. "Grounding Immigrant Generations in History: Cuban Americans and Their Transnational Ties." *International Migration Review* 36 (3): 799–837.

Eichenberger, Susan E. 2004. "'When Two or More Are Gathered': The Inclusion of Puerto Ricans in Multiethnic Parishes in Southeastern United States." PhD diss., University of Florida.

Enchautegui, María E. 2000. *Los determinantes de la inmigración dominicana a Puerto Rico*. Ensayos y monografías no. 104, Unidad de Investigaciones Económicas, Universidad de Puerto Rico, Recinto de Río Piedras. http://economia.uprrp.edu/ensayo%20104.pdf. Accessed September 7, 2009.

Erman, Sam. 2008. "Meanings of Citizenship in the U.S. Empire: Puerto Rico, Isabel Gonzalez, and the Supreme Court, 1898 to 1905." *Journal of American Ethnic History* 27 (4): 5–33.

Espino, María Dolores. 2010. "The Competitiveness of the Cuban Tourism Sector: Current Problems and Future Challenges." Paper presented at the Eighth Conference on Cuban and Cuban-American Studies, Cuban Research Institute, Florida International University, Miami, February 11–13.

Fagen, Richard, Richard A. Brody, and Thomas O'Leary. 1968. *Cubans in Exile: Disaffection and the Revolution*. Stanford, Calif.: Stanford University Press.

Falcón, Angelo. 1993. "A Divided Nation: The Puerto Rican Diaspora in the United States and the Proposed Referendum." In *Colonial Dilemma: Critical Perspectives on Contemporary Puerto Rico*, ed. Edgardo Meléndez and Edwin Meléndez, 173–80. Boston: South End.

———. 2004. *Atlas of Stateside Puerto Ricans*. Washington, D.C.: Puerto Rico Federal Affairs Administration.

———. 2007. "The Diaspora Factor: Stateside Boricuas and the Future of Puerto Rico." *NACLA Report on the Americas* 40 (6): 28–32.

Federal Communications Commission. 2010. *International Traffic Data*. http://www.fcc.gov/ib/sand/mniab/traffic. Accessed April 16, 2010.

Fernández, María Teresa (aka Mariposa). 2000. "Ode to the Diasporican: Pa' Mi Gente." *CENTRO: Journal of the Center for Puerto Rican Studies* 12 (1): 66.

Findlay, Eileen J. 2009. "Portable Roots: Latin New Yorker Community Building and the Meanings of Women's Return Migration in San Juan, Puerto Rico, 1960–2000." *Caribbean Studies* 37 (2): 3–43.

Fitzgerald, David. 2000. *Negotiating Extra-Territorial Citizenship: Mexican Migration and the Transnational Politics of Community*. Monograph Series no. 2. La Jolla, Calif.: Center for Comparative Immigration Studies.

Flores, Juan. 1993. *Divided Borders: Essays on Puerto Rican Identity*. Houston: Arte Público.

———. 2000. *From Bomba to Hip Hop: Puerto Rican Culture and Latino Identity*. New York: Columbia University Press.

———. 2008. *The Diaspora Strikes Back: "Caribeño" Tales of Learning and Turning*. New York: Routledge.

Foner, Nancy. 2005. *In a New Land: A Comparative View of Immigration*. New York: New York University Press.

Fouron, Georges Eugene, and Nina Glick Schiller. 2001. *Georges Woke Up Laughing: Long-Distance Nationalism and the Search for Home*. Durham, N.C.: Duke University Press.

Fresneda Camacho, Edel J. 2006. "Vivir con lo que me mandan: Las remesas y su impronta en la familia cubana." In *Informe final del concurso: Migraciones y modelos de desarrollo en América Latina y el Caribe*. Buenos Aires: Programa Regional de Becas CLACSO. http://bibliotecavirtual.clacso.org.ar/ar/libros/becas/2005/2005/migra/fresneda.pdf. Accessed September 12, 2009.

Friedman, Robert. 2004. "Exit Polls Show Kerry the Favorite for Stateside Puerto Ricans." *San Juan Star*, November 4.

Fritz, Sonia, dir. 1990. *Visa para un sueño*. Documentary film. San Juan: Isla Films.

Funkhouser, Edward, and Fernando A. Ramos. 1993. "The Choice of Migration Destination: Dominican and Cuban Immigrants to the Mainland United States and Puerto Rico." *International Migration Review* 27 (3): 537–56.

Fussell, Elizabeth. 2005. "The Initiation and Growth of Migration Streams from Communities in Five Latin American Countries." Paper presented at the Annual Meeting of the Population Association of America, Philadelphia, March 31–April 2. http://paa2005.princeton.edu/download.aspx?submissionId=50619. Accessed April 15, 2006.

García, María Cristina. 1996. *Havana USA: Cuban Exiles and Cuban Americans in South Florida, 1959–1994*. Berkeley: University of California Press.

García-Colón, Ismael. 2008. "Claiming Equality: Puerto Rican Farmworkers in Western New York." *Latino Studies* 6 (3): 269–89.

Georges, Eugenia. 1984. *New Immigrants and the Political Process: Dominicans in New York*. Occasional paper no. 45. New York: Center for Latin American and Caribbean Studies, New York University.

———. 1990. *The Making of a Transnational Community: Migration, Development, and Cultural Change in the Dominican Republic*. New York: Columbia University Press.

Giraud, Michel. 2002. "Racisme colonial, réaction identitaire et égalité citoyenne: Les leçons des expériences migratoires antillaises et guyanaises." *Hommes et migrations* 237: 40–53.

Glanton, Dahleen. 2000. "Hispanics Turn Florida into More of a Swing State." *Chicago Tribune*, November 26. http://www.ciponline.org/cuba/newsarchives/ november2000/ct112600glanton.htm. Accessed March 3, 2005.

Glick Schiller, Nina. 1999. "Transmigrants and Nation-States: Something Old and Something New in the U.S. Immigration Experience." In *The Handbook of International Migration: The American Experience*, ed. Charles Hirschman, Philip Kasinitz, and Josh DeWind, 94–119. New York: Russell Sage Foundation.

Glick Schiller, Nina, Linda Basch, and Cristina Blanc-Szanton, eds. 1992. *Towards a Transnational Perspective on Migration: Race, Class, Ethnicity, and Nationalism Reconsidered*. New York: New York Academy of Sciences.

Glick Schiller, Nina, Linda Basch, and Cristina Szanton Blanc. 1995. "From Immigrant to Transmigrant: Theorizing Transnational Migration." *Anthropological Quarterly* 68 (1): 48–63.

Goldring, Luin. 1996. "Blurring Borders: Constructing Transnational Community in the Process of Mexico-U.S. Migration." *Research in Community Sociology* 6: 69–104.

———. 2003. *Re-thinking Remittances: Social and Political Dimensions of Individual and Collective Remittances*. Working Paper Series, Centre for Research on Latin America and the Caribbean, York University. http://portal.rds.org.hn/download .php?id=558&sid=656903636730448d4ca43d0bD.C.8ba7cd. Accessed April 12, 2006.

Gómez, José Germán. 1993. "La organización y defensa de los derechos civiles de la comunidad dominicana en Puerto Rico." Paper presented at the Second Puerto Rican Congress on Civil Rights, Puerto Rican Bar Association, San Juan, January 16.

González, Nancy. 1970. "Peasants' Progress: Dominicans in New York." *Caribbean Studies* 10 (3): 154–71.

González-Corso, Mario A. 2007. "Cuban Monetary Reforms and Their Relation with Policies to Attract Remittances during the Special Period." In *Cuba in Transition*, vol. 18, ed. Association for the Study of the Cuban Economy, 315–28. http://lanic.utexas.edu/project/asce/pdfs/volume17/pdfs/gonzalezcorzo.pdf. Accessed January 8, 2009.

González Núñez, Gerardo. 2002. "¿Se encuentra Cuba en transición? Premisas y condicionantes de la encrucijada actual." In *El Caribe en la era de la globalización*, ed. Gerardo González Núñez and Emilio Pantojas García, 135–72. San Juan: Publicaciones Puertorriqueñas.

González-Pando, Miguel. 1998. *The Cuban Americans*. Westport, Conn.: Greenwood.

Graham, Pamela M. 1998. "The Politics of Incorporation: Dominicans in New York City." *Latino Studies Journal* 9 (3): 39–64.

———. 2001. "Political Incorporation and Re-incorporation: Simultaneity in the Dominican Migrant Experience." In *Migration, Transnationalization, and Race in a Changing New York*, ed. Héctor R. Cordero-Guzmán, Robert C. Smith, and Ramón Grosfoguel, 87–108. Philadelphia: Temple University Press.

Grasmuck, Sherri, and Patricia R. Pessar. 1991. *Between Two Islands: Dominican International Migration*. Berkeley: University of California Press.

———. 1996. "First- and Second-Generation Settlements of Dominicans in the United States: 1960–1990." In *Origins and Destinies: Immigration, Race, and Ethnicity in America*, ed. Silvia Pedraza and Rubén G. Rumbaut, 280–92. Belmont, Calif.: Wadsworth.

Graziano, Frank. 2006. "Why Dominicans Migrate: The Complex of Factors Conducive to Undocumented Maritime Migration." *Diaspora: A Journal of Transnational Studies* 15 (1): 1–33.

Greenbaum, Susan. 2002. *More than Black: Afro-Cubans in Tampa*. Gainesville: University Press of Florida.

Grenier, Guillermo J., and Lisandro Pérez. 2003. *The Legacy of Exile: Cubans in the United States*. Boston: Allyn and Bacon.

Grosfoguel, Ramón. 1994–95. "Caribbean Colonial Immigrants in the Metropoles: A Research Agenda." *CENTRO: Journal of the Center for Puerto Rican Studies* 7 (1): 82–95.

———. 2003. *Colonial Subjects: Puerto Ricans in a Global Perspective*. Berkeley: University of California Press.

———, ed. 2004. *Caribbean Migration to Metropolitan Centers: Identity, Citizenship, and Models of Integration*. Special issue of *Caribbean Studies* 32 (1).

Growers Association Files, Farm Labor Program, Migration Division, Department of Labor, Government of Puerto Rico. 1955–82. Microfilm reels 1–18; boxes 506–656. Records of the Offices of the Government of Puerto Rico in the United States. Centro de Estudios Puertorriqueños, Hunter College, City University of New York.

Grupo Areíto. 1978. *Contra viento y marea: Jóvenes cubanos hablan desde su exilio en Estados Unidos*. Havana: Casa de las Américas.

Guarnizo, Luis E. 1994. "*Los Dominicanyorks*: The Making of a Binational Society." *Annals of the American Academy of Political and Social Science* 533: 70–86.

———. 1995. "Regresando a casa: Clase, género y transformación del hogar entre migrantes dominicanos/as retornados/as." *Género y Sociedad* 2 (3): 53–127.

———. 1997. "The Emergence of a Transnational Social Formation and the Mirage of Return Migration among Dominican Transmigrants." *Identities* 4 (2): 281–322.

———. 1998. "The Rise of Transnational Social Formations: Mexican and Dominican State Responses to Transnational Migration." *Political Power and Social Theory* 12: 45–94.

———. 2000. "Notes on Transnational." Paper presented at the workshop on "Transnational Migration: Comparative Theory and Research Perspectives," University of Oxford, July 7–9.

———. 2003. "The Economics of Transnational Living." *International Migration Review* 37 (3): 666–99.

Guarnizo, Luis E., and Michael Peter Smith. 1998. "The Locations of Transnationalism." In *Transnationalism from Below*, ed. Michael Peter Smith and Luis Eduardo Guarnizo, 3–34. New Brunswick, N.J.: Transaction.

Hablando de Quisqueya en Borinquen. 1992. "Actividades institucionales: Casa Dominicana del Oeste informa." Vol. 1 (6): 14.

Hannerz, Ulf. 1996. *Transnational Connections: Culture, People, Places.* London: Routledge.

Haslip-Viera, Gabriel, Angelo Falcón, and Félix Matos-Rodríguez, eds. 2004. *Boricuas in Gotham: Puerto Ricans in the Making of Modern New York.* Princeton, N.J.: Markus Wiener.

Hendricks, Glenn. 1974. *The Dominican Diaspora: From the Dominican Republic to New York City — Villagers in Transition.* New York: Teachers College Press.

Henken, Ted. 2002. "'Vale Todo' (Anything Goes): Cuba's *Paladares.*" In *Cuba in Transition,* vol. 12, ed. Association for the Study of the Cuban Economy, 344–53. http://lanic.utexas.edu/project/asce/pdfs/volume12/henken.pdf. Accessed September 7, 2009.

———. 2005. "*Balseros, Boteros,* and *El Bombo*: Post-1994 Cuban Immigration to the United States and the Persistence of Special Treatment." *Latino Studies* 3 (3): 393–416.

Hernández, Rafael. 1995. "Cuba y los cubano-americanos: El impacto del conflicto EE.UU.-Cuba en sus relaciones presentes y futuras." *Cuadernos de Nuestra América* 12 (23): 4–22.

Hernández, Rafael, María Isabel Domínguez, Consuelo Martín, and Omar Valiño. 2002. "¿Por qué emigran los cubanos? Causas y azares." *Temas: Cultura, Ideología, Sociedad* 31: 73–91.

Hernández, Rafael, and Redi Gomis. 1986. "Retrato del Mariel: El ángulo socio-económico." *Cuadernos de Nuestra América* 3 (5): 124–51.

Hernández, Ramona. 2002. *The Mobility of Workers under Advanced Capitalism: Dominican Migration to the United States.* New York: Columbia University Press.

Hernández, Ramona, and Nancy López. 1997. "Yola and Gender: Dominican Women's Unregulated Migration." In *Dominican Studies: Resources and Research Questions,* by Luis Álvarez-López, Sherry Baver, Jean Weisman, Ramona Hernández, and Nancy López, 59–78. New York: Dominican Studies Institute, City University of New York.

Hernández Álvarez, José. 1967. *Return Migration to Puerto Rico.* Berkeley: Institute for International Studies, University of California.

Hernández Angueira, Luisa. 1990. "La migración de mujeres dominicanas hacia Puerto Rico." In *Los dominicanos en Puerto Rico: Migración en la semi-periferia,* ed. Jorge Duany, 73–89. Río Piedras, P.R.: Huracán.

———. 1997. "Across the Mona Strait: Dominican Boat Women in Puerto Rico." In *Daughters of Caliban: Caribbean Women in the Twentieth Century,* ed. Consuelo López Springfield, 96–111. Bloomington: Indiana University Press.

———. 2001. *Mujeres puertorriqueñas, "welfare" y globalización.* Hato Rey, P.R.: Publicaciones Puertorriqueñas.

Hernández Cruz, Juan E. 1994. *Corrientes migratorias en Puerto Rico/Migratory Trends in Puerto Rico.* San Germán, P.R.: CISCLA, Universidad Interamericana.

————. 2002. "La emigración puertorriqueña a Florida y el 'Mundo maravilloso de Disney.'" *Diálogo* (August), 29.

Herrera, Andrea O'Reilly, ed. 2007. *Cuba: Idea of a Nation Displaced*. Albany: State University of New York Press.

Herrera Mora, Myrna. 2008. *Mujeres dominicanas, 1930–1961: Antitrujillistas y exiliadas en Puerto Rico*. San Juan: Isla Negra.

History Task Force, Centro de Estudios Puertorriqueños, ed. 1979. *Labor Migration under Capitalism: The Puerto Rican Experience*. New York: Monthly Review Press.

Holgado Fernández, Isabel. 2000. *¡No es fácil! Mujeres cubanas y la crisis revolucionaria*. Barcelona: Icaria.

Hondagneu-Sotelo, Pierrette, ed. 2003. *Gender and U.S. Immigration: Contemporary Trends*. Berkeley: University of California Press.

Hondagneu-Sotelo, Pierrette, and Ernestine Avila. 1997. "'I'm Here, but I'm There': The Meanings of Latina Transnational Motherhood." *Gender and Society* 11 (5): 548–71.

Institute for Public Opinion Research, Florida International University. 2004. *Cuba Poll Final Results*. http://www.fiu.edu/orgs/cubapoll/index.html. Accessed September 14, 2009.

————. 2007. *2007 FIU/Cuba Poll*. http://www.fiu.edu/~ipor/cuba8/. Accessed September 12, 2009.

————. 2008. *2008 Cuba/U.S. Transition Poll*. http://www.fiu.edu/~ipor/cuba-t. Accessed September 12, 2009.

Inter-American Development Bank (IADB). 2004. *Sending Money Home: Remittances to Latin America*. http://idbdocs.iadb.org/wsdocs/getdocument. aspx?docnum=889459. Accessed September 12, 2009.

————. 2007. *Remittances to Haiti Topped $1.65 Billion in 2006, Says IDB Fund*. Press release, March 5. http://www.iadb.org/news/articledetail.cfm?language= en&artid=3637. Accessed May 20, 2008.

————. 2010. *Remittances to Latin America and the Caribbean 2009 (US$ Millions)*. http://www.iadb.org/mif/remesas_map.cfm?language=English. Accessed March 7, 2010.

International Labour Organization. 2009. *Main Statistics (Annual)*. http://laborsta .ilo.org/STP/guest. Accessed July 10, 2009.

Internet World Stats. 2010. *Cuba*. http://www.internetworldstats.com/car/cu.htm. Accessed July 24, 2010.

Irizarry Mora, Edwin. 2001. *Economía de Puerto Rico: Evolución y perspectivas*. Mexico City: Thomson Learning.

Iturrondo, Milagros. 1993–94. "'San Ignacio de la Yola' . . . y los dominicanos (en Puerto Rico)." *Homines* 17 (1–2): 234–40.

————. 2000. *Voces quisqueyanas en Borinquen*. San Juan: Camila.

Itzigsohn, José. 1995. "Migrant Remittances, Labor Markets, and Household Strategies: A Comparative Analysis of Low-Income Household Strategies in the Caribbean Basin." *Social Forces* 74 (2): 633–55.

————. 2006. "Immigrant Incorporation among Dominicans in Providence, Rhode Island: An Intergenerational Perspective." In *Latinos in New England*, ed. Andrés Torres, 253–72. Philadelphia: Temple University Press.

Itzigsohn, José, and Carlos Dore-Cabral. 2000. "Competing Identities? Race, Ethnicity, and Panethnicity among Dominicans in the United States." *Sociological Forum* 15 (2): 225–47.

Itzigsohn, José, Carlos Dore-Cabral, Esther Hernández Medina, and Obed Vázquez. 1999. "Mapping Dominican Transnationalism: Narrow and Broad Transnational Practices." *Ethnic and Racial Studies* 22 (2): 316–39.

Itzigsohn, José, and Daniela Villacrés. 2008. "Migrant Political Transnationalism and the Practice of Democracy: Dominican External Voting Rights and Salvadoran Hometown Associations." *Ethnic and Racial Studies* 31 (4): 664–86.

Junta de Planificación de Puerto Rico. 1970–2000. *Estadísticas socioeconómicas*. San Juan: Junta de Planificación de Puerto Rico.

————. 2001. "Movimiento de pasajeros entre Puerto Rico y el exterior: Años fiscales 1990–2000." Unpublished manuscript, Programa de Planificación Económica y Social, Negociado de Análisis Económico, Junta de Planificación de Puerto Rico.

————. 2000–2010. *Apéndice estadístico*. http://www.jp.gobierno.pr. Accessed April 13, 2010.

Kapur, Devesh. 2003. *Remittances: The New Development Mantra?* G-24 Discussion Paper Series, United Nations Conference on Trade and Development. http://www.unctad.org/en/docs/gdsmdpbg2420045_en.pdf. Accessed April 11, 2006.

Kearney, Michael. 1991. "Borders and Boundaries of State and Self at the End of Empire." *Journal of Historical Sociology* 4 (1): 52–74.

Knauer, Lisa Maya. 2001. "Afrocubanidad translocal: La rumba y la santería en Nueva York y La Habana." In *Culturas encontradas: Cuba y los Estados Unidos*, ed. Rafael Hernández and John H. Coatsworth, 11–31. Havana: Centro de Investigación y Desarrollo de la Cultura Cubana Juan Marinello/Centro de Estudios Latinoamericanos David Rockefeller, Universidad de Harvard.

————. 2003. "Remesas multi-direccionales y etnografía viajera." *Sociedade e cultura* 6 (1): 13–24.

Krauss, Clifford, and Larry Rohter. 1998. "Dominican Drug Traffickers Tighten Grip on the Northeast." *New York Times*, May 11. http://www.nytimes.com/1998/05/11/nyregion/dominican-drug-traffickers-tighten-grip-on-the-northeast.html. Accessed September 7, 2009.

La Fountain–Stokes, Lawrence. 2009. *Queer Ricans: Cultures and Sexualities in the Diaspora*. Minneapolis: University of Minnesota Press.

Laguerre, Michel S. 1998. *Diasporic Citizenship: Haitian Americans in Transnational America*. New York: St. Martin's.

Lamba-Nieves, Deepak. 2009. "Furthering the Discussions on the Migration-Development Nexus: A Closer Look at Dominican Hometown Associations and Their Development Impacts." First-year paper, Program in Urban Studies and Planning, Massachusetts Institute of Technology.

Laó-Montes, Agustín, and Arlene M. Dávila, eds. 2001. *Mambo Montage: The Latinization of New York*. New York: Columbia University Press.

Lapp, Michael. 1990. "Managing Migration: The Migration Division of Puerto Rico and Puerto Ricans in New York City, 1948–1968." PhD diss., Johns Hopkins University.

Larson, Eric M., and Teresa A. Sullivan. 1989. "*Cifras convencionales* en las investigaciones sobre migración: El caso de los 'dominicanos desaparecidos.'" In *Dominicanos ausentes: Cifras, políticas, condiciones sociales*, by Eugenia Georges, Eric M. Larson, Sara J. Mahler, Christopher Mitchell, Patricia Pessar, Teresa A. Sullivan, and Robert Warren, 67–114. Santo Domingo: Fundación Friedrich Ebert/Fondo para el Avance de las Ciencias Sociales.

Latin American Migration Project (LAMP). 2009. *Research*. http://lamp.opr .princeton.edu. Accessed September 7, 2009.

Leal Calderón, Zulima. 2010. "El otro lado de la moneda: Remesas y migración dominicana en Puerto Rico." Paper presented at the Institute of Caribbean Studies, University of Puerto Rico, Río Piedras, April 20.

Levitt, Peggy. 2001. *The Transnational Villagers*. Berkeley: University of California Press.

———. 2005. "Transnational Ties and Incorporation: Dominicans in the United States." In *The Columbia History of Latinos in the United States since 1960*, ed. David G. Gutiérrez, 187–228. New York: Columbia University Press.

Levitt, Peggy, and Rafael de la Dehesa. 2003. "Transnational Migration and the Redefinition of the State: Variations and Explanations." *Ethnic and Racial Studies* 26 (4): 587–611.

Levitt, Peggy, and Nina Glick Schiller. 2004. "Conceptualizing Simultaneity: A Transnational Social Field Perspective on Society." *International Migration Review* 38 (3): 1002–39.

Levitt, Peggy, and Ninna Nyberg-Sørensen. 2004. *The Transnational Turn in Migration Studies*. Global Migration Perspectives no. 6. Geneva: Global Commission on International Migration.

Levitt, Peggy, and Mary C. Waters, eds. 2002. *The Changing Face of Home: The Transnational Lives of the Second Generation*. New York: Russell Sage Foundation.

Lewis, Oscar. 1966. *La Vida: A Puerto Rican Family in the Culture of Poverty — San Juan and New York*. New York: Random House.

Lizza, Ryan. 2000. "Orlando Dispatch." *New Republic Online*, November 6. http:// www.thenewrepublic.com/110600/lizza110600.html. Accessed March 3, 2005.

López, Nancy. 2004. "Transnational Changing Gender Roles: Second-Generation Dominicans in New York City." In *Dominican Migration: Transnational Perspectives*, ed. Ernesto Sagás and Sintia E. Molina, 177–99. Gainesville: University Press of Florida.

López Carrasquillo, Alberto. 1999. "Prácticas de aceptación y rechazo de estudiantes dominicanos(as) en una escuela elemental en Puerto Rico." *Revista de Ciencias Sociales* (nueva época) 6: 41–64.

Lorenzo-Hernández, José. 1999. "The Nuyorican's Dilemma: Categorization of Returning Migrants in Puerto Rico." *International Migration Review* 33 (4): 988–1013.

Mahler, Sarah J. 1989. "La dinámica de la legalización en Nueva York: Un enfoque hacia los dominicanos." In *Dominicanos ausentes: Cifras, políticas, condiciones sociales*, by Eugenia Georges, Eric M. Larson, Sara J. Mahler, Christopher Mitchell, Patricia Pessar, Teresa A. Sullivan, and Robert Warren, 139–82. Santo Domingo: Fundación Friedrich Ebert/Fondo para el Avance de las Ciencias Sociales.

———. 1998. "Theoretical and Empirical Contributions toward a Research Agenda for Transnationalism." In *Transnationalism from Below*, ed. Michael Peter Smith and Luis Eduardo Guarnizo, 64–102. New Brunswick, N.J.: Transaction.

Mahler, Sarah J., and Katrin Hansing. 2005a. "Myths and Mysticism: How Bringing a Transnational Religious Lens to the Examination of Cuba and the Cuban Diaspora Exposes and Ruptures the Fallacy of Isolation." In *Cuba Transnational*, ed. Damián J. Fernández, 42–60. Gainesville: University Press of Florida.

———. 2005b. "Toward a Transnationalism of the Middle: How Transnational Religious Practices Help Bridge the Divides between Cuba and Miami." *Latin American Perspectives* 32 (1): 122–46.

Maldonado, Edwin. 1979. "Contract Labor and the Beginnings of Puerto Rican Communities in the United States." *International Migration Review* 13 (1): 103–21.

Marazzi, Rosa. 1974. "El impacto de la inmigración a Puerto Rico de 1800 a 1830: Análisis estadístico." *Revista de Ciencias Sociales* 18 (1–2): 1–42.

Marcus, George E. 1995. "Ethnography in/of the World System: The Emergence of Multi-Sited Ethnography." *Annual Review of Anthropology* 24: 95–117.

Marcus, Joseph. 1919. *Labor Conditions in Puerto Rico*. Washington, D.C.: U.S. Government Printing Office.

Martin, John Bartlow. 1966. *Overtaken by Events: The Dominican Crisis from the Fall of Trujillo to the Civil War*. Garden City, N.Y.: Doubleday.

Martín Fernández, Consuelo, Antonio Aja Díaz, Ángela Casaña Mata, and Magali Martín Quijano. 2007. *La emigración de Cuba desde fines del siglo XX y principios del XXI: Lecturas y reflexiones mirando a la Ciudad de La Habana*. http://www .uh.cu/centros/cemi/anuario%200708/2007/7%20Consuelo,%20Aja,%20 Angela%20y%20Magali%20LA%20EMIGRACION%20DE%20CUBA%20 DE%20FINALES%20DE%20SIGLO%20XX%20y%20PRINCIPOS%20DE%20 SIGLO%20XXI.pdf. Accessed September 28, 2009.

Martín Fernández, Consuelo, Maricela Perera, and Maiky Díaz Pérez. 2001. "Estrategias cotidianas en la crisis de los noventa." In *Anuario CEMI 1999–2001: Emigración Cubana*, ed. Centro de Estudios de Migraciones Internacionales, Universidad de La Habana. http://www.uh.cu/centros/ceap/estrategias.html. Accessed September 12, 2009.

Martín Fernández, Consuelo, and Guadalupe Pérez. 1998. *Familia, emigración y vida cotidiana en Cuba*. Havana: Editora Política.

Martínez, Milagros, Blanca Morejón, Antonio Aja, Magaly Martín, Guillermo Milán, Marta Díaz, Inalvis Rodríguez, Lourdes Urrutia, and Consuelo Martín.

1996. *Los balseros cubanos: Un estudio a partir de las salidas ilegales.* Havana: Ciencias Sociales.

Martínez, Samuel. 2003. "Identities at the Dominican and Puerto Rican International Migrant Crossroads." In *Marginal Migrations: The Circulation of Cultures within the Caribbean,* ed. Shalini Puri, 141–64. Oxford: Macmillan Caribbean.

Martínez Rosado, Raúl. 2006. *La travesía en yola: Odiseas a Puerto Rico.* Scott Depot, W.Va.: El Salvaje Refinado.

Martínez–San Miguel, Yolanda. 2003. *Caribe Two Ways: Cultura de la migración en el Caribe insular hispánico.* San Juan: Callejón.

———. 2007. "Puerto Rican Cubanness: Reconfiguring Caribbean Imaginaries." In *Cuba: Idea of a Nation Displaced,* ed. Andrea O'Reilly Herrera, 47–76. Albany: State University of New York Press.

Masud-Piloto, Félix. 1996. *From Welcome Exiles to Illegal Immigrants: Cuban Migration to the United States, 1959–1995.* Lanham, Md.: Rowman and Littlefield.

Matos-Rodríguez, Félix V., and Pedro Juan Hernández. 2001. *Pioneros: Puerto Ricans in New York City, 1896–1948.* Charleston, S.C.: Arcadia.

McIntyre, Frank. 1982 [1917]. "Memorandum for the Secretary of War, April 17." In *Sources for the Study of Puerto Rican Migration, 1879–1930,* ed. History Task Force, Centro de Estudios Puertorriqueños, 104–5. New York: Centro de Estudios Puertorriqueños, Hunter College.

Mejía Pardo, Diana. 1993. "Macroestructuras, superestructuras y proposiciones de opiniones en 17 relatos de puertorriqueños acerca de dominicanos." Master's thesis, Graduate Program in Linguistics, University of Puerto Rico, Río Piedras.

Meléndez, Edgardo. 1997. "Transnational Puerto Rican Politics: Unresolved Issues and Research Problems." Paper presented at the workshop, "The Caribbean Diaspora: The Current Situation and Future Trends," University of Puerto Rico, Río Piedras, May 2.

Meléndez, Edwin. 1993. *Los que se van, los que regresan: Puerto Rican Migration to and from the United States, 1982–1988.* Political Economy Working Paper Series no. 1. New York: Centro de Estudios Puertorriqueños, Hunter College, City University of New York.

———. 2007. "Changes in the Characteristics of Puerto Rican Migrants to the United States." In *Latinos in a Changing Society,* ed. Martha Montero-Sieburth and Edwin Meléndez, 112–31. Westport, Conn.: Praeger.

Mendible, Myra, ed. 2007. *From Bananas to Buttocks: The Latina Body in Popular Film and Culture.* Austin: University of Texas Press.

Merriam-Webster's Online Dictionary. 2009. "Diaspora." http://www.merriam-webster.com. Accessed October 14, 2009.

Mesa-Lago, Carmelo. 2007. "The Cuban Economy in 2006–2007." In *Cuba in Transition,* vol. 17, ed. Association for the Study of the Cuban Economy, 1–20. http://lanic.utexas.edu/project/asce/pdfs/volume17/pdfs/mesalago.pdf. Accessed September 28, 2009.

Migration News. 1997. "INS: Methodology and State-by-State Estimates." Vol. 3 (4) (March). http://migration.ucdavis.edu/mn/more.php?id=1196_0_5_0. Accessed September 7, 2009.

———. 1998a. "Caribbean/Central America." Vol. 4 (3) (July). http://migration. ucdavis.edu/MN/more.php?id=1574_0_2_0. Accessed September 28, 2009.

———. 1998b. "Cuba/Caribbean: Immigration, Remittances." Vol. 5 (1) (January). migration.ucdavis.edu/mn/more.php?id=1425_0_2_0. Accessed September 9, 2008.

———. 2009. *Remittances*. http://migration.ucdavis.edu/mn/data/remittances/ remittances.html. Accessed September 6, 2009.

Milia-Marie-Luce, Monique. 2002. "De l'Outre-mer au continent: Étude comparée de l'émigration puertoricaine et antillo-guyanaise de l'après-guerre aux années 1960." PhD diss., École des Hautes Études en Sciences Sociales, Paris.

———. 2007. "La grande migration des Antillais en France ou les années BUMIDOM." In *Dynamiques migratoires de la Caraïbe*, ed. GÉODE Caraïbe, 93–103. Paris: Karthala.

Milligan, Susan. 2000. "In Florida, Different Latino Group Now in Mix." *Puerto Rico Herald*, October 30. http://www.puertorico-herald.org/issues/vol4n44/ DiftLatinos-en.html. Accessed September 8, 2008.

Mills, C. Wright. 2000 [1960]. *The Sociological Imagination*. Fortieth anniversary ed. New York: Oxford University Press.

Mills, C. Wright, Clarence Senior, and Rose Kohn Goldsen. 1950. *The Puerto Rican Journey: New York's Newest Immigrants*. New York: Harper.

Ministerio de Relaciones Exteriores, Cuba. 2008. *Sitio cubano de la nación y la emigración*. http://www.nacionyemigracion.com/inicio.html. Accessed September 12, 2009.

———. 2009. *Informe de Cuba sobre la Resolución 63/7 de la Asamblea General de las Naciones Unidas*. http://www.cubavsbloqueo.cu/Informe2009/index. Accessed September 28, 2009.

MoneyGram International. 2004. *MoneyGram Services Expanded in Puerto Rico*. http://www.moneygram.com/MGICorp/PressReleaseNews/mgicorp_c_ci_pr_ mseipr. Accessed October 1, 2009.

Monreal, Pedro. 1999. "Las remesas familiares en la economía cubana." *Encuentro de la Cultura Cubana* 14: 49–62.

Monreal, Pedro, and Julio Carranza Valdés. 2000. "Los retos del desarrollo en Cuba: Realidades, mitos y conceptos." In *Cuba: Construyendo futuro — Reestructuración económica y transformaciones sociales*, ed. Manuel Monereo, Miguel Riera, and Juan Valdés, 109–38. Madrid: Viejo Topo.

Monserrat, Joseph. 1961. "Suggestions for a New Approach to Migration." Confidential Memorandum to Luis Muñoz Marín, February 9. Section 5: Governor of Puerto Rico, 1949–64; series 1: General Correspondence; box 137: Departments; folder 9: Labor — Migration Division. Fundación Luis Muñoz Marín, Trujillo Alto, P.R.

————. 1991. "The Development, Growth and Decline of the Puerto Rican Migrant Farmworkers Contract Program." Series: Subject Files; box 17; folder 2. Joseph Monserrat Papers, Centro de Estudios Puertorriqueños, Hunter College, City University of New York.

Morawska, Ewa. 2001. "Immigrants, Transnationalism, and Ethnicization: A Comparison of This Great Wave and the Last." In *E Pluribus Unum? Contemporary and Historical Perspectives on Immigrant Incorporation*, ed. Gary Gerstle and John Mollenkopf, 175–212. New York: Russell Sage Foundation.

Morris, Nancy. 1995. *Puerto Rico: Culture, Politics, and Identity*. Westport, Conn.: Praeger.

Muñoz Marín, Luis. 1946. "Foro público sobre el problema poblacional de Puerto Rico: Resumen de las soluciones ofrecidas por los ponentes en la sesión de julio 19, 1946." Memorandum to Max Egloff, September 28. Section 4: President of the Senate, 1941–48; series 2: Insular Government; subseries 1: Fortaleza; box 1B: Office of Information; folder 16. Fundación Luis Muñoz Marín, Trujillo Alto, P.R.

————. 1960. "Informe sobre Puerto Rico a los puertorriqueños residentes en Nueva York." Recorded on March 23 and broadcast on television on April 3. Section 5: Governor of Puerto Rico, 1949–65; series 9: Speeches; box 16: Status; folder 7. Fundación Luis Muñoz Marín, Trujillo Alto, P.R.

Mustelier Ayala, Sandra. 2006. *Ecos boricuas en el Oriente cubano: La diáspora de un ala*. San Juan, P.R.: Makarios.

Negrón-Muntaner, Frances. 2004. *Boricua Pop: Puerto Ricans and the Latinization of American Culture*. New York: New York University Press.

————, ed. 2007. *None of the Above: Puerto Ricans in the Global Era*. New York: Palgrave Macmillan.

Negrón-Muntaner, Frances, and Ramón Grosfoguel, eds. 1997. *Puerto Rican Jam: Essays on Culture and Politics*. Minneapolis: University of Minnesota Press.

Newby, C. Alison, and Julie A. Dowling. 2007. "Black and Hispanic: The Racial Identification of Afro-Cuban Immigrants in the Southwest." *Sociological Perspectives* 50 (3): 343–66.

Núñez Moreno, Lilia. 1997. "Más allá del cuentapropismo en Cuba." *Temas: Cultura, Ideología, Sociedad* 11: 41–50.

Oboler, Suzanne. 1995. *Ethnic Labels, Latino Lives: Identity and the Politics of (Re) Presentation in the United States*. Minneapolis: University of Minnesota Press.

O'Connor, Donald J. 1947. Letter to Luis Muñoz Marín, April 29. Section 5: Governor; series 2: Insular Government; subseries 1: Fortaleza; folder 22. Fundación Luis Muñoz Marín, Trujillo Alto, P.R.

————. 1948. "Mainland Labor Force Needs in 1948–49 and Puerto Rico's Opportunities to Exploit Them." Memorandum to Jesús T. Piñero and others, August 10. Section 4: President of the Senate, 1941–48; series 2: Insular Government; subseries 1: Fortaleza; 1C: Office of Puerto Rico in Washington; folder 18. Fundación Luis Muñoz Marín, Trujillo Alto, P.R.

Office of Global Analysis, Foreign Agricultural Service, U.S. Department of
Agriculture. 2008. *Cuba's Food and Agriculture Situation Report*. http://www.fas
.usda.gov/itp/cuba/CubaSituation0308.pdf. Accessed January 6, 2010.

Oficina Nacional de Estadística, República Dominicana. 2009a. *Portal de las
estadísticas dominicanas*. http://www.one.gob.do. Accessed December 10, 2009.

———. 2009b. "Remesas internacionales que reciben los hogares en República
Dominicana." *Panorama estadístico* 2 (20). http://www.one.gob.do/index.php?
module=articles&function=view&ptid=12. Accessed February 10, 2010.

Oficina Nacional de Estadísticas, Cuba. 2009. *Anuario estadístico de Cuba, 2008*.
http://www.one.cu/aec2008.htm. Accessed September 12, 2009.

Oficina Nacional del Censo, Dirección General de Estadística, República
Dominicana. 1958. *Tercer censo nacional de población, 1950*. Ciudad Trujillo,
Dominican Republic: Dirección General de Estadística.

Ojeda Reyes, Félix. 1992. *Peregrinos de la libertad: Documentos y fotos de exiliados
puertorriqueños del siglo XIX localizados en los archivos y bibliotecas de Cuba*. Río
Piedras, P.R.: Editorial de la Universidad de Puerto Rico.

Olwig, Karen Fog. 1997. "Hacia una reconceptualización de la migración y
transnacionalización." *Estudios Sociales* 30 (109): 53–75.

Oostindie, Gert, and Inge Klinkers. 2003. *Decolonising the Caribbean: Dutch Policies
in a Comparative Perspective*. Amsterdam: Amsterdam University Press.

Orozco, Manuel. 2002a. "Globalization and Migration: The Impact of Family
Remittances to Latin America." *Latin American Politics and Society* 44 (2):
41–66.

———. 2002b. *Remittances, Costs, and Market Competition*. http://www.the
dialogue.org/publications/country_studies/remittances/RemittancesCFRB.pdf.
Accessed September 7, 2009.

———. 2003. *Challenges and Opportunities of Marketing Remittances to Cuba*.
http://www.thedialogue.org/PublicationFiles/Challenges%20and%20
opportunities%20of%20marketting%20remittances%20to%20.pdf. Accessed
September 7, 2009.

———. 2004. *Remittances to Latin America and the Caribbean: Issues and Perspectives on Development*. Washington, D.C.: Organization of American States. http://
www.frbatlanta.org/news/CONFEREN/payments04/orozco.pdf. Accessed
April 11, 2006.

———. 2009a. *The Cuban Condition: Migration, Remittances, and Its Diaspora*.
http://www.thedialogue.org/PublicationFiles/cuban%20condition%20
migration%20remittances_FINAL.pdf. Accessed September 10, 2009.

———. 2009b. *Understanding the Continuing Effect of the Economic Crisis on Remittances to Latin America and the Caribbean*. Inter-American Dialogue, August 10.
http://idbdocs.iadb.org/wsdocs/getdocument.aspx?docnum=2100503. Accessed
January 21, 2010.

Orozco, Manuel, B. Lindsay Lowell, Micah Bump, and Rachel Fedewa. 2005.
*Transnational Engagement, Remittances, and Their Relationship to Development in
Latin America and the Caribbean*. Washington, D.C.: Institute for the Study of

International Migration, Georgetown University. http://www.thedialogue.org/
publications/2005/summer/trans_engagement.pdf. Accessed April 11, 2006.

Ortiz, Fernando. 1947. *Cuban Counterpoint: Tobacco and Sugar*. New York: Knopf.

Ortiz, Renato. 1996. *Otro territorio: Ensayos sobre el mundo contemporáneo*. Buenos
Aires: Universidad Nacional de Quilmes.

———. 1997. *Mundialización y cultura*. Madrid: Alianza.

Pabón, Carlos. 2002. *Nación postmortem: Ensayos sobre los tiempos de insoportable
ambigüedad*. San Juan: Callejón.

Padilla, Felix M. 1985. *Latino Ethnic Consciousness: The Case of Mexican Americans
and Puerto Ricans in Chicago*. Notre Dame, Ind.: University of Notre Dame Press.

Padilla, Heberto. 1968. *Fuera del juego*. Havana: Unión de Escritores y Escritores
de Cuba.

Pagán de Colón, Petroamérica. 1956. *Programa de trabajadores migratorios de Puerto
Rico a los Estados Unidos*. San Juan: Departamento del Trabajo, Estado Libre
Asociado de Puerto Rico.

Pantoja, Adrián D. 2005. "Transnational Ties and Immigrant Political Incorporation: The Case of Dominicans in Washington Heights, New York." *International
Migration* 43 (4): 123–44.

Pantojas-García, Emilio. 1990. *Development Strategies as Ideology: Puerto Rico's
Export-Led Industrialization Experience*. Boulder, Colo.: Lynne Rienner.

———. 2007. "'Federal Funds' and the Puerto Rican Economy: Myths and
Realities." *CENTRO: Journal of the Center for Puerto Rican Studies* 19 (2): 206–23.

Pascual Morán, Vanessa, and Delia Ivette Figueroa. 2000. *Islas sin fronteras:
Los dominicanos indocumentados y la agricultura en Puerto Rico*. San Germán,
P.R.: CISCLA/Revista Interamericana.

Pedraza, Silvia. 1996. "Cuba's Refugees: Manifold Migrations." In *Origins and
Destinies: Immigration, Race, and Ethnicity in America*, ed. Silvia Pedraza and
Rubén G. Rumbaut, 263–79. Belmont, Calif.: Wadsworth.

———. 2000. "The Last Wave: Cuba's Contemporary Exodus — Political or
Economic Immigrants?" In *Cuba in Transition*, vol. 10, ed. Association for the
Study of the Cuban Economy, 265–76. http://lanic.utexas.edu/la/ca/cuba/asce/
cuba10/pedraza.pdf. Accessed September 7, 2009.

———. 2006. "Assimilation or Transnationalism? Conceptual Models of the
Immigrant Experience in America." In *Cultural Psychology of Immigrants*, ed.
Ramaswami Mahalingam, 33–54. Mahwah, N.J.: Lawrence Erlbaum.

———. 2007. *Political Disaffection in Cuba's Revolution and Exile*. New York:
Cambridge University Press.

Pedraza, Silvia, and Rubén G. Rumbaut, eds. 1996. *Origins and Destinies: Immigration, Race, and Ethnicity in America*. Belmont, Calif.: Wadsworth.

Pedraza-Bailey, Silvia. 1985. *Political and Economic Migrants in America: Cubans and
Mexicans*. Austin: University of Texas Press.

Peralta, Reyna A. 1995. "Proyecto para la implantación de un Centro de Servicios
Múltiples para Inmigrantes (CENSERMI)." Master's thesis, Graduate School of
Planning, University of Puerto Rico, Río Piedras.

Pérez, Gina M. 2004. *The Near Northwest Side Story: Migration, Displacement, and Puerto Rican Families*. Berkeley: University of California Press.

Pérez, Lisandro. 1994. "Cuban Catholics in the United States." In *Puerto Rican and Cuban Catholics in the U.S., 1900–1965*, ed. Jay P. Dolan and Jaime R. Vidal, 147–247. Notre Dame, In.: University of Notre Dame Press.

———. 2001. "Growing Up in Cuban Miami: Immigration, the Enclave, and New Generations." In *Ethnicities: Children of Immigrants in America*, ed. Rubén G. Rumbaut and Alejandro Portes, 91–125. Berkeley: University of California Press.

Pérez, Louis A., Jr. 1978. "Cubans in Tampa: From Exiles to Immigrants." *Florida Historical Quarterly* 57 (2): 129–40.

———. 1999. *On Becoming Cuban: Identity, Nationality, and Culture*. Chapel Hill: University of North Carolina Press.

———. 2006 [1988]. *Cuba: Between Reform and Revolution*. 3rd ed. New York: Oxford University Press.

Pérez, María E. 2008. "El precio de la revitalización: El desplazamiento de la comunidad latina de las zonas urbanas en Miami — circa 2007." In *Orbis/urbis latino: Los "hispanos" en las ciudades de los Estados Unidos*, ed. Cardenio Bedoya, Flavia Belpoliti, and Marc Zimmerman, 121–33. Houston: Global CASA/LACASA.

Pérez, Marvette. 1996. "La 'guagua aérea': Política, estatus, nacionalismo y ciudadanía en Puerto Rico." In *América Latina en tiempos de globalización: Procesos culturales y transformaciones sociopolíticas*, ed. Daniel Mato, Maritza Montero, and Emanuele Amodio, 187–200. Caracas: CRESALC.

Pérez Firmat, Gustavo. 1994. *Life on the Hyphen: The Cuban-American Way*. Austin: University of Texas Press.

Pérez López, Jorge. 2006. "The Cuban Economy in 2005–2006: The End of the Special Period?" In *Cuba in Transition*, vol. 16, ed. Association for the Study of the Cuban Economy, 1–13. http://info.lanic.utexas.edu/project/asce/pdfs/volume16/pdfs/perezlopezj.pdf. Accessed September 28, 2009.

Pérez López, Jorge, and Sergio Díaz-Briquets. 2005. "Remittances to Cuba: A Survey of Methods and Estimates." In *Cuba in Transition*, vol. 15, ed. Association for the Study of the Cuban Economy, 396–409. http://lanic.utexas.edu/project/asce/pdfs/volume15/pdfs/diazbriquetsperezlopez.pdf. Accessed September 12, 2009.

Pérez Memén, Fernando. 1989. "Panorama histórico de las emigraciones dominicanas a Puerto Rico." In *Los inmigrantes indocumentados dominicanos en Puerto Rico: Realidad y mitos*, ed. Juan Hernández Cruz, 7–34. San Germán, P.R.: Centro de Publicaciones, Universidad Interamericana de Puerto Rico.

Pessar, Patricia R. 1995. *A Visa for a Dream: Dominicans in the United States*. Boston: Allyn and Bacon.

Pessar, Patricia R., and Sarah J. Mahler. 2003. "Transnational Migration: Bringing Gender In." *International Migration Review* 37 (3): 812–46.

Portes, Alejandro. 1969. "Dilemmas of a Golden Exile: Integration of Cuban Refugee Families in Milwaukee." *American Sociological Review* 34 (4): 505–18.

———. 1996. "Global Villagers: The Rise of Transnational Communities."
American Prospect 25. http://www.prospect.org/cs/articles?article=global_
villagers. Accessed September 7, 2009.

———. 2001. "Introduction: The Debates and Significance of Immigrant Transnationalism." *Global Networks: A Journal of Transnational Affairs* 1 (3): 181–94.

Portes, Alejandro, and Robert L. Bach. 1985. *Latin Journey: Cuban and Mexican
Immigrants in the United States.* Berkeley: University of California Press.

Portes, Alejandro, Juan M. Clark, and Robert L. Bach. 1977. "The New Wave:
A Statistical Portrait of Recent Cuban Exiles to the United States." *Cuban Studies/
Estudios Cubanos* 7: 1–32.

Portes, Alejandro, Juan M. Clark, and Robert D. Manning. 1985. "After Mariel:
A Survey of the Resettlement Experiences of 1980 Cuban Refugees in Miami."
Cuban Studies/Estudios Cubanos 15 (2): 37–59.

Portes, Alejandro, Cristina Escobar, and Renelinda Arana. 2009. "¿Lealtades divi-
didas o convergentes? Informe sobre la incorporación política de inmigrantes
latinoamericanos en los Estados Unidos." In *Nuevos retos del transnacionalismo
en el estudio de las migraciones,* ed. Carlota Solé, Sonia Parella, and Leonardo
Cavalcanti, 49–89. Madrid: Observatorio Permanente de la Migración, Gobi-
erno de España.

Portes, Alejandro, Cristina Escobar, and Alexandria Walton Radford. 2005.
Immigrant Transnational Organizations: A Comparative Study. CMD Working
Paper no. 05–07. Princeton, N.J.: Center for Migration and Development,
Princeton University.

Portes, Alejandro, and Luis E. Guarnizo. 1991. *Capitalistas del trópico: La inmigración
en los Estados Unidos y el desarrollo de la pequeña empresa en la República Dominicana.* Santo Domingo: FLACSO.

Portes, Alejandro, Luis E. Guarnizo, and Patricia Landolt. 1999. "The Study of
Transnationalism: Pitfalls and Promises of an Emergent Research Field." *Ethnic
and Racial Studies* 22 (2): 217–37.

Portes, Alejandro, William Haller, and Luis E. Guarnizo. 2002. "Transnational
Entrepreneurs: The Emergence and Determinants of an Alternative Form of
Economic Adaptation." *American Sociological Review* 67 (2): 278–98.

Portes, Alejandro, and Leif Jensen. 1989. "The Enclave and the Entrants: Patterns
of Ethnic Enterprise in Miami before and after Mariel." *American Sociological
Review* 54 (6): 929–49.

Portes, Alejandro, and Rubén G. Rumbaut. 2006. *Immigrant America: A Portrait.*
3rd ed. Berkeley: University of California Press.

———, eds. 2001. *Legacies: The Story of the Immigrant Second Generation.*
Berkeley: University of California Press.

Portes, Alejandro, and Alex Stepick. 1993. *City on the Edge: The Transformation of
Miami.* Berkeley: University of California Press.

Portes, Alejandro, and Min Zhou. 1993. "The New Second Generation: Segmented
Assimilation and Its Variants." *Annals of the American Academy of Political and
Social Science* 530 (1): 74–96.

Poyo, Gerald E. 1989. *"With All, and for the Good of All": The Emergence of Popular Nationalism in the Cuban Communities of the United States, 1848–1898.* Durham, N.C.: Duke University Press.

Price, Patricia. 2007. "Cohering Culture on *Calle Ocho*: The Pause and Flow of *Latinidad.*" *Globalizations* 4 (1): 81–99.

Prieto, Yolanda. 2009. *The Cubans of Union City: Immigrants and Exiles in a New Jersey Community.* Philadelphia: Temple University Press.

Puerto Rican Forum. 1964. "Puerto Rican Community Development Project Training Institute." Section 5: Governor of Puerto Rico, 1949–64; series 1: Personal Correspondence; subseries: Proposals; folder 326. Fundación Luis Muñoz Marín, Trujillo Alto, P.R.

Puerto Rican Legal Defense and Education Fund (PRLDEF). Various dates. "*Vazquez v. Ferre.*" Box 7: Legal Division; Litigation Files. Puerto Rican Legal Defense and Education Fund Papers. Centro de Estudios Puertorriqueños, Hunter College, City University of New York.

Ramos-Zayas, Ana Y. 2003. *National Performances: The Politics of Class, Race, and Space in Puerto Rican Chicago.* Chicago: University of Chicago Press.

Reeves, Terrence, and Claudette Bennett. 2003. *The Asian and Pacific Islander Population in the United States: March 2002.* http://www.census.gov/prod/2003pubs/p20–540.pdf. Accessed September 8, 2008.

Regional and Field Office Farm Labor Files, Farm Labor Program, Migration Division, Department of Labor, Government of Puerto Rico. 1958–83. Microfilm reels 30–37; boxes 856–73. Records of the Offices of the Government of Puerto Rico in the United States. Centro de Estudios Puertorriqueños, Hunter College, City University of New York.

Reports, Farm Labor Program, Migration Division, Department of Labor, Government of Puerto Rico. 1956–92. Microfilm reels 38–50; boxes 874–93. Records of the Offices of the Government of Puerto Rico in the United States. Centro de Estudios Puertorriqueños, Hunter College, City University of New York.

Reyes, Xaé Alicia. 2000. "Return Migrant Students: Yankee Go Home?" In *Puerto Rican Students in U.S. Schools*, ed. Sonia Nieto, 39–68. Mahwah, N.J.: Lawrence Erlbaum.

Ricourt, Milagros. 1998. "Patterns of Dominican Demography and Community Development in New York City." *Latino Studies Journal* 9 (3): 11–38.

———. 2002. *Power from the Margins: The Incorporation of Dominicans in New York City.* New York: Routledge.

———. 2007. "Reaching the Promised Land: Undocumented Dominican Migration to Puerto Rico." *CENTRO: Journal of the Center for Puerto Rican Studies* 9 (2): 324–43.

Ricourt, Milagros, and Ruby Danta. 2003. *Hispanas de Queens: Latino Panethnicity in a New York City Neighborhood.* Ithaca, N.Y.: Cornell University Press.

Ríos, Palmira. 1992. "Acercamiento al conflicto domínico-boricua." *CENTRO: Journal of the Center for Puerto Rican Studies* 4 (2): 44–49.

————. 1995. "Citizenship, Nationality, and Transnational Public Policies in Latin America and the Caribbean." Paper presented at the conference "Caribbean Circuits: Transnational Approaches to Migration," Yale University, New Haven, Conn., September 21–23.

Rivera-Batiz, Francisco L., and Carlos E. Santiago. *Island Paradox: Puerto Ricans in the 1990s*. New York: Russell Sage Foundation.

Rivera Ortiz, Ángel Israel. 1996. *Puerto Rico: Ficción y mitología en sus alternativas de status*. Río Piedras, P.R.: Aurora.

Rivera Román, Jenilda. 2004. "Características sociodemográficas de la población inmigrante que participa en la fuerza laboral de Puerto Rico, 1990." Master's thesis, Graduate School of Public Health, University of Puerto Rico, Medical Sciences Campus.

Rivero, Yeidy M. 2004. "Caribbean Negritos: Ramón Rivero, Blackface, and 'Black' Voice in Puerto Rico." *Television and New Media* 5: 315–37.

Rodríguez, Clara E. 1989. *Puerto Ricans: Born in the U.S.A.* Boston: Unwin Hyman.

————. 2000. *Changing Race: Latinos, the Census, and the History of Ethnicity in the United States*. New York: New York University Press.

Rodríguez, Magdalys. 1997. "Pedido de libre tránsito." *El Nuevo Día*, March 14, 12.

Rodríguez Chávez, Ernesto. 1997. *Emigración cubana actual*. Havana: Ciencias Sociales.

————. 2000. "Determinantes de la emigración cubana actual y su impacto en la redefinición del fenómeno." Paper presented at the Twelfth International Congress of the Latin American Studies Association, Miami, March 16–18.

Rodríguez de León, Francisco. 1998. *El furioso merengue del norte: Una historia de la comunidad dominicana en los Estados Unidos*. New York: n.p.

Rohter, Larry, and Clifford Krauss. 1998. "Dominicans Allow Drugs Easy Sailing." *New York Times*, May 10. http://www.nytimes.com/1998/05/10/world/dominicans-allow-drugs-easy-sailing.html. Accessed September 7, 2009.

Romero Anico, Flavia A. 1984. "La migración dominicana: Sus implicaciones para Puerto Rico." Master's thesis, Graduate School of Public Administration, University of Puerto Rico, Río Piedras.

Rosaldo, Renato. 1989. *Culture and Truth: The Remaking of Social Analysis*. Boston: Beacon.

Rosario Natal, Carmelo. 1983. *Éxodo puertorriqueño: Las emigraciones al Caribe y Hawaii, 1900–1915*. San Juan: n.p.

————. 1990. "Para la historia de las relaciones intermigratorias entre Puerto Rico y la República Dominicana: Primeras etapas." *Revista de la Universidad de América* 2 (1): 20–25.

————. 1995. "Puerto Rico y la República Dominicana: Emigraciones durante el período revolucionario (1791–1850)." *Revista de la Universidad de América* 7 (1): 107–14.

Rosenthal, Mona. 1997. *Inside the Cuban Revolution: Everyday Life in Socialist Cuba*. Ithaca, N.Y.: Cornell University Press.

Rouse, Roger. 1995. "Thinking through Transnationalism: Notes on the Cultural Politics of Class Relations in the Contemporary U.S." *Public Culture* 7 (2): 353–402.

Ruggles, Steven, Matthew Sobek, Trent Alexander, Catherine A. Fitch, Ronald Goeken, Patricia Kelly Hall, Miriam King, and Chad Ronnander. 2010. *Integrated Public Use Microdata Series: Version 4.0.* Minneapolis: Minnesota Population Center. http://usa.ipums.org/usa. Accessed November 16, 2010.

Rumbaut, Rubén G. 2004. "Ages, Life Stages, and Generational Cohorts: Decomposing the Immigrant First and Second Generations in the United States." *International Migration Review* 38 (3): 1160–1205.

Safran, William. 1991. "Diasporas in Modern Societies: Myths of Homeland and Return." *Diaspora: A Journal of Transnational Studies* 1 (1): 83–99.

Sagás, Ernesto, and Sintia E. Molina, eds. 2004. *Dominican Migration: Transnational Perspectives.* Gainesville: University Press of Florida.

Sainz, Rudy Anthony. 1990. "Dominican Ethnic Associations." PhD diss., Columbia University.

Saldívar, José David. 1997. *Border Matters: Remapping American Cultural Studies.* Berkeley: University of California Press.

Salgado, César A. 2009. "CubaRícan: Efectos de la capilaridad colonial." *La Habana Elegante* (segunda época, Fall/Winter). http://www.habanaelegante. com/Fall_Winter_2009/Invitation_Salgado.html. Accessed September 24, 2009.

Sana, Mariano. 2003. "International Monetary Transfers: Three Essays on Migrant Decision-Making." PhD diss., University of Pennsylvania.

Sana, Mariano, and Douglas S. Massey. 2005. "Household Composition, Family Migration, and Community Context: Migrant Remittances in Four Countries." *Social Science Quarterly* 86 (2): 509–28.

Sánchez, Luis. 2009. *The New Puerto Rico? Identity, Hybridity and Transnationalism within the Puerto Rican Diaspora in Orlando, Florida.* Saarbrücken, Germany: Verlag Dr. Müller.

Sánchez, Luis Rafael. 1994. *La guagua aérea.* Río Piedras, P.R.: Cultural.

Sánchez Korrol, Virginia E. 1994. *From Colonia to Community: The History of Puerto Ricans in New York City.* 2nd ed. Berkeley: University of California Press.

Sassen, Saskia. 1998. *Globalization and Its Discontents: Essays on the New Mobility of People and Money.* New York: New Press.

———. 1999. "Beyond Sovereignty: De-Facto Transnationalism in Immigration Policy." *European Journal of Migration Law* 1 (2): 177–98.

Sawyer, Mark Q. 2006. *Racial Politics in Post-revolutionary Cuba.* New York: Cambridge University Press.

Secretaría de Estado de lo Interior y Policía, República Dominicana. 1923. *Censo de la República Dominicana.* Santo Domingo: n.p.

Selman Fernández, Ana F., Glenés Tavarez María, and Rafael Puello Nina. 1990. "La emigración ilegal de los dominicanos hacia Puerto Rico." *El Caribe Contemporáneo* 20: 91–100.

Senior, Clarence. 1947. *Puerto Rican Emigration*. Río Piedras, P.R.: Social Research Center, University of Puerto Rico.

Smith, Benjamin. 1999. "The Self-Employed in Cuba: A Street Level View." In *Cuba in Transition*, vol. 9, ed. Association for the Study of the Cuban Economy, 49–59. http://lanic.utexas.edu/la/cb/cuba/asce/cuba9/smith.pdf. Accessed September 7, 2009.

Smith, Michael Peter. 1994. "Can You Imagine? Transnational Migration and the Globalization of Grassroots Politics." *Social Text* 39: 15–34.

Smith, Michael Peter, and Luis Eduardo Guarnizo, eds. 1998. *Transnationalism from Below*. New Brunswick, N.J.: Transaction.

Smith, Robert Courtney. 2006. *Mexican New York: Transnational Lives of New Immigrants*. Berkeley: University of California Press.

Sørensen, Ninna Nyberg. 1994. "Telling Migrants Apart: The Experience of Migrancy among Dominican Locals and Transnationals." Unpublished manuscript, Institute of Anthropology, University of Copenhagen.

———. 1996. "'Nueva York es tan sólo otra capital dominicana — Madrid es otro mundo': Prácticas espaciales y culturales de desplazamiento entre migrantes dominicanos en Nueva York y Madrid." *Género y Sociedad* 4 (1): 160–220.

———. 1997. "Género, etnicidad y cruce de fronteras: ¿Cambios en la identidad genérica dominicana?" *Estudios Sociales* 30 (109): 77–105.

Sørensen, Ninna Nyberg, and Karen Fog Olwig, eds. 2002. *Work and Migration: Life and Livelihoods in a Globalizing World*. London: Routledge.

Soto-Crespo, Ramón E. 2009. *Mainland Passage: The Cultural Anomaly of Puerto Rico*. Minneapolis: University of Minnesota Press.

Sotomayor, Orlando. 2000. "Análisis comparado de las estructuras de salarios de Puerto Rico y los Estados Unidos." *Revista de Ciencias Sociales* 9 (nueva época): 106–35.

Soto Toledo, Rosalinda. 1998. "Emigración de puertorriqueños a Santo Domingo: 1900–1930." Master's thesis proposal, Department of History, University of Puerto Rico, Río Piedras.

Spadoni, Paolo. 2004. "U.S. Financial Flows in the Cuban Economy." *Transnational Law and Contemporary Problems* 14: 81–117.

Stepick, Alex, Guillermo Grenier, Max Castro, and Marvin Dunn. 2003. *This Land Is Our Land: Immigrants and Power in Miami*. Berkeley: University of California Press.

Stinson Fernández, John. 1996. "Hacia una antropología de la emigración planificada: El Negociado de Empleo y Migración y el caso de Filadelfia." *Revista de Ciencias Sociales* (nueva época) 1: 112–55.

Suki, Lenora. 2004. *Financial Institutions and the Remittances Market in the Dominican Republic*. New York: Earth Institute, Columbia University. http://www.iadb.org/mif/v2/files/Suki_NYNov04.pdf. Accessed April 11, 2006.

Taylor, Henry Louis, Jr. 2009. *Inside El Barrio: A Bottom-Up View of Neighborhood Life in Castro's Cuba*. Sterling, Va.: Kumarian.

Thompson, Lanny. 1990. "La migración en una semi-periferia incipiente: Aspectos económicos y socio-culturales de la migración en Puerto Rico." In *Los dominicanos en Puerto Rico: Migración en la semi-periferia*, ed. Jorge Duany, 89–121. Río Piedras, P.R.: Huracán.

Tölölyan, Khachig. 1991. "The Nation-State and Its Others: In Lieu of a Preface." *Diaspora: A Journal of Transnational Studies* 1 (1): 3–7.

Toro-Morn, Maura. 1995. "Gender, Class, Family, and Migration: Puerto Rican Women in Chicago." *Gender and Society* 9 (6): 712–26.

Toro-Morn, Maura, and Marixsa Alicea. 2003. "Gendered Geographies of Home: Mapping Second- and Third-Generation Puerto Ricans' Sense of Home." In *Gender and U.S. Immigration: Contemporary Trends*, ed. Pierrette Hondagneu-Sotelo, 194–214. Berkeley: University of California Press.

Torres, Andrés. 1995. *Between Melting Pot and Mosaic: African Americans and Puerto Ricans in the New York Political Economy*. Philadelphia: Temple University Press.

Torres, María de los Angeles. 1999. *In the Land of Mirrors: Cuban Exile Politics in the United States*. Ann Arbor: University of Michigan Press.

Torres-Padilla, José L., and Carmen Haydée Rivera, eds. 2008. *Writing Off the Hyphen: New Perspectives on the Literature of the Puerto Rican Diaspora*. Seattle: University of Washington Press.

Torres-Saillant, Silvio. 1999. *El retorno de las yolas: Ensayos sobre diáspora, democracia y dominicanidad*. Santo Domingo: Trinitaria/Manatí.

———. 2000. *Diasporic Disquisitions: Dominicanists, Transnationalism, and the Community*. Dominican Studies Working Papers Series 1. New York: CUNY Dominican Studies Institute.

Torres-Saillant, Silvio, and Ramona Hernández. 1998. *The Dominican Americans*. Westport, Conn.: Greenwood.

Tweed, Thomas A. 1997. *Our Lady of the Exile: Diasporic Religion at a Cuban Catholic Shrine in Miami*. New York: Oxford University Press.

Ugalde, Antonio, Frank D. Bean, and Gilbert Cárdenas. 1979. "International Migration from the Dominican Republic: Findings from a National Survey." *International Migration Review* 13 (2): 235–54.

Unión de Escritores y Artistas Cubanos and Universidad de La Habana, eds. 1995. *Cuba: Cultura e identidad nacional*. Havana: Unión.

University of Sussex, Development Research Centre on Migration, Globalisation and Poverty. 2007. *Global Migration Origin Database. Updated March 2007.* http://www.migrationdrc.org/research/typesofmigration/global_migrant_origin_database.html. Accessed October 25, 2009.

Uriarte, Miren. 2002. *Cuba: Social Policies at the Crossroads. Maintaining Priorities, Transforming Practice*. Boston: Oxfam America.

U.S. Bureau of Statistics. 1868–92. *Annual Report on the Commerce and Navigation of the United States*. Washington, D.C.: U.S. Government Printing Office.

U.S. Census Bureau. 1933–50. *Statistical Abstract of the United States*. Washington, D.C.: U.S. Government Printing Office.

————. 1953. *Census of Population: 1950.* Vol. 2, *Characteristics of the Population,* parts 51–54, *Territories and Possessions.* Washington, D.C.: U.S. Government Printing Office.

————. 1961. *U.S. Census of Population: 1960. General Population Characteristics, Puerto Rico.* Washington, D.C.: U.S. Government Printing Office.

————. 1973. *Census of Population: 1970. Characteristics of the Population.* Part 53, *Puerto Rico.* Washington, D.C.: U.S. Government Printing Office.

————. 1984. *1980 Census of Population: General Social and Economic Characteristics. Puerto Rico.* Washington, D.C.: U.S. Government Printing Office.

————. 1993. *1990 Census of Population: Social and Economic Characteristics. Puerto Rico.* Washington, D.C.: U.S. Government Printing Office.

————. 2009a. *Census of Population and Housing.* http://www.census.gov/prod/ www/abs/decennial/index.htm. Accessed September 8, 2009.

————. 2009b. *Hispanic Population of the United States.* http://www.census.gov/ population/www/socdemo/hispanic/about.html. Accessed September 11, 2009.

————. 2010. *American Factfinder.* http://factfinder.census.gov. Accessed September 29, 2010.

U.S. Citizenship and Immigration Services. 2002–9. *Yearbook of Immigration Statistics.* http://www.dhs.gov/files/statistics/publications/yearbook.shtm. Accessed April 9, 2010.

————. 2003–8. *Profiles on Legal Permanent Residents.* http://www.dhs.gov/files/ statistics/data/dslpr.shtm. Accessed October 25, 2009.

U.S. Coast Guard. 2009. *Alien Migrant Interdictions.* http://www.uscg.mil/hq/cg5/ cg531/AMIO/FlowStats/FY.asp. Accessed December 27, 2009.

U.S. Commission on Civil Rights. 1976. *Puerto Ricans in the Continental United States: An Uncertain Future.* Washington, D.C.: U.S. Government Printing Office.

U.S. Commissioner-General of Immigration. 1893–1932. *Annual Report of the Commissioner-General of Immigration.* Washington, D.C.: U.S. Government Printing Office.

U.S.-Cuba Trade and Economic Council. 1999. *1999 Commercial Highlights.* http:// www.cubatrade.org/99hlights.html. Accessed September 12, 2009.

————. 2000. *2000 Commercial Highlights.* http://www.cubatrade.org/2000hlights .html. Accessed September 12, 2009.

U.S. Department of Justice, Immigration and Naturalization Service. 1942–77. *Annual Report of the Immigration and Naturalization Service.* Washington, D.C.: U.S. Department of Justice.

————. 1978–95. *Statistical Yearbook of the Immigration and Naturalization Service.* Washington, D.C.: U.S. Department of Justice.

————. 1996–2001. *Statistical Yearbook of the Immigration and Naturalization Service.* http://www.dhs.gov/files/statistics/publications/archive.shtm. Accessed September 9, 2009.

U.S. Department of the Treasury, Office of Foreign Assets Control. 2009. *List of Authorized Providers of Air, Travel, and Remittance Forwarding Services to Cuba.*

http://www.treas.gov/offices/enforcement/ofac/programs/cuba/cuba_tsp.pdf. Accessed September 12, 2009.

Vargas-Ramos, Carlos. 2006. *Settlement Patterns and Residential Segregation of Puerto Ricans in the United States.* Policy Report 1, no. 2. New York: Centro de Estudios Puertorriqueños, Hunter College, City University of New York.

Vázquez Calzada, José L. 1979. "Demographic Aspects of Migration." In *Labor Migration under Capitalism: The Puerto Rican Experience*, ed. History Task Force, Centro de Estudios Puertorriqueños, 223–38. New York: Monthly Review Press.

Vázquez Calzada, José L., and Zoraida Morales del Valle. 1979. "Características sociodemográficas de los norteamericanos, cubanos y dominicanos residentes en Puerto Rico." *Revista de Ciencias Sociales* 21 (1–2): 3–37.

Vertovec, Steven. 2009. *Transnationalism.* New York: Routledge.

Vidal Alejandro, Pavel. 2009. "La macroeconomía cubana en 2008: Datos de cierre de año." *Cuba Siglo XXI* 93. http://www.nodo50.org/cubasigloXXI/economia/alejandro_310109.pdf. Accessed September 29, 2010.

Viguié Films. N.d. *Los beneficiarios.* Film produced for the Migration Division of the Department of Labor, Government of Puerto Rico. Records of the Offices of the Puerto Rican Government in the United States. Centro de Estudios Puertorriqueños, Hunter College, City University of New York.

Villarrubia-Mendoza, Jacqueline. 2007. "The Residential Segregation of Puerto Ricans in New York and Orlando." *Latino(a) Research Review* 6 (1–2): 119–31.

———. 2010. "Characteristics of Puerto Rican Homeowners in Florida and Their Likelihood of Homeownership." *CENTRO: Journal of the Center for Puerto Rican Studies* 22 (1): 154–73.

Waldinger, Roger. 2007. *Between Here and There: How Attached Are Latino Immigrants to Their Home Countries?* Washington, D.C.: Pew Hispanic Center. http://pewhispanic.org/reports/report.php?ReportID=80. Accessed May 15, 2008.

Waldinger, Roger, and David Fitzgerald. 2004. "Transnationalism in Question." *American Journal of Sociology* 109 (5): 1177–95.

Weissert, Will. 2009. "Despite Crisis, Cuba Says GDP Rose 1.4% in '09." *Puerto Rico Daily Sun*, December 21. http://www.prdailysun.com/index.php?page=news.article&id=1261383681. Accessed January 8, 2010.

Weyland, Karin. 1998. "Dominican Women 'Con un pie aquí y otro allá': International Migration, Class, Gender, and Cultural Change." PhD diss., New School for Social Research.

Whalen, Carmen Teresa. 2001. *From Puerto Rico to Philadelphia: Puerto Rican Workers and Postwar Economies.* Philadelphia: Temple University Press.

———. 2005. "Colonialism, Citizenship, and the Making of the Puerto Rican Diaspora." In *The Puerto Rican Diaspora: Historical Perspectives*, ed. Carmen Teresa Whalen and Víctor Vázquez-Hernández, 1–42. Philadelphia: Temple University Press.

Whalen, Carmen Teresa, and Víctor Vázquez-Hernández, eds. 2005. *The Puerto Rican Diaspora: Historical Perspectives.* Philadelphia: Temple University Press.

Whitehead, Laurence, and Bert Hoffman, eds. 2007. *Debating Cuban Exceptionalism*. New York: Palgrave Macmillan.

Wimmer, Andreas, and Nina Glick Schiller. 2002. "Methodological Nationalism and Beyond: Nation-State Building, Migration, and the Social Sciences." *Global Networks* 2 (4): 301–34.

World Bank. 2008. *Migration and Remittances Factbook 2008*. http://econ.worldbank .org/WBSITE/EXTERNAL/EXTDEC/EXTDECPROSPECTS/0,,contentMDK:2135 2016~pagePK:64165401~piPK:64165026~theSitePK:476883,00.html. Accessed May 16, 2008.

———. 2009. *Data and Research*. http://econ.worldbank.org/WBSITE/EXTERNAL/ EXTDEC/0,,menuPK:476823~pagePK:64165236~piPK:64165141~theSit ePK:469372,00.html. Accessed July 11, 2009.

Yager, Arthur. 1912. "Fundamental Social and Political Problems of Porto Rico." In *Report of the Thirtieth Annual Lake Mohonk Conference of Friends of the Indians and Other Dependent Peoples*, 145–53. Lake Mohonk, N.Y.: Lake Mohonk Conference of Friends of the Indians and Other Dependent Peoples.

Zentella, Ana Celia. 2003. "Returned Migration, Language, and Identity: Puerto Rican Bilinguals in Dos Worlds/Two Mundos." In *Perspectives on Las Américas: A Reader in Culture, History, and Representation*, ed. Matthew G. Gutmann, Félix V. Matos Rodríguez, Lynn Stephen, and Patricia Zavella, 245–58. Malden, Mass.: Blackwell.

Index

El Barrio (East Harlem), 49, 55, 66, 67, 105

Employment and Migration Bureau (Puerto Rico), 84, 85, 90, 238 (n. 5). *See also* Migration Division

Entrando por la cocina (television comedy), 206

Espaillat, Adriano, 182, 183

Espino, María Dolores, 239 (n. 8)

Estado Libre Asociado. *See* Commonwealth of Puerto Rico

Ethnic humor, 205–6

Ethnic tourism. *See* Tourism

Ethnographic fieldwork, 9, 10, 103, 136, 144, 175, 227

Ethnosurvey, 215–16

Exiles: Cuban, 42, 43, 45, 75, 139, 141, 143; definition of, 138; Dominican, 55, 180, 189; Puerto Rican, 48

External vote. *See* Voting abroad

Falcón, Angelo, 106, 213

Farm Labor Program (Puerto Rico), 52, 83, 87, 88, 89–103

Farmworkers, Puerto Rican: diet of, 91, 96–97, 102; health problems of, 91, 95; housing conditions of, 91, 95–96; language barrier against, 90, 99, 102, 103; working conditions of, 91, 93–94

Female-headed households, 69, 72, 177, 204

Fernández, José, 185

Fernández, Leonel, 185, 191

Fernández, María Teresa (aka Mariposa), 125

Fernós-Isern, Antonio, 85

Ferré, Luis A., 92

Ferré, Rosario, 15

Figueroa, Sotero, 48

First-generation immigrants, 17, 29, 53, 75, 116–18, 120, 149, 174, 210, 235 (n. 4)

Fitzgerald, David, 30, 138, 141

FIU Cuba poll, 146, 148, 149

Flores, Juan, 2, 3, 228

Foner, Nancy, 29

Fortune, 140

"Freedom Flights," 44

Fuera del juego (Padilla), 236 (n. 7)

Fundación Luis Muñoz Marín (Puerto Rico), 10

Funkhouser, Edward, 240 (n. 2)

Fussell, Elizabeth, 213

García-Colón, Ismael, 101

Gender and transnationalism, 31, 82, 204–5, 223

Georges, Eugenia, 201

Glassboro Service Association, 90, 92, 97

Glick Schiller, Nina, 7, 9, 18, 19, 20, 21, 22, 25, 28, 135, 229

Globalization, 19, 23, 28, 30, 32, 33, 227, 228

"Golden Exiles," 11, 13, 42–43, 235 (n. 3)

Goldring, Luin, 181

González, Elián, 76, 136

González, José Luis, 189

Graham, Pamela M., 170, 171

Green Giant Company, 96

Grenier, Guillermo J., 135–36

Grito de Lares (Puerto Rico), 48

Grosfoguel, Ramón, 27, 81

"Guagua aérea, La" (Sánchez), 52

Guantánamo (Cuba): U.S. naval base in, 46, 47, 157

Guarnizo, Luis E., 20, 22, 71, 100, 170

Haitians: in Dominican Republic, 78, 183, 206, 211, 212; in United States, 79, 138

Hart-Celler Act, 38

Helms-Burton Act, 154

Henríquez Ureña, Camila, 55

Henríquez Ureña, Pedro, 55

Heredia, José María, 39

Hernández, Carmen Dolores, 15